Damned Agitator

Damned Agitator

A Michael Gold Reader

Edited and with an Introduction by

Patrick Chura

Photograph of Michael Gold in the 1910s. © Aaron Granich. Source: Granich family.

Published by State University of New York Press, Albany

Printed in the United States of America

For information, contact State University of New York Press, Albany, NY
www.sunypress.edu

Library of Congress Cataloging-in-Publication Data

Names: Gold, Michael, 1893–1967 author. | Chura, Patrick, 1964– editor.
Title: Damned agitator : a Michael Gold reader / edited by Patrick Chura
Description: Albany : State University of New York Press, [2023] | Includes bibliographical references and index.
Identifiers: LCCN 2023009077 | ISBN 9781438495330 (hardcover : alk. paper) | ISBN 9781438495347 (pbk. : alk. paper) | ISBN 9781438495354 (ebook)
Classification: LCC PS3513.O29 M55 2023 | DDC 813/.54—dc23/eng/20230412
LC record available at https://lccn.loc.gov/2023009077

10 9 8 7 6 5 4 3 2 1

Contents

Part Three

Part Four

Part Five

Part Six

*These works have not appeared in previous collections of Gold's writings.

Introduction

In December 2020, SUNY Press published my *Michael Gold: The People's Writer*, the first extensive study of a radical artist whose signature achievements were a long-running newspaper column under the title "Change the World" and a best-selling novel of 1930, *Jews Without Money*. As its author, I argued for Gold's overdue recognition as a consequential writer and called for an understanding of his oppositional life as a representative American journey.

The book and its arguments were well received. "Anyone who professes to represent a progressive point of view owes no small debt to Gold, who, since the early 1950s, has gone largely unrecognized," wrote Woody Haut in the *Los Angeles Review of Books*. In the scholarly journal *American Communist History*, Randi Storch celebrated Gold's rehabilitation as hopeful evidence that "the American academy is increasingly ready to treat seriously U.S. radical writers." *American Literary History* noted poignantly that Gold's life "pays testament to the courage of a man who accepted the limitations imposed by the present in order to hasten the arrival of a different kind of future. This lesson should not be lost."

Such responses were gratifying, but the book also elicited outrage. Editors of several conservative journals reviled Mike Gold while attacking the very idea of a sympathetic biography of a communist artist, thereby reminding us that Cold War fears and orthodoxies linger, and that Gold still agitates. Even today he riles the reactionaries.

One review of *The People's Writer* did the most to spark this new anthology. "Is it time to release Michael Gold from his personal gulag to range free in the pastures of 20th-century American literature?" Jim Hoberman asked in *The Nation* in May 2021. It was the right question, and its answer was implicit: Free Mike Gold. A week later I was contacted by

Richard Carlin of SUNY Press, who said he'd seen Hoberman's piece and would be very interested in a book that gives an introduction to Gold's work in various genres.

Initially I hesitated. Significant portions of Gold's writing had already been collected and anthologized—by Robert Forsythe in 1936, Samuel Sillen in 1954, and Michael Folsom in 1972. As I thought it over, it struck me that all of these anthologies appeared under the imprint of International Publishers, the semiofficial press of the US communist movement. As a result, they were largely denied the recognition they deserved and did not long remain in print. I felt also that each was limited. Folsom passed over Gold the journalist to focus solely on his "literary" work; Sillen overlooked Gold the playwright; Forsythe's collection appeared three decades before the end of the author's career. This book, then, is the first Gold anthology by a scholarly press, the first to include the full range of Gold's work in all genres, and the first in more than fifty years.

That half century has been marked not only by the end of the Cold War and fall of the Soviet Union, but by the stunning rise of fascist authoritarianism in the United States. In this context, I felt that the job of reevaluating Gold's body of work would be a compelling project with the potential to reach a new readership. If millennials and Gen Z know of Gold, it is probably only as an obscure figure associated with a strangely titled novel. Certainly not everyone is aware that Gold wrote plays, stories, avant-garde poetry, personal essays, criticism, proletarian chants, and historical analysis—or that his contributions to literary theory are undervalued. I recall five years ago when I was asked to write an article-length critical summary of Gold's career for the Gale American Writers series, edited by Jay Parini. When I submitted the article, even Parini, one of the most erudite scholars I've known, was surprised. "I had no idea there was so much!" he said.

The title of this anthology is *Damned Agitator* because Gold wrote a fine short story with that title, but really because that's what Mike Gold was. He was born Itzhok Isaac Granich in New York in 1893, the first surviving son of impoverished Eastern European Jewish immigrants. Growing up in the slums of the Lower East Side, he quit school at age twelve to support his family with a series of menial jobs. In spring 1914, Gold, then using the name Irwin Granich, became involved in the labor movement when, after losing his job as a factory worker and shipping clerk, he wandered into a protest rally in New York's Union Square and heard passionate anticapitalist speeches. The crowd was attacked by police and he was beaten with other demonstrators when he attempted to help an injured woman. Soon afterward he bought his first copy of the radical journal *Masses* and began submitting revolutionary poetry to editors Floyd Dell and Max Eastman. Recalling the incident years later, Gold stated, "I have always been grateful to that cop and that club. He introduced me to literature and the revolution." Gold's first published poem, "Three Whose Hatred Killed Them," espoused violence in the cause of radical labor by extolling three activists killed by a bomb they had manufactured for use against industrialists.

Only a few months after his political awakening, Gold was given the opportunity to attend Harvard as a "special student." To support himself while studying he wrote an anonymous daily column for the *Boston Journal* about his experiences with elite education. When the columns became critical of the great university, they were canceled, forcing Gold to drop out of school after only a few months. Ever afterward he was suspicious of the elitists, purists, and professors, the "book-proud intellectuals" and smug arbiters of literary taste.

By the end of 1914 Gold was living in Boston, where he survived for months as a homeless street beggar before taking a room in an anarchist flophouse. In early 1916 he accepted an assignment from the anarchist newspaper *Blast* to report on a strike at the Plymouth cordage factory, where he met Bartolomeo Vanzetti and produced his first article about the radical labor movement. A decade later he was arrested along with other literary activists during protest demonstrations to save Sacco and Vanzetti from the "lynchers in frockcoats" of respectable Boston when the case culminated in the execution of the two immigrant anarchists.

In the late 1910s, Gold found a creative outlet as a member of the Provincetown Players, contributing three one-act plays that were produced along with those of Eugene O'Neill, Susan Glaspell, and Edna St. Vincent Millay at the Provincetown Playhouse in New York. The best of these one-acts, a play titled *Money* (included in this anthology), portrayed starving immigrants who, in Gold's words, "achieve a certain greatness as all men must."

With American entry into the Great War, Gold moved to Mexico to avoid the draft. One of his first short stories, a powerful antiwar screed published under the title "First Aid" (also reprinted in this anthology), helps explain that decision. While living in Mexico in 1918–19 he received news of the Palmer Raids: the widespread arrests and detentions of leftists by the US Department of Justice. Upon his return to New York, he adopted the name Michael Gold as both a protective pseudonym and a symbol of his revolutionary rebirth. The new name was taken from a person known to him, a Jewish friend of his father who had been a corporal in the Civil War, fighting for the North in the liberation struggle against the Southern slavocracy. He kept the name for the rest of his life.

In 1921 Gold was elected to the editorial board of *The Liberator*, the successor journal to the suppressed *Masses*, and a year later became its coeditor with Black poet Claude McKay. In this role Gold encouraged and published works from the "mass poets" of the working classes to counter what he termed the "ego-poets" of the bourgeoisie. In the February 1921 issue he published the seminal essay "Towards Proletarian Art," an impassioned manifesto in which he broke with the liberal-individualist aesthetic theory of his mentors, Dell and Eastman. Citing Walt Whitman as "the heroic spiritual grandfather" of proletarian culture, Gold called for heightened social consciousness in literature and asserted that "a mighty national art cannot arise save out of the soil of the masses." The new art, Gold implied, would express the experience of the poor and without exception be created either by the poor themselves or artists who had lived sympathetically among them. The American currency of the term "proletarian literature" dates from the publication of this article, a major document in radical literary theory.

One of Gold's best poems from the 1920s, "The Strange Funeral in Braddock," focuses on three reactions to the horrific death of Jan Clepak, an immigrant worker who is buried alive by an avalanche of molten steel. One observer at the funeral chooses self-destructive despair, but Clepak's widow pledges never to let her children work in a mill and vows to use the death transformatively: "I'll make myself hard as steel, harder, I'll come some day and make bullets out of Jan's body, and shoot them into a tyrant's heart!" Journalist Art Shields called this elegiac piece "the most tragically beautiful poem that has come out of the United States class struggle."

During the decade following the 1929 stock market crash, Gold was a controversial national figure as a best-selling novelist, committed communist, and vocal advocate of the literary genre he labeled "proletarian realism." Two essays from 1930 sum up Gold's theory and the intense debates it incited. "Wilder: Prophet of the Genteel Christ," a scintillating *New Republic* review of several novels by Thornton Wilder, scandalized readers and touched off a nationwide "Gold-Wilder controversy" that played out for several years. Gold's economic interpretation of literature saw Wilder as "the poet of the genteel bourgeoisie," whose "irritating and pretentious" novels lacked contemporary relevance because within them "nobody works in a Ford plant, and nobody starves looking for work." *New Republic* editor Edmund Wilson, who had commissioned the review, gave Gold credit for exposing "the insipidity and pointlessness of most literary criticism" and for making it "very plain that the economic crisis [the Great Depression] was to be accompanied by a literary one."

In a second important article, his September 1930 *New Masses* editorial column (later given the title "Proletarian Realism"), Gold enumerated the essential elements of a "new form" of literary expression: "Proletarian realism deals with the real conflicts of men and women who work for a living. It has nothing to do with the sickly mental states of the idle Bohemians, their subtleties, their sentimentalities, their fine-spun affairs." Writers of this genre, Gold insisted, must be workers or must "have the courage of proletarian experience."

Gold's authority for making these declarations was based on his recent publication of a successful piece of literature that met his stated criteria. *Jews Without Money*, Gold's only novel and by consensus his best work of fiction, has been described by Alfred Kazin as "a great piercing cry of lament and outrage" over the struggles of the working classes. A loosely narrated series of sketches from Gold's childhood, the novel is self-announced as a "truthful book of poverty" that spares no detail in cataloging slum misery while identifying its causes in capitalism: "America is so rich and fat," Gold writes, "because it has eaten the tragedy of millions of immigrants."

Aside from its central emphasis on the class war, the work is a perceptive critique of urban America, theorizing racism, sexism, and the costs of assimilation for Jewish immigrants struggling with cultural identity in the United States. Appropriately, the only light in the book's dark, brutalizing world is the potential for systemic social revolution. The novel ends, and the life of teenaged Mikey Gold is given purpose, when he hears and responds to a speech from "a man on an East Side soap-box" about a world movement to abolish poverty: "O workers' Revolution, you brought hope to me, a lonely suicidal boy. You are the true Messiah. . . . O Revolution, that forced me to think, to struggle and to live. O great Beginning!"

Jews Without Money reached a wide audience, going through eleven printings in 1930 alone. In that year Sinclair Lewis mentioned Gold in his Nobel Prize acceptance speech, crediting *Jews Without Money* for revealing "the new frontier of the Jewish East Side." By 1950 the book had seen twenty-five printings and been translated into sixteen languages. In Germany, as Gold notes in his preface to the 1935 edition, the translated novel was used as "a form of propaganda against the Nazi anti-Semitic lies." The author was proud to have helped counteract anti-Semitism in Germany, but he reminded readers that the US had its own Hitler-like demagogues.

The World War II years required US communists to adapt rapidly to shifts in the national consensus. They were staunchly antiwar until events of 1941, primarily Hitler's invasion of the USSR, drove immediate changes in position and rhetoric.

After Pearl Harbor, American communists gained some temporary protection from persecution by virtue of the need for US-Soviet wartime unity against the common fascist enemy. Still, in a December 1941 column, "They Hate the Soviets More than They Love America," Gold warned that many American politicians preferred fascism to an alliance with the USSR. He had a point. Already the red-baiters were parroting the Dies Committee and calling for the suppression of Gold's column: "You would never know from their speeches that we were under attack from Hitler and Japan, and it wasn't the *Daily Worker* that had bombed Pearl Harbor," Gold quipped.

For their part, US communists like Gold recognized common cause with national war goals and largely sublimated their revolutionary agenda for the duration. These political fluctuations softened Gold's message in his "Change the World" columns at a time when his family life, including his commitments as a father of two young boys, demanded increasing time and attention.

Of course Gold spent the McCarthy years blacklisted and broke. His wife Elizabeth held down several jobs while he stayed home and did the cooking in their cold-water flat in the Bronx. Alone all day with his health deteriorating and FBI agents parked outside, he wrote poems that questioned whether he and his "petty troubles" could "outlast Wall Street America." One year he got an idea for a business, the "Mike Gold Writers' Workshop," which he advertised as "a place where students can grow in the craft of writing by means of constant experiment, mutual criticism, and advice and inspiration from an experienced leader. The atmosphere will be not that of a classroom, but of a group of craftsmen helping each other." Tuition for the ten-week class was a dollar a week. Few students registered.

The crisis and transition came in 1956, a terrible time in communist history. In June the *New York Times* published the text of Khrushchev's "secret speech," fully revealing the immeasurable horrors of Stalin's rule.

That October Mike, Elizabeth, and their younger son Carl moved to San Francisco, settling into an apartment at 448 Waller Street. Simultaneously came news of the Hungarian crackdown—in which Soviet troops forcefully put down a prodemocracy movement, turning the situation into a bloody revolt. The brutal repression sent shock waves through the Soviet bloc but was just as devastating to the organized Left worldwide. Within weeks, thirty thousand US communists quit the party. Most of those who remained were bewildered.

At the San Francisco offices of the leftist *People's World* newspaper, the effect was immediate. Circulation fell to a nadir of six thousand. But among the many goodbyes and dispirited turmoil as the *People's World* staff disbanded, there was, according to longtime editor Al Richmond, "one brave hello." This was from Gold, who appeared in the newspaper's offices one day to offer his services. The younger Richmond remembered Mike as the prophet of proletarianism and guiding light of the thirties. He resurrected the once-famous "Change the World" column and managed to put together a small syndication for the articles, guaranteeing his aging comrade fifty dollars a week.

Given the chance to earn a living again, the damned agitator seized the day. The fresh iteration of Gold's journalism ran from 1957 to 1966, during which he only occasionally reminisced about the heyday of the old Left. Mainly he showed how young he still was. His tone was not bombastic as in the thirties, yet still oppositional, charged with antifascist resistance and optimistic about a socialist future. Unlike most of the literary leftists of his generation, Michael Gold did not eventually disavow his radicalism, nor did he ever seek wealth or adopt a bourgeois lifestyle. He also refused to soft-pedal his artistic or political opinions, in the process earning enemies in the cultural establishment. Perhaps more brazenly (or naively as some would have it), he never abandoned the cause of what he termed "world socialism," instead retaining throughout his life the hope expressed in the epiphanic ending of *Jews Without Money*, that a workers' messiah would come. What Mike Gold explained about his spirit and temperament at the advent of his fame in 1921 was just as true in the author's final days: "The tenement is in my blood. When I think it is the tenement thinking. When I hope it is the tenement hoping. I am not an individual; I am all that the tenement group poured into me during those early years of my spiritual travail."

Since the publication of Gold's biography in 2020, an encouraging number of writer-activists and graduate students have contacted me either to ask questions or express solidarity. Recently I've been informed of a budding Mike Gold Collective of younger progressive activists and journalists in Columbus, Ohio. Before that, Massachusetts folk singer Bob Feldman sent a video of a "biographical song" he'd written after reading about Gold. Its refrain—"What workers write/ What workers sing/ Professors don't let you learn/ But Mike Gold/ The People's Writer/ His columns the workers loved"—sums up an aesthetic Gold encouraged and cultivated. I heard as well from some of Gold's actual contemporaries, including Beatrice Lumpkin, an activist, writer, and onetime union organizer who recently reached the age of 104. Looking back on Gold's glory days, Lumpkin wrote, "I am happy that Mike Gold is coming back. His *Jews Without Money* was a big influence in my life. Gold spoke to our student group around 1935, and I wish I could remember more. Fortunately, his books speak for him."

These testimonies are signs that Gold may be returning from exile, perhaps sooner than some believed he would. Reacting to Gold's death in 1967, journalist Robert Shaw wrote a letter to one of Gold's great advocates, Mike Folsom, in which Shaw declared, "He could have done a newspaper or magazine column that would have made him rich and famous. But my prediction is that when all the hired apologists for the status quo are dead and forgotten, the name of Mike Gold will be known to millions of people around 2067." As a step toward the fulfillment of Shaw's centenary prophecy, here are sixty-eight pieces, spanning the period from 1914 to 1966. Over half of these works have not seen the light of day since their original publication. Several selections, like the excerpts from Gold's unfinished memoirs and the powerful scene from his circa-1950 play, *The Honorable Pete*, have never been published in any form.

From Gold's early career, there are several of his anonymous columns about Harvard, alongside his first strike journalism in the anarchist *Blast*. From the 1930s there is a key scene from *Battle Hymn*, Gold's important play about the life of abolitionist John Brown. From the post–World War II years there are the three columns Gold wrote about the death of his younger brother George. These reveal the most intimate reaches of the author's character and the deep sources of his political passions. From the dark days of McCarthyism there are two manifesto-like pieces: "The Rosenberg Cantata," an excruciating lament about the most brutal moment of the Cold War, and "The Troubled Land," a touching personal essay about Gold's national speaking tour of 1954.

From Gold the activist artist there are short stories, poetry, drama, and a chapter from his novel. From Gold the political journalist there are commentaries, personal essays, and cultural criticism. You will notice a variety of genres and a variety of messages that are nevertheless shot through with a clear uniformity of voice and purpose. From World War I to Korea and Vietnam, from the 1914 Ludlow Massacre to the 1963 Birmingham church bombing, Gold consistently embodied an art best defined as the direct expression of a man who is angry about something.

But the contents of this book are only a fraction of an astonishingly large output. In this volume it's especially pleasing to include the forgotten trove of columns from the author's late-career stint with the San Francisco *People's World* (articles that were previously collected only by the FBI). From these columns we learn that Gold saw clearly what was happening in Vietnam and knew how it would end. Within them we witness Gold in his early seventies, walking with civil rights marchers in the streets of San Francisco and siding with the beatniks and hippies in their battle against the military-industrial complex. I'm glad to offer these selections to a generation that came of age long after Gold's death.

At the close of my biography of Gold, I stated: "In a period of corporate control, wealth disparity, and the mainstreaming of proto-fascism, Michael Gold should be more than ever of interest to a cultural establishment whose attention to his work has been insufficient." Since 2020 the situation has worsened and we're no longer talking about "proto" anything.

While working in Mike Gold's archived papers at the University of Michigan almost a decade ago, I came across the barely legible manuscript of *Song for Roosevelt*, a play in three acts and a prologue. This interesting drama is too long to include in full in this anthology, but I want the world to know about it. The script was completed in 1948 in France, where the author self-exiled because the Cold War was closing in and he foresaw the McCarthy era's persecutions. As I transcribed the play, I realized that Gold also foresaw what's happening now.

Song for Roosevelt reminds us that American fascism is a deep-rooted phenomenon and offers guidelines for opposing it. Though Gold's characters suffer intimidation that is both race-based and class-based, they ultimately find hope in *community-based* democratic activism. The drama is set in the neighborhood Gold knew best, Manhattan's Lower East Side. The action begins on April 12, 1945, the day of Franklin Roosevelt's death. The spokespersons for the playwright's message are two resilient young women who've lived through separate tragedies in the fight against fascism: Theresa is a twenty-six-year-old war widow and single mom, her husband killed in the 1944 battle against Axis forces at Anzio. Hannah is a refugee from Nazi Germany whose entire family—parents and two siblings—died in Hitler's gas chambers.

Adopted by the Shuster family, Hannah had arrived in New York severely traumatized, "afraid of every cop in the street" and panic-stricken when left alone. She enters the play as "a vivid, rather shy girl of 20, carrying books and flowers" but also bearing a question many are asking today: "*I can see America is different from Germany. It could never be another Germany. Just the same, fascism is growing here, also. How can that be?*"

The answer to Hannah's question follows from a depiction of New York social history. One of the forces Gold addresses is the Christian Front, an organization (composed mainly of followers of radio priest Charles Coughlin) that fomented violence against Jews. In 1945 anti-Semitic attacks were frequent enough to become the subject of an Oscar-winning short film, *The House I Live In*, starring Frank Sinatra and written (by leftist screenwriter Albert Maltz) to counteract the brutality.

Early in the play, anti-Semites emboldened by Roosevelt's death attack a barbershop co-owned by Hannah's adoptive father, Louis Shuster, after which the elderly man collapses from a stroke. Months later Louis's son Bernie, twenty-five, returns from the war against Hitler to learn that his father is comatose. He vows to avenge the assault, but Hannah pleads with him to forgo this plan and recommit to his ambition of becoming a great chemist. One way to defeat intolerance, Hannah knows, is to live a meaningful life.

While in Europe, Bernie too had witnessed the horrors of the concentration camps. Realizing that even New York is unsafe, he weighs questions about how democracies die: "How can we end the Christian Front and Blackshirts in New York? What protects them in a democracy?" He says he can't understand the dismissive attitude of some politicians toward violent hate crimes.

"It was like that in Berlin," Hannah responds ominously.

"And the South, too," adds Randy, an African American porter who dreams of becoming an inventor. He relates the story of his father's lynching, after which the police arrested his mother rather than the white murderers.

In the play's last scene, a neighborhood meeting is held in the kitchen of the Shuster tenement. Before it begins, Max Gottlieb, Louis's partner in the barbershop, wearily reminds everyone that, as "a bunch of nobodies," they are no match for the fascists. Theresa enters, "dressed for a summer night, a flower in her hair," and confidently outlines a plan: "Forget the big shots and appeal to the people of the neighborhood. Organize them." Max calls this strategy "childish," but Theresa is unfazed and offers specifics: "Parades, mass meetings, pressure on the politicians—the whole works—the same things we did to fight the black market and elect Roosevelt. Organize the people, and everything else will begin. It's like unlocking a big dam, freeing the water so it comes rushing down to turn the big dynamos that make power and light for the world!"

Cold War critics never forgave Gold his communist views. He probably knew no audience would ever hear Theresa's speech, at least in his lifetime. But when my university classes studied the play last year, its lessons resonated. One student wrote, "The strength of *Song for Roosevelt* is its message of empowerment, the encouragement to unite and fight against tyranny."

The moment seems right for Gold's message. Something Hannah says in Gold's play makes this more certain. When Bernie vows solitary vengeance for the assault on his father, Hannah challenges him to see the bigger picture: "You are a Hamlet and want to avenge," she says, "but *Hamlet* is an old story. It does not fit our time! It is too personal. It does not seek the causes of the murder, the causes of fascism, and fight that."

Only through collective action will today's fight against fascism get anywhere. And as Hannah implies, our models aren't always found in navel-gazing art, or in escapism, or in poets who only poeticize. Instead, we should be talking and teaching about people's poets like Gold, because the clock is ticking.

Part One

"Three Whose Hatred Killed Them"

Irwin Granich, *The Masses*, August 1914

On April 11, 1914, the day before he turned twenty-one, something happened to Irwin Granich that would later become central to the personal legend of Mike Gold. He became involved in the radical labor movement when he wandered into an unemployment protest in New York's Union Square, heard passionate anticapitalist speeches, and witnessed an authoritarian crackdown on the right to free assembly. The crowd was attacked by police and Irwin was beaten along with other demonstrators as he attempted to help an injured woman who reminded him of his mother. After this event, it did not take him long to place his first poem in a large-circulation magazine: "Three Whose Hatred Killed Them" appeared in Masses *in August 1914 and marked the beginning of the author's long association with that journal. The poem espouses violence in the cause of labor liberation by extolling three anarchists who were accidentally killed in a New York tenement by a bomb they had made for use against enemies of the working class. In reminding his audience that "they hated, but it was the enemy of man they hated," Irwin referred to the probable intended target of the bomb, John D. Rockefeller, who had hired heavily armed militia to crush a strike in his Colorado coal mines. On April 20, 1914, Rockefeller's private army set fire to strikers' tents, killing thirteen women and children, in the horrific Ludlow Massacre. Here Irwin Granich—who would six years later assume the name Mike Gold—documents a grave setback to the anarchist cause but eventually finds hope, treating the "undisciplined warriors" as political descendants of John Brown and precursors to renewed radical ardor.*

~

These wild, bitter men, whose iron hatred burst too soon,
Judge them not harshly, O comrades.
Forgive them their sin, for they loved much.
They hated, but it was the enemy of man they hated.
They lusted for man's blood, but it was the blood of those who shed man's blood they lusted for.
They thought to spoil God's clay, but it was to save much more of that sacred stuff that they thought this.

Think of them, dear comrades, as fellow soldiers too impatient to await the signal.
Undisciplined warriors, aflame for battle and loath to bide the issue
Until came reinforcements, fresh troops by love and reason recruited,
Singing as they came to join us, the Army of the Brotherhood of Man.

"A Freshman at Harvard"

By One of Them

Irwin Granich, *Boston Journal*, October–November 1914

In September 1914 Granich applied to Harvard University as a "special" or provisional student and was surprised to be admitted. He pretended ignorance of the fact that his provisional admission did not give him the privilege to register for regular undergraduate courses. As Dean of Admissions John Hart explained, his acceptance meant only that he could take a few classes in a specific discipline (in Irwin's case, journalism). Nevertheless, Irwin's account of his hardships—his father's death, his factory work from the age of twelve, his family's poverty—convinced the dean to grant the earnest East Side boy access to the full Harvard undergraduate course catalog.

But from the moment of his arrival in Cambridge, his studies were undercut by the fact that after paying ninety dollars for tuition and buying books, he was broke. Desperate for income and subsisting on a diet of bread and coffee, Irwin finagled an interview with the editor of the Boston Journal newspaper and pitched an idea for an anonymous column called "A Freshman at Harvard" and based on his experience as a class interloper. The editor liked the angle and miraculously offered him a salary of fifteen dollars for a six-day-per-week column.

The resulting articles, in which the alter ego "Dan Marvin" represents Irwin's thoughts and feelings, offered an insightful assessment of higher education from a working-class perspective. The column was more subversive than the Journal editors could tolerate, and the series was abruptly canceled after twenty-nine installments, forcing the anonymous freshman to leave Harvard only a few months after he'd arrived. It was the first but certainly not the last time Mike Gold paid a price for bringing discerning judgments to bear on the establishment.

~

October 19

I have never applied to Washington for a patent, nor have I enjoyed the pleasure of being in Germany in wartime, nor have I, finally, as the records will show if examined, ever given my pedigree to one gentleman in official blue while another blithely separated me from my auburn locks.

But I have just finished entering Harvard, and I think I know what the above experiences must be like. Harvard has just put me through the entrance examinations in the "Personal History of Myself," and I am feeling much as Bill Sikes must feel immediately after he has been rechristened "Number 999."

I confess I do not like all this elaborate machinery, with its cold, unhuman and mechanical mill of forms and cards and receipts of one kind or another. I realize that a great corporation like Harvard must in financial self-defense build up a complex system of administration, but I feel strongly that any such development in a university can be nothing but deplorable.

Lacking in Warmth

Education, the relation of master to learner, of teacher to pupil, has always seemed to me to be the most sacred and personal of relationships, and I am sorry to see it become so lacking in warmth and humanity. I cannot conceive of any higher good accruing from this formalization of the process of education. I do not question, however, in all fairness as to Harvard, that much of this dehumanization is but another symptom of the quantitative age we are living in.

I went with my room-mate, Dan Marvin, to the secretary's office the other day to see about Dan's admission. Dan left grammar school to go to work, not because he wanted to, but because he was too poor to have any choice in the matter. Dan has always read and thought deeply. Now he has saved some money from his wages as a printer, and he wants to get a few years of college work without undergoing any tedious schoolboy preparation for it.

Demanded Personal History

He was given a blank at the office which demanded his reasons for wanting to enter Harvard, the minute details of his personal and academic history, the names of several references and a volume of other information which it distressed Dan to contemplate.

"Look at all this," Dan said out of a wry mouth, a melancholy twist in his level blue eyes. "They must know that I'm a rough neck printer with no right to be here. Do you think I ought to tell them the truth about that grandfather of mine who was hung as a horse thief? Or do you think it might prejudice them against me?"

I smiled and tried to console Dan. "They use this blank on every special student, Dan. They haven't gotten it up just for you." "Yes, I suppose that's so," he answered. "But I sort of think they should have gotten one up for me. And why should they ask me for my reasons for wishing to enter? Don't you think they ought to give me reasons instead telling why I ought to enter?"

Professor Was Kind

But Dan finally made the blank out, giving as his reason the statement that he "wanted to learn just what the world was all about from men who knew." Professor J.G. Hart, who has charge of admissions and is a fine but over-worked gentleman, gave Dan a little kindness out of his overtaxed store, and Dan was admitted three days later, after a purely formal permission had been granted for his admittance by the various professors whose courses he was taking.

I do not suppose Dan would have ultimately been refused admission. Harvard, within its limitations, is sound and comprehending, as far as its faculty goes. But the institution itself is big, it is swollen, it has grown from the friendly, intimate center of Holmes and Emerson into a colossal machine—I would say a commercial machine if I did not yet hope to find the old beautiful spirit burning at the core of it.

[. . .] But I wish that the old days were back, when Dan might have possibly entered with no other examination but that of a heart-to-heart talk with some kindly old professor. I wish that somehow Dan might have found a warm, understanding, personal greeting awaiting him as he came from the shop with his work-worn hands and his thirsty brain. Walt Whitman and Abraham Lincoln and John Burroughs and Mark Twain and a host of other great hearts might thus be welcomed if professors possessed the gift of prophecy. And it is thus that I would have every man welcomed who is seeking the light, whatever his antecedents, and whatever promise he might hold forth. For that would be no more than that new evolving passion we call democracy, which many people think of as Christianity.

November 10

There is a certain type of businessman who brings the problems of his desk to the dinner table, the theatre, the dance party and all the other places man has dedicated to the sacred uses of play. We tolerate this species of bore as best we may, and if he has a trainer, she usually lectures him when the curtains are drawn and adjures him to refrain from "shop talk" in company.

There is a manner of shop talk, however, which can be made very acceptable, even entertaining. This is the kind a broad-minded, well-informed man knows how to indulge in—a man who can see the general outlines of the work he is in, and knows how they are correlated to the affairs of the world.

The other description of shop talk never does, however. It is this latter narrow type that one hears principally within the academic environs of a university. There have been very few student conversations that I have heard or overheard which did not center chiefly in marks and examinations. I have yet failed to hear a spontaneous discussion of the intrinsic values of the subject the discussers were debating. I have never yet heard men argue hotly the pros and cons of a question they had just left in the classroom. There seems to be no interest apparently in the inherent worth of the college courses—they are discussed only as means to an end.

[. . .] I do not know whether to credit this to the marking system or to the type of student who may require a marking system to keep him straight. I know students and a university where knowledge and not marks are the end sought. This is the People's Institute at Cooper Union in New York city. Every night approximately three hundred workingmen gather in its rooms for lectures and discussion in economic, sociological, literary and scientific courses. They come voluntarily, the act of regstration being the only formula of admittance. There is no espionage of any sort for the purpose of forcing these students to fulfill their part in the educational relation.

And yet, any night after 10, one may go in front of Cooper Union and find little knots of these men gathered in fervent prolongation of the discussions that were interrupted in the class room by the closing bell. Sometimes the instructor is with them—as keenly vibrant with the living touch of his subject as are they.

These men are in the main workingmen who are employed from eight to twelve hours daily at monotonous and physical tasks. Most of them come to the courses, which are collegiate in standard, with no other preparation than the rudiments of the grammar school. I have not the slightest doubt in the world that if they had the leisure for self-development with which the college student is gifted, they would produce some of the finest intellects in the country. The potentiality and the will are certainly to be found among them.

I wonder why college students may not be taught on this basis. Is it because they are not as eager to learn as are these hampered workingmen? If that is the case, something is wrong somewhere. Society, for its self-preservation, must use its best material to the ends that will best serve it. If these workers contain precious possibilities that are being dulled irretrievably at the bench and the machine and the counter, something must be done. And if these boys at college are so indifferent to the feast spread before them that they have to be coerced to eat, more grateful and more hungry banqueters should be sought.

November 14

The Harvard method of education seems to call for a stunning amount of outside reading. A man who is taking a full number of courses is supposed to go through an average daily total of about 100 solidly-packed pages.

It is shameful, though, that there should be so little discussion between the professor and students of the subject matter thus assimilated. Some of the courses have what are called conferences, but they are usually recitations for the purpose of ascertaining how much of the reading the students have done. There is almost no conference in the sense in which Bacon once used it. It is just the report of probationers to their probation overseer.

"Darn it all!" Dan says of this phase of higher education, "the whole process reminds me of one of the big Hoe newspaper presses. You put your roll of white paper in, you get your forms on, start the motor and then go round to the other end to get your neatly folded extras. We're the white paper, Charlie, and the profs are the type forms. That is how they seem to feel about it anyway. They think that by just letting us come into contact with their stereotyped sides we ought to take their imprints as easily and as readily as the white paper does the inked plates. It's fundamentally wrong though, Charlie, because it isn't human. We're more than machines, and they should be more than such to meet us."

November 16

I am sitting under Bliss Perry, in a course on Lyric Poetry, and for the past month he has been discussing the philosophical nature of esthetics and poetry. Bliss Perry is the editor of the *Atlantic Monthly*, and a conspicuous figure in American letters.

I must confess to the criminal fact that I have not over-enjoyed the past month. It is not the fault of Professor Perry, probably, so much as it is mine. I do not like this analytic and microscopic examination of the operations of beauty and poetry. It fulfills no practical end, it seems to me, for no laws have ever nor ever will be thus formulated for the guidance of future artists, who will always have to work, as did their predecessors, by the light of their own inward fires. This process of taking a man's work apart in the tacit assumption that one may thus surprise the secret of his genius reminds me of nothing so much as the small boy who takes apart the works of a watch and then finds he must leave them so.

[. . .] Professor Perry is a man of medium stature, with a broad, keen face that is engraved with lines of thought and responsibility, and sharp eyes that easily turn humorous. He pushes his head out from his shoulders while he is lecturing, which is a mannerism that gives him an air of intense earnestness.

Of course, he is an authority on the subject he is handling, "Lyric Poetry." But I cannot help thinking that all the warm pulsing life in that great body of emotion called Poetry has died for Bliss Perry. Vivisection usually carries death with it.

November 17

There was a thoughtful, slow smile on Dan's face Saturday morning as he opened an envelope in his mail and shook from it a sheet of notepaper to which was pinned a dollar bill. Dan read the note with the same little smile, then handed it to me. It was written in a painful scrawl on coarse white paper. In labored, unfamiliar phrases the note tried to convey what was evidently a profound and unutterable gratitude for the loan of the dollar to the writer.

I made Dan explain the circumstances of the loan to me. He was reluctant at first. Then he told me how two or three days before he had been walking on Massachusetts Avenue about three miles away from the college when a little lame man with a haggard face and brown, defeated eyes accosted him.

"Am I headed in the direction of Waltham?" Dan says he wearily asked. Dan didn't know, of course. He had a vague idea that Waltham was a goodly distance away, however. It seemed curious that the little man should be planning to walk there. So he suggested in an offhand fashion that Waltham would be quite a long walk. Yes, the man said, it would be six or seven miles distant. He thanked Dan abruptly and started to limp painfully away. Dan intercepted him, however, and asked him why he didn't ride. The man muttered some surly answer. Dan came up to him and put his arm across the man's shoulder. The little lame man broke down miserably and cried like a heartsick child.

He told Dan his story. He was a cotton mill hand whose home was in Worcester. There had been a strike there, and he had been one of the prominent union men. For this he had been blacklisted by the larger mills. The smaller ones let him have occasional work, however. This work had given out some three or four weeks before.

The little man had a wife and children to support. So he decided to go to Lawrence in search of work. For this he had taken all the money there had been in the shrunken family exchequer. He stayed at Lawrence two weeks, eating up his meager funds and not finding anything to do in the interim. Then, when all his money had been spent, sick, beaten, disheartened, he had attempted to return to Worcester. He had just enough money to get him into Boston, where he hoped to find friends. He found no friends.

Of course, Dan took him out for a meal and then set him on a car for home.

"I shall never forget the change that came over him as he gradually felt that he was being treated as a human being again," Dan said.

> He had been bitter and warped with hate when I met him. He had snarled at me when I asked him whether he intended walking to Waltham. But under the warm meal and the democratic acceptance I gave him, he thawed back to humanity. It is wonderful and strange to see the Holy Ghost enter men by way of their bellies, Charlie. The little man expanded to heroic proportions when all traces of his grief had been temporarily flooded away. And he was a hero, relatively. In his circumscribed circle of living, the little man had played a hero's part. I am not quite sure that either of us could have risen to his stature in the same conditions. I wonder whether either of us could be great enough to throw up a job and lead a strike when a beloved family at home depended for its life on what we brought it daily. I wonder whether we would dare to walk fifty miles with a crippled leg because those we had counted on had bruised our spirits and betrayed our trust. I wonder whether either of us could detach ourselves from our pressing personal crisis in the same great manner as did this little lame man, who discussed world philosophies and political economy and German literature with me—a man who had merely loaned him a few pennies.
>
> It was ennobling, Charlie, to be with him. A little shabby man he was, in rough clothes and a flannel shirt, and shoes broken and muddied. One of the coarse, yearning people who had stretched out his hands toward the light in the only expression vouchsafed him—a violent strike, for which he was now paying the price. One of the wistful, betrayed people, rude children forgetting for long intervals and then remembering with impassioned starts the high heritage of manhood awaiting their claim.
>
> Oh, Charlie, it made me love the people to see him sitting there, so big and brave in his sea of troubles. It reassured me of the hope I have in them, of their ultimate maturity, of the finest growth of the race they must become, because they are so much longer in development. It made me feel afresh that all this sacrifice will not have been in vain, that it is molding

and impregnating with nobility the force that must one day redeem all the world from its thralldom of hatred and strife.

You know, Charlie, I wished that it were somehow possible to have gotten the little man to lecture my economics class on the social problem. I know that he could give more than any professor. I know he would clarify all the maladjustments and brutal disproportions that prevail in our economic scheme of distribution. Do you think that any professor could present more vividly the social problem than he could in his short and simple annals?

Why was he poor, we might ask him? Was it not because of some deficiency in his character? Did not the best men always climb to the top in this equitable world of ours?

Then he would tell the class, as he had told me, how he had been born into a weaver's family, how he had gone to work when he was 11, how he had never dreamed that there was anything but looms and shops in this world until the labor propaganda had revealed to him the fact that he was more than a machine for weaving cloth—he was a man.

If we were at all disposed to be in sympathy with him we might read through the lines of his story. We might add to it the fact that he was no more than a normal, commonplace human being, who had been born into an environment that laid certain conditions upon him in exchange for life. He must be a weaver if he would live. There was no other choice offered him. And of course, he wanted to live. If he had had any unusual talents that insisted upon expression—if he had been musically or intellectually gifted the choice would have been still harder. He would have had to starve and be miserable in the pursuit of his ideal, or ultimately give it up in despair as a vain dream.

But he had not been gifted especially. He was just a normal, humble individual as are the majority of us, and so he had adapted himself as best he might to the environment into which he was born. He had never been tried and found wanting in the battle for the greater things of life. He had never been given the chance to enter that battle. He hadn't even realized before his awakening that there was anything more than bread and butter worth fighting for.

> The miracle and the sign unto the generation was that in spite of all the crushing forces about him he was able to respond to the awakening touch. He finally did learn to think of all his comrades in the abstract—he did learn to feel that he was but an atom in the solidly packed mass of labor—he did come to appreciate that even though an atom, his thinking and his efforts would be eternally valuable.

Charlie, this is a tremendous age. It is the race's zenith so far as we are able to read, I believe. Many great achievements must be credited it in the pages of the books to come. But, Charlie, when its sum total is balanced I feel that achievements such as the transformation of the little lame man from a machine to a man will lead all the rest. Human values will eternally be the greatest values, and the humanizing and emancipation of this great submerged portion of the race known as labor will be the most glorious chapter in the race's history. Just as America dates her greatness from the year of independence, so will the world revere one of the years of the twentieth century for its universal dawn of freedom. Charlie, it's worth fighting for.

~

The "Freshman at Harvard" columns continued for twenty-nine installments but were abruptly canceled, undoubtedly because the Boston Journal *editors got much more than they wanted. They had introduced the series with a front-page lead-in that suggested conventional amusement: "Here's a new story of life at Harvard—a freshman's experiences, a freshman's views of the great institution, told day by day as he comes in contact with the varied activities." What amusement the pieces actually delivered was decidedly subversive. Here is the final installment.*

~

November 21

The tone of Harvard today is unrecognizably different from that which prevailed in its golden age during the stirring days that revolved about the Civil War. Harvard was then a university which emphasized first, last and all the time the humanistic culture. Emerson, Holmes, Lowell, Longfellow, Agassiz, James, and the other planets of that dazzling galaxy created a wide, universal temper that enfolded all knowledge and made the heart of as much value in character building as the head. The sympathies were not allowed to wither while the intellect expanded. In the warm sunshine of the love suffused by this poet hierarchy there was grown a body of men who took all humanity as their province and who subordinated learning to living.

With ex-President Eliot the change came. He was a professor of chemistry when the responsibility of guiding the destinies of the huge institutions fell on his 35-year-old shoulders. He introduced his scientific ideals into the administration of the university and he introduced them so effectually that no corner of the university is left unpermeated by them.

"A man, to be a scholar, must have learned to give up his interest in the common occurrences of life, in the political and religious controversies of his countrymen and in everything not connected with his single aim," he said.

This was essentially the ideal of scientific Germany, and it was with German methods that President Eliot gave substance to it. That is why Harvard is now known as a Germanized university, and that is why its principal danger lies in that it has a tendency to turn out two extreme types of men—uninspired businessmen and uninspired pedants.

President Eliot used to believe that the methods of science held equally true in all divisions of knowledge and that physiology and poetry might both be taught in the same manner. He believed in the foremost value of research work and he directed the expenditures of the university with that goal ever in view.

As a result of his policies, Harvard now finds itself in possession of a scheme of administration that has isolated each of the departments, so that the professors and students comprised in them revolve in the narrow circle of the department's single aim. There is no correlation; in fact, as one of my professors said when he assigned some reading to us the other day, "There is a continuous sharp competition going on between the departments for the attention of the student."

I cannot see the prospect of good in such an internecine conflict. It must inevitably prove fatal to the development of the full, complete man the university is designed to produce. The university owes a large debt to knowledge, but I cannot see how it can avoid its debt to the community.

Dan grows impatient with this short-sightedness of the university. "Great Scott," he said the other night, when we were discussing this, "what do they want to make of a university—just one great, dreary laboratory where men enter never to depart? Science is indispensable, and pioneers in it are needed all the time, too. But, Charlie, how about the millions who never come inside a university, and who do the chores of mankind so as to leave the university free for its work? Isn't there something due them?

"There are 5000 or less students on this side of the Charles getting the advantages of civilization. What are they doing and what will they do, Charlie, to transmit this accumulated wealth to the less fortunate millions on the other side of the Charles? How is the university training them to do this? Or is it training them?

"I have always thought, Charlie, that every college man ought to go out a missionary of culture. Just as the doctor leaves his school and the divinity student his, to carry their knowledge to the world, just so ought the college man.

"I know this all sounds like the commencement day bunk, but gee, how little those two hours of baccalaureate oratory do compared to the four years they are meant to counteract!

"Why doesn't the university make it a point to practice this advice all through the college life of the undergraduate? Why, for instance, shouldn't every man be obliged to give a prescribed number of hours every week to teaching at some night school or settlement? Why isn't he trained in some form of service as part of his collegiate work? Why is the teaching allowed to become so disrupted that there is no channel through which the social conscience of the student can be developed?

"I suppose that if I were to speak to President Lowell of this he would say, 'But what would you suggest?' I don't see why anyone should suggest anything. It is enough to point out to the university that it is derelict in its duties. It is up to the university officials to remedy the deficiency.

"What good are all these individual dynamos of mental power going to be if they are not being trained to work for the community? None that I can see, other than to themselves. It reminds me of the way Dr. Elliott of New York characterized this blind spot in the university training.

"For four years these men are trained by the college to grow strong, powerful individuals. Then, on commencement day, before the cheering crowds, the university president makes a long scholarly and inspiring address, the tenor of which is briefly this—"Sic 'Em."

"Do you blame this all on President Eliot's scientific ideals?" I asked Dan.

"No," he answered, "there is one other reason."

"What is it?" I asked.

Dan jingled the quarters in his pocket and smiled significantly.

THE END

"Anarchists in Plymouth"

Irwin Granich, *Revolt*, February 5, 1916

Down and out on the streets of Boston following his Harvard misadventure, Gold discovered and embraced philosophical anarchism. Five decades later, in interviews with Mike Folsom, he vividly recalled the circumstances that led to his first piece of strike journalism:

> *"A short powerful Ukrainian house painter, with the blue luminous eyes of a child, said to me in his Slavic accent one day, "We are going to Plymouth. There is a big strike in a cordage factory, and we thought you might like to write it up for the Revolt." This was a little anarchist paper published in New York by Hyppolite Havel. Anarchist leaders all over New England were going to go along with us. Police had threatened any anarchist who came into the city with arrest, and old Luigi Galleani had taken up the challenge. Galleani had made so many eloquent speeches on the subject in little Italian halls around Boston, the meeting places of the anarchists. He had frightened the citizens so badly that it was said that the whole city was buying revolvers.*
>
> *"We got out at the station in Plymouth to walk into the biggest police parade I had ever seen. It must have been a hundred cops, some of them with tommy guns. They lined the pavement, and we walked through them with very many mixed feelings. I looked at our little band of young anarchists, innocent and non-aggressive people of that type of sentimentality that chooses the stake rather than a gift of a million dollars from some crazy millionaire. They were idealists and nobody was more idealistic*

at any time than a believing anarchist. It was the thing that had attracted me to the movement, its innocence."

~

Plymouth, if you remember the rubbish taught at school, is where the joy-hating Puritans landed. Now it is a smirchy industrial centre, sprawling and smoke-belching and hideous with the vile sores of capitalism. One of its principal products is cordage, and the Plymouth Cordage Company pays three-fourths of the town taxes. Two weeks ago, the helots who make the cordage rose in rebellion, and REVOLT will rejoice to know that anarchist tactics and leaders are the spirit of the uprising.

The company has for the past ten years been paying eight percent dividends on highly watered stock. It has multiplied its assets more than fifty-fold, and recently put half a million dollars into a new venture in Canada. Yet one slave, who has been with the company for thirty-three years, still receives the nine dollars a week he began with. He has not collected a penny of prosperity, and in all those years he and his fellow-workers have never had the guts to holler. Maybe this is because the masters are so kind, and of the enlightened capitalistic ilk. They have given the faithful serfs a cunning little club house, with real shower baths and ping pong tables, and a reading room which furnishes the *Youth's Companion* and other uplifting literature. They have given yearly free "fellowship" banquets and have always praised the honest laboring man in their annual reports.

But under the tutelage of a fringe of uncompromising anarchists, the men have at last become class conscious. There are two thousand men and women in all, mainly Italians, and they are saying to their charitable masters, "To hell with your damned ping pong games. Give them to your feeble-minded sons at Harvard. We must have bread and more liberty."

The strike was not agitated; it began quite spontaneously, as the result of a petty squabble between a foreman and two workers in the baling division. Labor interests are puzzled by the deep-rooted aversion of the strikers to any form of organization. A. F. of L. and I.W.W. leaders have been in, but can do nothing with the men. The anarchists control all. Through Luigi Galleani, the Nestor of Massachusetts anarchism, they say that the problems of every strike are unique and cannot be solved by the generalizations of a large labor body. They despise centralized per capita organizations of every kind, and affirm loyalty to labor as a whole, not to any particular faction of it. They cry that solidarity and not organization wins strikes, and are content therefore to trust to the undoubted solidarity that exists.

They may win. They ask for $12 for men and $9 for women, instead of the $9 and $6 now prevailing. Probably a compromise will be reached, for the bosses are afraid of physical violence, and the workers are flat broke.

"First Aid"

Irwin Granich, *New York Call*, July 9, 1916

Gold left New York for Mexico in 1918 to evade the World War I draft. The decision had a long political gestation, as evidenced by one of his first short stories, written about ten months before the US declaration of war on Germany.

I heard this story at a fashionable meeting for "preparedness" held here in Boston's Back Bay. The man who told it was a lean, virile, superb young Harvard patrician who had just returned from a year's service in a French ambulance corps. The war had been a divine lark for him, a cosmic picnic, where fun and nobility had been interwoven in a great pattern of chivalrous nights and days. He was very gallant and jolly, exactly like a schoolboy telling his folks at home of some big football match he had distinguished himself in. He vibrated with sheer boyish joy as he told of the rough, jovial comradeship of the trenches, or the tragic-comic accidents that befall men under fire. He was full of scraps of scarlet romance and intimate viewpoint of the Great War and he knew how to tell them pungently and well. It was all very fine, and it made the hundred or more children in the room yearn to play in the jolly game that war seemed to be.

The fashionable matrons had collected all their children on this evening and were giving what they called a "junior preparedness night." Pictures of army officers were all about the walls, framed patriotic editorials from the Hearst papers, unsheathed swords, charts and maps demonstrating the nation's inadequate defenses, rifles of various historical epochs, gaudy

Plattsburg posters, one or two lithographed battle scenes and an endless display of red, white, and blue in bunting or creamy-soft woolen flags.

There were also several glass cases crowded with relics picked up on the European battlefields, already historical though a few months old. Great shells were placed in three or four parts of the room, and a real machine gun pointed ominously from a corner.

One of the strangest contrasts was to see the impotent, amiable cackling faces of the society women against this stern background of death. One marveled at the hold this new fashion of "preparedness" had taken on them that they could move amid such suggestions with equanimity. Only the thought that the best circles were in this thing must have braced these squeamish, soft spines to the fierceness of militarism.

The Harvard man made the wrinkled, matronly eyes gleam with doting pride. He was so obviously of their "set" that his exploits reflected back upon them, and in their simple, shallow souls they gurgled with the class-conspicuousness that this hero was of their flesh and blood.

"Isn't he splendid? And isn't war ennobling? We must really import some of this for America," was what was fluttering through their minds.

He was an extremely well-bred young man with soft, sliding accents and that roundabout habit of rhetoric which is the leisure class's most stinging rebuke to the inferiors who sweat for their bread and have no time for any but blunt and direct ways.

His manners were perfect, but he made one serious faux pas during the night. It was when he told them the story I am repeating here. He should not have told it. It was too real, too true, too terrible in its nakedness for these people who had lived among lies so long. It pricked the rainbow bubble of war somehow, and revealed it for what it was—a monstrous, meaningless bath of insanity and blood.

Here is the story. It is as cruel a snapshot of the red face of Mars as any I know.

"One of the tragic sides of war for the soldier is the manner in which he loses his friends," said the patrician.

You make a pal in the trenches, some pleasant chap who is your intellectual and social equal. You spend many days and nights very close to him, talking and exchanging experiences and views on life. You get nearer each other than peace would ever bring you, and then—

Then, out of a clear sky a bomb or dart will drop into your trench or the enemy will begin hurtling shells into it and you see your friend shattered to a million bits before your eyes. You may even hear his last frantic cry, or his entrails maybe bespatter you in a red shower.

Well, it is war, and in a fight one only thinks of winning, and these things are, therefore, borne stoically and without sentiment.

I knew an officer who had to kill his own friend amid the most excruciating circumstances. It was at Verdun, during the first days of that great holocaust which is still raging. The Germans were attacking the first line trench in which the comrade-officers were stationed. For two days they bombarded ineffectually but on the third day they found the range and then a series of terrible shells fell into the trench tearing it mercilessly to pieces and burying most of the men in a great crater.

One of the two officers managed to escape with a few fortunate others, but his pal and boyhood friend was left behind cut up with big, fatal, wounds.

Soon the Germans came pouring into the trench, and a sharp fight followed for a few minutes in which the remaining French were annihilated.

Then, as the Germans were about to make ready for complete proprietorship, the French guns broke into a furious bombardment that made permanent occupation impossible. So the Germans retreated in their turn leaving their wounded and dying and dead indistinguishably mixed up with the French fallen.

And so there all of them lay huddled in that giant crater, waiting for the sun and the flies to cease torturing them and hoping of the cooling stars and relief. But no relief could be brought them, because the Germans did not dare come back and the French had shifted to another position in the battle line. Orders had come from headquarters to relinquish the trench without a struggle.

Only the officer I knew came back to find his friend. With one private he stole out under truce of night and crawled about a mile back till he found the crater with its stack of twisted groaning flesh. It must have been a nightmare spectacle, for high-explosive shells reek awful havoc where they strike. They rip men in two or shatter their heads or twist off whole limbs, or gouge away faces, till nothing is left but raw, running red meat.

The two men burrowed in the horrible reek till they found the officer's friend. From under a mound of fragmentary figures he answered weakly when they called his name.

He was wounded beyond repair. His right leg hung on a thread of skin, he was without his left arm, his chest bones stuck grotesquely through his uniform, and his chin and neck were slashed away.

When they lifted his head he screamed, then wept abjectly, "Shoot me!" he gasped to his friend, "Shoot me—for God's sake, shoot me!"

They tried to pick him from the ground, but it was impossible he was so disjointed and tattered of flesh.

"Shoot me, Frank," he wept again and again.

Suddenly a hand clutched the foot of the officer who had come to save his friend. He looked down and saw a German officer staring at him with fevered, pleading eyes.

"Shoot me, too!" the German cried in broken French. "Shoot us all, for Jesus's sake! No one will ever come to get us here. Shoot us, shoot us, shoot us!"

The officer considered what chance these men had for being rescued. Then he came to a decision. Above the mingled moans and curses of the hundred-odd men in the crater he lifted his voice high and shouted: "How many here wish me to end their misery?"

He was taking a majority vote. About ten of the wounded were able to answer with a painful yes; a few lifted their hands or tried to shake their head, many answered with their tortured eyes.

> So my friend the captain said good-by to his pal and climbed out of the pit and went back to the camp. Here he and the private gathered armfuls of hand grenades and went back to the crater. Standing at the edge, they tossed one hand grenade after the other into the cavity until they had exhausted their supply.
>
> The smoke and the echoes died away, and they listened. The soft silence of the night surged back, and that was all. No sound of life from the pit. The men were all quiet in the international peacefulness of death.

~

And that was the story. The Harvard man seemed to sense how beastly poor in taste it was at a "preparedness" meeting and he started to apologize.

"I know this is not a fitting story to be telling you young people, but war is like that," he stammered limply. "War isn't a drawing room affair, you know. And, really, what does this story prove if not that America must build up the best army and navy in the world. For only thus may she be assured that such things as these will not overtake her sons, I believe."

But the damage was irretrievably done, and nothing could bring back the holiday feeling of war to the little audience. Nobody seemed to take any more pleasure in the real machine gun or the battlefield relics. The stately Madame Cahillady shook her rosy chins determinedly and tried to whip up the belligerency of the meeting again with a request that they sing the "Star Spangled Banner."

But the words seemed to stick in everybody's throat, and the piano thumped on without an accompaniment through many mournful places.

All the little girls who had come to hear how nobly they would sew bandages in war time were as pale as the bandages. The amiable dowagers were abnormally still; not a saving superficiality could they bring to their lips. And the Boy Scouts grew hushed as if weighted down with knowledge too great to bear. In the hush one little fellow in khaki suddenly fell a-weeping.

"To One Dying"

Irwin Granich, *New York Call*, August 13, 1916

Near the end of his life Gold recalled his first impulse toward poetry: "I was a shipping clerk in a place on lower Broadway in the cotton goods district. I used to deliver heavy bundles that a truck horse would have rejected. My boss was so stingy he would not even get a hand truck. So we had to carry these heavy bundles which often weighed a hundred pounds on our backs and shoulders. I wrote a poem, on the boss's time, called 'Nails,' and I remember this scrap of paper and the lead pencil that I used then and that I still use for poetry."

Gold believed that millions of scraps of this sort of writing were produced every day by workers, but no one observed it. What mattered was that the impulse for such literary efforts was natural, born "not out of theory but out of struggle, out of the actual tortured flesh" of working people: "What else would you call it but proletarian?" he asked, "and what sort of stuff was it made of . . . but life itself?"

~

Like me, when young, your heart was
 a drum beating for revolution.
And to its roll you marched down the
 white-hot years, a soldier of
 Light.
Never faltering, Old Man, never straggling
 where fields were cooler
 than the roadway,

Never yielding to the glittering lures
of sophistry.
Ever fearless, valorous, wistful, ever
marching to a rose-red high
dawn.
And now Death.
Death in a bleak hole of poverty,
Away from the seas and the skies,
Trumpets and the war of men.
So long, Old Man, it is death, and,
though I weep for you,
I must kiss you once and bid you
farewell.
You must bury yourself, for you are
the past,
And your place in the van waits and
calls me with cries, calls with
cries!

"A Damned Agitator"

Irwin Granich, *New York Call*, March 4, 1917

One of the last persons Gold saw during his first visit to the Soviet Union in 1924–25 was "Big" Bill Haywood, the great IWW leader who had fled into exile in 1921 after his conviction and sentencing to twenty years in prison on Espionage Act charges. The two had a long talk one evening in the kitchen of Haywood's dingy Moscow apartment. Undeniably it was a bleak and lonely last phase of Haywood's life; overweight, largely immobile, and addicted to alcohol, he had lost his vigor but not his will. The meaning of the labor leader's struggle, clearly nearing its end, deeply impressed Gold.

"A Damned Agitator" is based in part on Haywood's exploits as an organizer of notorious labor actions including the legendary pre–World War I textile strikes in Lawrence, Massachusetts and Paterson, New Jersey. When Moscow party officials proposed a Russian-language edition of the 1924 pamphlet, The Damned Agitator and Other Stories, *Gold suggested that Haywood write the introduction. In the title story, revised and republished several times between 1917 and 1929, Haywood surely discerned echoes of his own experience. This is the earliest version.*

~

THE STRIKE was now smoldering into its seventh week, and, perhaps, it would soon be a bitter ash in the mouths of the men. For funds were at an ebb, scabs were coming in like a locust plague, the company officials were growing more and more militant in their self-righteousness, and the strikers themselves were drifting into a settled state of depression and dangerous self-distrust. Their solidarity was beginning to show fissures and aching cracks.

All these woeful conditions beat in like a winter sea on the tired brain of Kurelovitch with the bleak morning light that waked him. He lifted his throbbing head from the pillow, looked about the dingy bedroom with his bleary, sleep-glazed eyes, and heaved a long, troubled sigh out of his pain.

At a meeting of company executives once Kurelovitch had been denounced as a dangerous agitator, whose pathological thirst for violence had created and sustained the strike.

"The man is a menace, a mad dog, whose career ought to be stopped before he does more mischief," said one venerable director, his kind, blue eyes developing a pinkish glare that would have horrified the women folk of his family.

"The scoundrel's probably pocketing half of the strike funds," declared another director with plump, rosy gills and a full, bald head that glittered like a sunset cloud, as he stunned the long table with a blow of his balled fist.

But Kurelovitch was not a mad dog, and he was not waxing fat with industrial spoils, as so many of the directors had. He was really a tall, tragic, rough-hewn Pole, who had been suddenly hammered into leadership by the crisis of the strike, by reason of his unquenchable integrity and social fire. He had deep, blue, burning eyes, a rugged nose and moustache, and his hands and form were ungainly, work-twisted symbols of the life of drudgery he had led.

Now he was thinking wearily of all the thorny problems that would be heaped upon him that day in the course of the strike. As he extricated himself from the bedclothes and sat up to dress, the problems writhed and clamored in his jaded brain for solution. For seven weeks now he had risen almost at dawn and had labored till midnight at the Titan task of wringing a fifteen per cent increase out of capitalism for his fellow workers. He had grown gaunt and somber and wise in the process; skeptical of man and of God. He had seen plans collapse, heads broken unjustly, sentences inflicted by corrupt judges, babies and women starving. He had heard himself assailed as a monster by the other camp and as a weakling and tool by the more embittered of his own side.

His wife heard him sigh, and she called from the kitchen, where she was already stirring. "There ain't no coffee for you this morning, Stanislaw," she announced in a sullen voice, in which there was also anger and scorn. "And there ain't no nothin' else to eat, only a few hunks of old bread."

Kurelovitch stumbled wearily to his feet and entered the malodorous kitchen. Greasy pans and platters and sour garbage were strewn about, and in an opaque cloud of smoke his wife was hovering over the stove, their fourth child mewing in the nest of her arms. She was heating all the milk she had for the infant, and when her husband came in she turned on him with swift virulence.

"No, not a taste of food in the house, damn you," she spat. "And the kids went to bed last night without hardly any supper."

"But it's not my fault now, is it, Annie?" the big man returned humbly as he went over to her and put an arm over her shoulder. She cast it off with fierce contempt, and stood him off with a volley of words that were like poisoned arrows, each piercing straight to his vital parts.

"It is your fault, you clumsy fool, you," she screamed out of her over-laden heart. "You were one of the first men to go out on strike, even though we hadn't a penny in the house at the time. And last week when the company wanted the men to come back you talked them out of it, and so we're all still starving, thanks to you."

"But, Annie—" the tall man attempted gently.

"Don't Annie me, or try to fool me with one of your speeches. You know the strike's lost as well as I do, and that after it you'll be blacklisted in every mill town in New England. But you don't care if your children starve, do you? You'd be glad to see us all dead wouldn't you?"

The man had crumpled under the attack, and he seemed as small almost as his infuriated wife. But then he straightened in the dusty pallor of the kitchen, and moved to the door.

"I'll see that you get a lot of groceries and things from headquarters this morning," he said huskily, as he went out into the dark, bitter streets.

Kurelovitch shivered at his contact with the gray, sharp air. A thin ash of snow had fallen through the night, and was now a noisome slush, after its brief experience with the mill town, which degraded everything it touched. The muddy ooze squirmed through the vulnerable spots in his shoes, and started the gooseflesh along Kurelovitch's spine. Across the river in the drab morning he could see the residential heights where the rich dwelt, and they reminded him of the village of his youth, with its girdle of snow-crowned hills and peaceful cottages. He remembered a Polish lullaby his mother used to sing to him, and shivered the more.

From the rough bridge which bound the split halves of the town he could see the mill, glowering and blocking shadows deep as ignorance on the rotting ice of the river. The resplendent emblem of America gleamed and waved from a staff on the low, sprawling structure as if to sanctify all that went on beneath. And now Kurelovitch had traversed a morass of decaying huts and offal-strewn streets and was directly within the massive shadow of the mill. Two or three of his fellow-workers recognized him, and came hurrying forward from the picket line. Kurelovitch's day had begun.

"The damned gunmen are out for fight this morning," said a sombre, chunky Pole, swathed in old burlap and a tremendous fur cap that had come from Europe.

"Yes, they must have gotten more booze than usual last night," said another striker between his chattering teeth.

A young picket with brooding, dark eyes burst out with a hot voice, "Well, we'll give them any fight they want, the dirty lice. We're not afraid." Kurelovitch put his hand on the young chap, and then the three went with him to where about fifty or more of the strikers were shifting slowly up and down the length of the wide mill gate.

There were men and women in the line, all dark and silent and seeming more like a host of mourners than anything else in the world of bitter sky and slush-laden earth. They were muffled to the chins in grotesque rags, and their breaths went up like incense in the chill morning. A mood of sadness and suspense hung about them, and whenever they passed the knot of gunmen at the gate they turned their eyes away almost in grief.

Two of the gunmen had detached themselves from the evileyed mob huddled, like a curse, at the gate. They carried clubs in their hands, and at their hips could be seen bulging the badges of their mission in life, which was to break strikes and to murder.

They came up to Kurelovitch and sneered at him with sadistic eyes. As he walked up and down in the sluggish picket line, they dogged him and used their vilest art to taunt him into resistance.

About an hour later, as he was departing from the line, the two gunmen still followed him. A little group of pickets, therefore, formed themselves in a cordon about Kurelovitch and escorted him to the strike headquarters, burning all the way with repressed rage. Kurelovitch was a marked man in the strike zone, and his maiming was a subject of much yearning and planning by the gunmen.

The daily meetings of the strikers were held in a great barnlike structure in the center of the tangled streets and alleys of the mill-workers' quarter. A burst of oratory smote Kurelovitch as he entered the great room and a thousand faces, staring row on row, orientated to the leader as he marched in.

"Kurelovitch, Kurelovitch has come," ran a murmur like wind through a forest.

Kurelovitch leaped on the rough stage, where others of the strike committee were sitting, and whispered in consultation with a fellow Pole.

He learned that there was nothing of moment that day—no sign from the bosses nor funds from sympathizers. It was merely another of the dark days of the strike.

"But many of the Russians are getting restless," the man whispered. "Raviloff has been at them, and yesterday their priest told them to go back. Give 'em hell, Kurelovitch!"

Kurelovitch came to the edge of the platform in a hush like that of an operating room, looking out over a foam of varied faces. They were faces that had blown into the golden land on the 12 winds of the world, though about nine-tenths of the faces were the broad-boned, earthy, beautiful faces of mystic Slavdom. Daylight struggled through large, smutty windows and dusted the heads and shoulders of the strikers with a white, transcendent powder. A huge oilcloth behind Kurelovitch proclaimed in big, battering letters, "We Average $9 a Week and We Are Demanding 15 Per Cent More. Are You With Us?"

The air tightened as Kurelovitch loomed there, a sad hero, stooped and gaunt with many cares. Finger-deep hollows were in his cheeks, and, with his blazing eyes and strong mouth, he seemed like some ascetic follower of the warrior Mohammed.

"Fellow workers . . ."

In low, thrilling Polish he began by disposing of the secular details of the strike, as on every day. Then something would come over Kurelovitch, a strange feeling of automatism, as if he were indeed only the voice that this simple-hearted horde had created out of their woe. The searing phrases would rush from his lips in a wild, stormy music, like the voice of a gale, and as mystic and powerful.

With both hands holding his breast, as if it were bursting with passionate vision, Kurelovitch lifted his face in one of his superb moments and flamed up like an Isaiah.

"Fellow workers," he chanted, giving the words a value such as cannot be transmitted by mere writing, "we can never be beaten, for we are the workers on whose shoulders rest the pillars of the world and in whose hands are the tools by which life is carried on. Life, liberty and happiness—let us not rest till we have gotten these for ourselves and our children's children! Let us not permit the accidents of a strike to stay us on our journey toward the beautiful city of freedom, whose grace is one day to shine on all the world.

"We are beginning to starve, some of us, but let us starve bravely, for we are soldiers in a greater and nobler war than that which is bleeding Europe. We are soldiers in the class war which is finally to set mankind free of all war and all poverty, all bosses and hate. Workingmen of the world, unite; we have nothing to lose but our chains; we have a world to gain!"

Kurelovitch ended in a great shout, and then the handclapping and whistles rose to him in turbulent swirls. He found himself suddenly weary and limp and melancholy, and his deepest wish was to go off somewhere alone to wait until the hollow places inside were refilled. . . .

But, with the others of the strike committee, he left the platform and fused into the discussions that were raging everywhere. Everybody tried to come near Kurelovitch, to speak to him. He was a common hearth at which his people crowded and shouldered for warmth, his starving, wistful people who believed him when he said they could wipe out the accumulated woe of humanity. . . .

He was treated to long recitals of the workings of the proletarian soul in this time of want and panic and anger. He heard a hundred tales of temptation, of desperate hunger, of outrages at the hands of gunmen. Kurelovitch listened to it all like a grave, kind father confessor, untying many a Gordian knot with his clear-eyed strength and understanding.

And then came to him Raviloff, the leader of the Russians, a short, black, wrinkled man, with slow eyes that became living coals of fire when passion breathed on them.

He was angry to impotence now. "You said in your speech that I was a traitor, Kurelovitch," he shouted fiercely. "You lie; I am not. But we Russians think this strike is lost, and that we'd all better go back before it's too late."

"It's not lost," Kurelovitch replied slowly. "The mills can't work full time until we choose to go back. And, Raviloff, I say again that you're a scab and traitor if you go back now."

Raviloff flushed purple with wrath, and rushed upon the tall Pole as if to devour him. But Kurelovitch did not lift his stern, calm gaze from the other's face, and a light like that of swords came and went in his blue eyes. The Russian surged up and touched him, chest to chest, and then Kurelovitch intrigued the other into a sensible discussion that served to keep the Russian on the firing line. . . .

And thus it went. So Kurelovitch passed his day, moving from the swooning brink of one crisis to another. He sat with the strike committee for many hours in a smoky room and agonized over ways and means. He addressed another large meeting at headquarters in the afternoon. He went out on the picket line and was singled out for threats and taunts again by the gunmen, so that he felt murder boiling in his deeps and left. Then he had to return later to the picket line because word was rushed to him that five of the pickets had been arrested in a fight finally precipitated by the gunmen. Kurelovitch spent the rest of the afternoon scurrying about and finding bail for the five.

Toward night he had a supper of ham sandwiches and coffee, and then he and three of the strike committee went to a meeting of sympathizers about fifteen miles away. Kurelovitch made his third passioned address of the day, and stirred up a large collection. The long, dull, wrenching ride home followed.

He got off the trolley car near his house about midnight, his brain whirling and hot, his heart acrid and despairing. The urgency of the fight was passed, and nothing was left to buoy him against his weariness. He walked in a stupor; the day had sucked every atom of his valor and strength. He wished dumbly for death; he was the cold ashes of the flaming Kurelovitch of the day. Had gunmen come now and threatened him he would have cringed and then wept.

There was a feeble light waning and wavering in the window of his little three-room flat, and when he had fumbled with the lock and opened the dilapidated door he found someone brooding with folded arms near the stove. It stood up awfully and turned on him with baleful eyes, like a wild beast in its cave. "You rotten dog!" his wife screamed at Kurelovitch in the vast quiet of the night. "You mean and dirty pig!"

"Annie, dear—"

"To go away in the morning and leave us to starve! To send food to others' families and then to forget us! Oh, you'd be glad if we all died of starvation! You'd laugh to see us all dead, you murderer!"

Kurelovitch was too sorrowful to attempt an answer. He went to the bedroom where he and two of the children slept and shut the door behind him. His wife took this for a gesture of contempt, and her frenzy mounted to a blood-curdling crescendo that ran up and down the neighborhood like a ravaging blight. Heads popped out of windows and bawled to her to cease for Christ's sake. And, finally she broke down of sheer exhaustion and Kurelovitch heard her shuffling into bed.

There was anguished silence, and then Kurelovitch heard his poor, overburdened drudge of a wife weeping terribly, with gulping sobs that hurt him like knives. . . .

And now he could not sleep at all, even after her sobbing had merged into ugly snoring. He tossed as in a fever, as he had on so many other nights of the seven frantic weeks of the strike.

He went blindly for relief to the window, beyond which reigned the cold, inimical night. The shabby slum street dwindled to an obscure horizon, and the mass of the mill building could be seen dominating over the ragged houses. No being was abroad in the desolate dark; he saw a chain of weak lanterns casting morbid shadows, and the vicious wind whipping up the litter of the streets. The stars were white and high overhead, as distant as beauty from the place where Kurelovitch burned with sleeplessness. He heard the rattling, gurgling snore of his wife.

Kurelovitch ached with his great need of forgetfulness. As he twitched on his humid bed the days that had gone and the darker days to come ranged about and taunted him like fiends. The feeling that he held the fate of the strike in his hand rested on him monstrously, and his starving children made him gasp and cry like one drowning.

In dumb anguish he prayed unconsciously to the power of the righteousness, to God or whatever fate it was that had brought him into the world. But no relief came that way, and, finally, after a struggle, he groped with all his pangs to a little dresser in the room, where he searched out a brandy bottle. This he took to bed with him, and drank and drank and drank again, till the past and the more terrible future were blurred in kindly night, and the great dark wings of peace folded over him and he sank into the maternal arms of oblivion.

On the morrow he would wake and find the ring of problems haunting him again, and he would grapple them again in his big, tragic fashion till his soul bled with many fresh wounds as he stumbled home in the night. And thus he would go on and on till he was broken or dead, for Kurelovitch had dared to spit into the face of the beast that reigns mankind, and never for this sin would he be permitted to know sweetness or rest under the wide shining range of the heavens.

"Birth: A Prologue to a Tentative East Side Novel"

Irwin Granich, *The Masses*, November–December 1917

An early draft of the autobiographical material that eventually became Jews Without Money *(1930).*

~

I was born (so my mother once told me), on a certain dim day of April, about seven in a morning wrapped in fog. The streets of the East Side were dark with grey, wet gloom; the boats of the harbor cried constantly, like great, bewildered gulls, like deep, booming voices of calamity. The day was somber and heavy and unavoidable, like the walls of a prison about the city. And in the same hour and the same tenement that bore me, Rosie Hyman the prostitute died, and the pale ear of the same doctor heard my first wails and the last quiverings of her sore heart.

I saw it all afterward through the simple words of my mother, a strange and mournful picture. The doctor had stayed at my mother's bedside all through the night, for her labors had come on her soon after she had disposed of the supper dishes, suddenly, dreadfully.

"Ay, ay, when does it end, dear doctor?" she had moaned all night, while the newly-bearded young practitioner rested his tired, anemic face on his hand and stole moments of sleep.

He would flutter his eyelids to show her he was alert and sympathetic.

"Patience, only patience," he mumbled over and over in Yiddish, as he pressed her hand. He was not long out of school, and had not grown too professionally familiar with the vast misery which is the physician's East Side.

All through my mother's travail my father sat under a jaundiced gas-jet in the kitchen, drinking *schnapps* and weeping; this was all he was fit for in time of strain or sorrow. My father was a slim, cleanshaven, unusual kind of Jew, who had been the gay blacksheep of his family in Rumania, loving joy and laughter as only young thoughtless people can love them. He had capped a career of escapades by running away to America and freedom at the age of nineteen, and had struggled unhappily since then. He had a broad nose, cheek bones wide as twin hills, and black proud eyes. He must have been a dancing flame of life in his youth, for once I saw him at a wedding where he shook off the years and flashed with a glad, wild, imaginative revelry such as I had never beheld in him. The poverty of the golden, promised land had eaten his joy, however, and mostly I knew him as a sad, irritable, weakly sort of father, who drank in the troubled times when the family needed him, and who loved us all to maudlinity.

"And now how is she, Herr Docktor?" my father whispered anxiously every fifteen minutes through the door, for the doctor had detected his fundamental pessimism and had barred him from the sick room.

"She is well, she is all right, please go away!" the doctor would call back impatiently. My father would wring his hands, and would creep back like a doleful, homeless dog to his vigil by the stove in the kitchen. All night he sat there like a mourner at an orthodox funeral, weeping and drinking and despairing of the harshness of life, and the pain God had put into the world for reasons unknown.

"It is so hard to live, so hard!" my father would sigh in his sad, tearful voice. He was always saying this, I remember, and in a hurt, wondering voice, as if it were a fresh discovery with him every day. My father was never anything but a child, and hunger and pain and toil and meanness he never grew accustomed to, as grown men must. He hated them without understanding them, as a child hates the rod.

The night ebbed away slowly, the hours moving over the East Side with the solemn pace of a funeral cortege. Dawn came on. It grew like a pallid mushroom in the spaces between the tenements, the great heads of the houses lifting themselves languorously in the light, like monstrous vegetation, and a few early men and women hurrying in the shadows as the white lances pricked them. Bakers' wagons lumbered through the fog; there were throaty grumblings of distant elevated trains, gongs, a horn, and other strange, cloaked morning sounds. The light spread like an infection; ashy clouds of it rolled through the windows and lay on my tortured mother, and the leaden-eyed doctor, and my father with his *weltschmerz* and brandy under the gas flame.

My mother breathed easier with the dawn, and she stirred in her humid bed and called through the door, "Rueben, you are sleeping?"

My father sprang up theatrically. "No, no, how could I?" he cried with passion. "You are feeling better, my dear little heart? Soon it will be over, my sweet little bird?"

"Yes, yes," was my mother's impatient reply. "And now get some coffee and rolls for the poor doctor here!"

So my father puttered about with various utensils in his vague way, till the brown coffee was bubbling like a happy fountain on the stove, and rich, odorous steam filled all the air with promise.

"I can find no milk!" my father wailed after one of his puerile searches. "Where is the milk, Yettala?"

"One goes out and gets it at the grocery, fool!" my mother said. "I think you would starve to death if there was no one near to tell you the simplest things, Rueben. And get some rolls; *Wiener* rolls, tell them!"

So my father threw his musty old coat over his shoulders, peasant-wise, and stamped out into the unwholesome dark of the tenement. There must have been tiny gems of gaslight glowing on every floor, as there still are in early dawn on the East Side, and strange shadows must have brooded in every corner and risen and followed him as he moved through the queer gloom, his nostrils filled with the packed odors of crowded bedrooms, old cooking, garbage and faulty sanitation, the immemorial mingled smell of poverty.

On the stoop of our tenement (so my mother told me), my father stumbled on a huddled thing that rose and accosted him. There was the dingy morning light to see by, and under an enfolding shawl my father beheld the great, sad, bewildered eyes of Rosie Hyman, the prostitute.

The East Side was rampant with prostitution then; Jewish "daughters of joy" beckoned openly from every tenement doorway during all the hours of day and night. So numerous were they that they did not even lose caste with their more respectable and hard-working neighbors; for their way of life was charged to the general corrupting influence of America, where the children of Israel break the Sabbath, eat of the unholy pig, and otherwise neglect the God of their fathers. My mother was one of Rosie Hyman's best friends.

"Rosie, you are up too early! What is wrong?" my father exclaimed, seeing some tragedy in her brooding eyes.

"I could not sleep," the girl answered, almost painfully. "It is too warm in my room."

"Too warm?" my father cried. "When everyone is shivering in this devil's weather?"

"Yes," the girl said shortly. "How is Mrs. Gottlieb now?"

"Ach, the same," my father sighed, shaking his head piteously. "It is so terrible to bring a child into the world! All night I have been weeping for my Yettala!"

"It is terrible," the girl said, her face darkening. "Why did you do it, then?"

My father's cheeks ran with tears. "Because I am weak, God curse me! Am I not weak, Rosie, say? Already I have two children, and here is another who will have to suffer with them. Am I not a murderer?"

Rosie had always been kind, and now she tried to comfort my father. She raised a hand through her great, red shawl and touched his shoulder.

"We are all weak before love," she said softly. "And it is not our fault, Mr. Gottlieb. God made us so."

My father wept on. "God made us so, and then He punishes us for it," he uttered with choked voice.

"Yes, that is life," the girl said. "And we poor will only be happy in the grave, Mr. Gottlieb."

"Yes, yes, yes," my father sighed, moving away as he remembered his errand. "And now go back to bed and snatch a little sleep, Rosala."

She did not answer, but stood looking after him with great, sad eyes, like a dying thing taking its last fill of vision.

When my father returned from the grocery he found her a twisted heap on the stoop, writhing like a cut worm when he reached down and touched her.

"Rosala, Rosala, what is the matter?"

Nothing coherent came from her, and my father sped and brought back the sleepy doctor. Now she was stark and silent. The doctor put down her wrist with an air of finality.

"She is dead," he announced in his young and pompous way, fingering an empty phial he had found near her. "Why do you think she did it?"

"The man she loved left her, I think," my father said. "Doctor, it is very hard to live!"

"Um-m," the doctor muttered, and went back to my mother. The news could not be kept from her, and she wept and lamented in the heart-rending Jewish manner for more than half an hour.

Then I was born.

My father hurried to tell all the neighbors, and brought back some of the women to act as nurses. It was about noon when the doctor was finally able to leave.

My father offered him three shabby one-dollar bills for his fee.

"And is this all?" the young man cried fiercely, waving the green, ragged things in a gloved hand.

"It is all we have, Herr Docktor," my father said feebly, with a shamed, red face.

"Beggars!" the doctor stormed, throwing the poor bills on the table contemptuously, and sweeping out of the door. "Buy food with it!" he shouted over his shoulder on the landing.

My father picked the bills up and regarded them long and sadly. Then he shrugged his shoulders, and went into the room where my mother was still weeping with pain.

Money

By Michael Gold

Money was performed by the Provincetown Players on a bill with works by Edna Ferber and Djuna Barnes in January 1920 and was published nine years later in One-Act Plays, *an anthology of short drama intended for use in secondary schools. One of the editors who selected* Money *for publication just before the 1929 stock market crash wrote prophetically of the play as a "typically American" drama that "succeeded in throwing light on one of our most complex sociological problems."*

Describing the plot and subject matter much later, Gold acknowledged Maxim Gorky as a strong influence. The immigrant Jews who "starve and suffer in an old basement as many of them did at the time" resemble the down-and-out characters in Gorky's 1902 drama The Lower Depths.

~

CHARACTERS

MOISHA, *a cobbler*
YONKEL, *a peddler*
ABRAM, *a porter*
HYMAN, *a peddler*
MENDEL, *a factory worker*
POLICEMAN

SCENE: *A gloomy East Side cellar, a cobbler's shop by day, now in the deep of night, the sleeping place of five weary men. In the darkness their forms are seen vaguely, like queer distorted sacks flung on these old mattresses. No sheets cover them, and they are dressed in undershirts and pants. Some wear socks, others are barefooted. Three or four wooden steps, seen through a glass window, lead up to the East Side street of tenements and night. A faint shaft of light from an arc lamp breaks through the glass window of the door and illuminates the cellar with a goblin glow.*

Four of the men are sleeping; one of them snores. But the fifth, REB MOISHA, *the cobbler himself, is sitting up on his mattress and uttering mournful sighs. He is a thin, pale man, with a reddish beard, feverish eyes, and shoulders hunched by long years at the bench.*

MOISHA. (*in a low voice, so as not to disturb the others*) Gottenu, Gottenu, Gottenu! (*He sighs again, then slowly lifting himself, and stepping softly as a thief, he lights a candle and looks around the shop, sighing all the while. One of the sleepers stirs restlessly and MOISHA stands stock still. A moment later he is searching again.*) Where is it? Where can it be? (*He feels about the walls, under and above his cobbler's last, everywhere. He wrings his hands.*) Is it really gone? Gottenu, gone?

(*The restless* SLEEPER *stirs again, and then sits up and looks at* MOISHA. *He is a very thin little Jew, a shoelace peddler, with anemic body and a black wiry beard that stands out sharply on his pallid face.*)

YONKEL. Again you wake me, Moisha. I am a weak man; I must sleep; the doctor of the big hospital said I need rest.

MOISHA. I know—forgive me, Yonkel. You know what I am looking for.

YONKEL. But why should you wake me? Is it right? And for a whole week it has been—for a whole week. Every night I must lie here and listen to you looking—looking—looking.

MOISHA (*humbly*) It comes on me, Yonkel. All day I work and put it out of my head. I say, "Well it is past, the money is gone, now I will begin another struggle." But in the night, when there are no shoes to be mended, when I am alone, then it comes. I must look. I cannot help it.

YONKEL. But the money is gone, Moisha. You are looking for a shadow. You lost it somewhere, in the street or somewhere. Be a man. Go to sleep, and stop worrying.

MOISHA. (*eagerly*) No, it is here. It *must* be here. How *could* it be any other place? See how I came to lose it, Yonkel, and tell me whether the money could have been lost any place else but in this cellar. Listen. This is how it was: it was seven o'clock that night, and I sat here alone counting the money, one hundred dollars in bills, five-dollar and ten-dollar bills, twelve dollars in silver, one hundred and twelve dollars in all. As I was counting, I heard a customer coming down the steps, so I quickly tied up the money in my handkerchief and put it—

YONKEL. (*impatiently*) I have heard all this before, Moisha. What do you want of my life? Sleep, in God's name, sleep! (*He lies down himself.*)

MOISHA. (*mournfully, sitting down on his mattress*) Yes, I will do as you say. I will try to sleep, Yonkel. I will shut my eyes and maybe peace will come. (*Shuts his eyes for a moment.*) But it is no use, Yonkel!

YONKEL. Ai, let me alone.

MOISHA. (*mumbling, then rising to wail*) No use. One cannot shut out the world and its troubles by shutting one's eyes. It is here Yonkel, in my blood, in my brain, in my heart. It is a disease only death can cure. Yes, O God, let me die. Be kind. When a cat or dog is very sick, men kill it. Be as kind, O God. My heart is broken, and you let me live on and suffer. Why is this, oh God? Why—

ABRAM. (*A stout, outright sort of Jew, a carpenter with sparse, black beard and big voice, wearing a red flannel undershirt. He turns on his mattress and looks at* MOISHA *sleepily.*) Why is what, Moisha? Did you speak to me?

YONKEL. Ai, he is looking for his money again, Abram!

ABRAM. Can't you sleep, Moisha?

MOISHA. How can I? You understand.

YONKEL. (*sharply*) How can we? We have our troubles, many as great as yours. No man is happy. See, I have been sleeping, and I know that in a few years I may die. The doctor said so, but what can I do?

MOISHA. The money *must* be here somewhere. Any one can see that.

YONKEL. (*in a loud voice*) Moisha, I swear it, I swear it on my mother's grave, that if you keep me awake another night, I will take my mattress and move. I pay you a dollar a month rent, and I have my rights. I will stand no more.

ABRAM. (*putting up his hand*) Shah, Yonkala, shah, not so loud. You seem to take Moisha's wandering at night more bitterly than all of us. It is not necessary.

YONKEL. I am sorry for him, Abram, But he must not be a fool. And I am a sick man, God knows, and I must have fresh air and good food and rest, the doctor said.

ABRAM. All right, just let him alone and he will go to bed. Won't you, Moisha?

MOISHA. (*taking up candle and looking at them pitifully*) Just once more I will look for the money and then I will not bother you again. Just once. It must be here. Money is not like water, to run away into the cracks or be dried up into the air. It *must* be here. Gottenu, it must be—(*His voice goes off into a pitiful mumbling, as he taps and feels about the cellar in its corners with the candle in his hand.*)

ABRAM. (*calling after him*) Moisha, what is the use, there is nothing to do. The money is gone, so take up your burden again and be brave. This will not help.

MOISHA. (*mumbling*) Yes, Abram. Yes, Abram. (*But he continues looking.*)

ABRAM. (*whispering to the peddler* YONKEL) Did you see the look in his eyes? Like a fire, Yonkel, that burns him up. He will go crazy.

YONKEL. No, he will get over it, with God's help.

ABRAM. I am afraid for our poor Moisha, Yonkel. I fear for him.

YONKEL. Men have lost money before.

ABRAM. Yes, but it is a terrible thing to work a whole year for the devil. And see what the money meant to Moisha. We would weep, too, if we had lost it.

YONKEL. Yes, it meant everything to him.

ABRAM. We all know you love money, Yonkel, but not for the same reasons as Moisha. You would not need to suffer so much if you had lost—how much was it he lost, Yonkel?

YONKEL. (*indifferently*) About one hundred and twelve dollars, he said.

ABRAM. (*musing*) One hundred and twelve dollars! To Rothschild it would mean nothing. And for Moisha it means life and death. Everything is so different for the rich and the poor. I think God made two worlds for us to live in. (*The Carpenter sighs in his beard.*)

YONKEL. Better call him again, Abram.

ABRAM. Yes, we must get him to bed. Moisha!

MOISHA. (*looking up*) Just a minute. I will look in this other corner, and then come.

ABRAM. Ai, let him look. Let him hope. It is better than nothing.

YONKEL. But hope won't find his money. And there isn't a hole or corner or spider's web of this old cellar he hasn't searched.

ABRAM. If we could only help him! If we only knew where the money is! How do you think it was lost, Yonkel?

YONKEL. How should I know? Am I a fortune teller?

ABRAM. Well, what do you think anyway?

YONKEL. (*indifferently*) I don't know. He lost it in the street maybe; or maybe it was stolen from him. Who can tell?

ABRAM. (*musingly*) Stolen? How do you know? I never thought of that. Yes, it might have been stolen. But how? Who would have done such a thing?

YONKEL. (*annoyed*) Why do you ask me? I didn't say I knew it was stolen. I only said I *thought* so. It is—

(*They hear a loud crash.* MOISHA *has stood up suddenly and has thrown over two empty packing cases in the back of the room. He is coming toward them excitedly, the candle fluttering. The two other sleeping Jews have been roused by the sound and are looking around them dazedly.*)

MENDEL. (*one of the two, a young, sickly man with a slight moustache; a sweatshop worker*) What was that?

ABRAM. (*to* MOISHA, *who stands over him*) Have you found it, Moisha?

MOISHA. No, no, but I heard what Yonkel just said! Is it true Yonkel?

HYMAN (*the other of the two sleepers, a white-haired old man, with a feeble, high voice*) God in heaven, the money again? You are like an owl, Moisha, crying as soon as it is dark.

MOISHA. (*almost hysterical with excitement*) Yes, but listen, Hyman, Yonkel has just told me something new. He says the money was stolen. Perhaps we will find it now. Oh, who stole my money, Yonkel, who was it stole my money?

MENDEL. (*in a despairing wail*) God in heaven, no sleep again.

YONKEL. (*fiercely, like a trapped beast*) What is the matter with you two? Are you both crazy? Or are you trying to drive me crazy? I drop a word and you make a mountain of it. Have I said I knew the money was stolen, Abram? I said it might have been stolen. That was all. Now let me alone.

MOISHA. But it is true, it is plain, it is clear. Yonkel just said—

ABRAM. (*soothing him*) No, he only said he *though*t the money was stolen. That is true, Moisha.

HYMAN. Why did you put such a thought in his head, Yonkel?

MOISHA. (*obsessed now by the idea*) Abram, it is plain as day to me now. Why have I not seen it before? Have my brains been stolen, too? It does not matter what Yonkel said, but I know now the money was not lost. It was stolen.

ABRAM. Ai, now you have a new worry. Forget this idea.

MOISHA. (*very eager, his hands waving*) Listen, Abram. I see how it all happened. I was sitting that night, all alone here by the candlelight, counting my money, one hundred and twelve dollars; in bills, one hundred dollars; in silver twelve dollars. It was about seven o'clock, and none of you were yet home. Then as I am counting—

HYMAN. You have told us this many times, Moisha.

MOISHA. (*almost screaming in his excitement*) Listen! Listen! Now it is clear! I am counting the money, and as I am counting I hear a step on the stair. I put the money quickly away, here in a hole in the mattress where I always kept it. The door opens and a customer enters. It is a boy with a pair of shoes to be heeled, and he sits down, takes them off, and waits, while I work on them. As I work Mendel comes in, then Hyman and Abram. You eat your suppers. Hyman had herring and bread, I remember, and Mendel corned beef sandwiches. I finish the shoes and the boy leaves. Then we sit and talk a little, Yonkel and I. Abram and Mendel play cards, Hyman reads a newspaper. Then I blow out the candle and we go to bed. I remember it all like yesterday. In the morning, at about six, I awake. Abram has already gone to work, as always. The others are still sleeping. I go to open the door to let in the fresh morning air. I come back and look in the mattress for my money. I do not find it. It is gone. It has vanished like a cloud. Now, how could I have lost it? It must have been stolen; there was no other way! Abram, am I right?

ABRAM. (*slowly*) You know what you are saying, Moisha?

MOISHA. Yes.

ABRAM. You mean, then, Moisha, that one of us stole it?

MOISHA. (*perplexed and tearful*) What else can I believe? There was no one else in the cellar all that night. Tell me, is there anything else to believe?

(*The other men look at each other blankly.*)

HYMAN. You see what you have done, Yonkel.

ABRAM. Can there really be a thief among us?

MENDEL. But didn't you go out for rolls, Moisha? You might have taken your money with you then.

MOISHA. I hadn't gone for the rolls yet. No.

HYMAN. (*earnestly*) No one here would have taken your money, Moisha.

ABRAM. Yes, it is impossible. You didn't think of it till now; don't believe it anymore.

MOISHA. (*throwing out his hands*) But where is my money?

HYMAN. It *must* have been lost, Moisha.

MOISHA. Where could I have lost it? I went nowhere.

ABRAM. (*solemnly*) Moisha, we are all of us poor men. And we are weak men, and bad men, bad as the rest. For a little money we have to work and pay with our blood and sweat. It would be easy to tempt us. But, look at us, Moisha. Can you really believe one of us would have robbed you of what meant so much to you?

MOISHA. (*weeping*) No, I do not believe it. I did not even dream of it before, until Yonkel spoke of it. But was there any other way the money could have disappeared that night, unless someone stole it? Tell me, Abram.

ABRAM (*depressed, a frown on his bluff face*) I don't know what to think, Moisha.

HYMAN. (*shrilly*) I can't believe it! It would have been like stealing a man's child, to steal that money from you.

MOISHA. (*wailing mournfully, in the orthodox Hebrew singsong*) Yes, it was my child, you all knew that. It was the wife and children in Poland I have not seen for five years. I have starved and struggled to save enough to send for them, and now the money is gone. Oh, you are Jews, you have suffered and been lonely, in this strange land! Who of you could have done this?

ABRAM. (*staunchly*) I swear it, Moisha, no one—

MOISHA. (*throwing his arms about him and weeping*) Good, kind, beloved Abram, who has always been true as gold to me, was not the door locked all that night? Were not only we five here? What have they done to me? Why have they taken my life, my hope away?

MENDEL. (*eagerly*) He can search us, Abram. I know I have not touched his money.

ABRAM. (*sadly*) Do you want to do that, Moisha?

MOISHA. Oh, what will it help? It is a week now the money is gone, and searching will not find it. No, give it back to me. Have pity, pity, pity! (*weeps with face in hands.*)

ABRAM. (*in despair*) I don't know what to do. What can we do for him, Hyman?

HYMAN. (*timidly*) Moisha—

MOISHA. (*looking at them wildly, his voice high and despairing*) No, I will not search you! No, I will ask you each, in the name of the God of Israel, in the name of your own brothers and sisters, your own wives and children in Poland, did you take it? I weep before you, I throw my tired old body on the ground before you, I ask you again and again: Did you take my money? What does a man live for, I ask you? Does he live only to work, to make shoes in a dark hole away from the sun? No, he lives for his children, to see them grow up strong and happy, and to reach greater things than he himself has reached. That is what a man lives for. But you have taken my children away from me. Oh, who has taken my life away from me? Did you take it Hyman? Hyman, dear, I beg you, have you taken my children from me? Tell me, I will forgive you if you did. Did you?

HYMAN. (*sorrowfully*) How can you ask that, Moisha? Strip me to the skin; search everything I have.

MOISHA. What can I believe, Hyman? Was it you, Mendel? Did you do it? Have you my money? Give it back; only give it back; I will not reproach you; I shall be glad to forget. Mendel, did you?

MENDEL. What are you saying to me, Moisha?

MOISHA. Did you?

MENDEL. (*passionately*) No, no. How could I?

MOISHA. Abram, did you? I must know, I must find my money. Would you have done such a thing to me, Abram? Or you, Yonkel? Tell me, in God's name. Tell me.

ABRAM. (*slowly*) Moisha, I sooner would have cut off my right hand. You know that.

YONKEL. (*lifting his face from his hands*) I did not take it, Moisha.

MOISHA. You have never known wife or children, Yonkel. But you saw your brother killed by the Cossacks, and you know what it is to lose loved ones. Don't you know where my money is, Yonkel?

YONKEL. (*tears running down his pale face, his voice broken*) Why do you ask me again? I have told you I don't know.

MOISHA. (*desperate and wild*) So what can I do? Where can I turn now? You say none of you took my money. But it was stolen from me, I know that.

HYMAN. Before you were sure you forgot or lost the money somewhere; now you are sure it was stolen. Don't you see how mad this all is, Moisha?

MOISHA. (*his mood growing to an hysterical anger*) It is not mad. Don't you try to put me off, Hyman. One of you must have it. Or all of you took it and are keeping it from me. That is the way you stole it; you did it together. You must give it up now, do you hear?

ABRAM. (*to* YONKEL) Now he is really mad. I told you it would drive him mad.

YONKEL. (*his face in his hands*) Oh, don't speak to me, Abram.

MOISHA. (*pacing the floor, while the others watch him in awe*) Yes, you have all been plotting against me. I can see that now! It is clear. But you will not succeed, do you hear? I will not be killed so easily. I will fight. I will make you give it up. I will—

ABRAM. (*trying to restrain him*) Moisha!

MOISHA. (*screaming as he breaks away from* ABRAM'S *hand*) Let me be! I know what I am doing. And I know how to make you give it up! I will lock the door on all of you, and go for a policeman. That is what I will do. He will make you tell the truth, he will make you give up my money! You will listen to his club, you hard-hearted men who wouldn't listen to my tears. And how I trusted you all, how I believed you were my friends! Now you have stabbed me in the heart; you have taken what is only a little money to you, but to me it is life! Murderers, give me back my money! For the last time, give me back what I have suffered for, give me back my wife and children!

ABRAM. (*going to door and standing by him*) Don't shout, Moisha. Moisha, be reasonable, listen to us!

MOISHA. No, I have listened long enough! I have asked for the truth from thieves long enough. I am going to call a policeman now. I will show you. I will make you all confess I—(*he starts to go out.*)

ABRAM. (*holding him*) Moisha, for God's sake, what would you do?

MOISHA. (*struggling*) Ah, it is you, Abram? You whom I trusted most of all?

ABRAM. What do you mean?

MOISHA. (*in mad, exulting voice*) See, he trembles already! He is afraid of the policeman; it was he that took the money! Now we know—now we know—Abram—(*He turns white and half faints into* ABRAM'S *arms.*) Ah, my heart! (ABRAM *takes him to the cobbler's bench and seats him there.*)

ABRAM. Bring some water, Mendel! Quick! (*They press the water on* MOISHA. *He sips it, and opens his eyes slowly.*) Quiet, Moisha, quiet!

MOISHA. (*sobbing in a low, heartrending voice*) I cannot do it over again, I tell you! You see how my heart has failed me. I have not the strength to starve, to wait another five years in this cellar. No.

HYMAN. Moisha—

MOISHA. Yes, it is all over for me. Ai! Ai! It is over—my sun and moon have gone out. I wish I could die.

ABRAM. Shah, Moisha dear! (*He takes* MOISHA'S *hand. There is a little space of quiet. Then* MOISHA *looks up with big, staring eyes.*)

MOISHA. (*tensely*) Listen. I have solved it all. I do not need the money. Some night when I am alone I will take my cobbler's knife and cut my throat. That will be best.

ABRAM. What are you saying? Moisha, do not—

MOISHA. (*in fresh burst of tears*) But what else can I do? Am I not dead now? I have no strength, no hope, to begin again. It is over for me. I will cut my throat. I will kill myself. I will not wait for God to be kind. I will end it all.

HYMAN, Moisha, dear!

(MOISHA *becomes weak again. They give him more water. He shuts his eyes and gasps, while the tears flow down his cheeks.*)

MOISHA. (*weakly and pitifully*) Dear, kind, good friends, Jews who know what it is to be a Jew and suffer, why have you done this to me? Why have you killed me? Have I ever injured one of you? Have I ever taken from you one thing that was yours? Have I not lain here with you night after night, and been one of you? I am no stranger. And you saw—

YONKEL. (*Suddenly springing up from the mattress where he has been moodily sitting all through this. He looks wildly at Abram and clutches at his shirt.*) My God. Moisha! (*The rest look at him startled. His long pale face is white as a madman's. His eyes burn with fever.*)

HYMAN. What is wrong, Yonkel?

YONKEL. I can't stand this, I can't stand this! (*He sits down on his mattress again.*)

MOISHA. Yes, what shall I do Yonkel? You see how terrible life has become for me. It is hopeless. Yonkel, you remember when you were sick and lay a month here night and day. I charged you no rent, and tended you, and now see what has become of me. What shall I do? Shall I—

YONKEL. (*springing up*) Stop! Stop, Moisha! Here is your money! (*He pulls out a small canvas bag from where it was tied by a string around his neck, next to the skin. As he hands the bag to* MOISHA, *he is seized by a violent fit of coughing.* MOISHA *seizes the money eagerly, uttering gurgling sounds of joy, and counts the contents of the bag. Meanwhile* ABRAM *comes over to the coughing* YONKEL *and hits him a hard blow on the jaw.* YONKEL *falls, coughing in an uncontrollable spasm that shakes his whole frame.*)

ABRAM. (*in a roar of disgust*) You louse!

MENDEL. (*shaking his head*) And this is God's world!

HYMAN. (*mildly, as he strokes his white beard*) Better leave him alone now, Abram. His coughing is on him again.

ABRAM. (*fiercely, as he pushes* YONKEL'S *body aside with his foot*) The thief! The louse! It is no Jew, no man here, it is a mean little blood sucking louse!

HYMAN. (*patiently*) He is very sick. We had better put him on the mattress.

ABRAM. I won't help a louse! I would rather kill it!

HYMAN. Here, Mendel, help me. (*They lift* YONKEL, *who is still coughing, onto his mattress. They give him MOISHA'S water.*)

MOISHA. (*coming over to* ABRAM) The money is all here, thank God! One hundred and twelve dollars, all here!

ABRAM. (*forgetting his black rage*) And now you are happy again, yes, Moisha?

MOISHA. (*sadly*) No, when was I happy before? And I will not see them yet—my family. I need sixty dollars more, and it will take many months to save it. But I will eat less, I will work more, I will save, save, save!

ABRAM. Shah, Moisha, you will strain your heart again. Lie down on the mattress and rest!

MOISHA. Yes, yes, I must rest. (ABRAM *helps him to lie down.*) Abram, you will forgive what I said to you before? I did not mean it; I was half crazy.

ABRAM. I understand, Moisha.

MOISHA. It has all been like a bad dream to me. (YONKEL *begins coughing again.*)

ABRAM. Yes, a bad dream, but not yet ended for some. A policeman will be here yet, and we will see what a louse gets for stealing.

HYMAN. (*slowly*) I think, Abram, we should let him alone now! He is very sick.

YONKEL. (*sitting up and coughing*) No, he is right; Abram is right, Hyman.

ABRAM. I am right, am I?

YONKEL. (*weeping*) Yes, Abram. I deserve everything.

ABRAM. (*standing over him*) So why did you do it? You know it was wrong now, so how could you have done it? You knew why Moisha was saving, was starving himself to a shadow.

YONKEL. (*coughing*) I—I—saw how—

ABRAM. (*fiercely*) Don't explain. I will tell you why you did it. I have met your kind before. It is because you are one of those Jews who have a lust for money. It is the food of your soul, like blood is the food of the louse. Don't tell me, I know. Suck-suck-suck, suck till you've sucked all your brothers dry. What a man! Hah! (*He spits in disgust.*)

YONKEL. (*weakly*) Yes, Abram.

ABRAM. (*fiercely*) Yes, Yonkel! "Yes," you whine, "it is true, Abram!" You admit you are one of those whose religion is to steal and lie and kill and betray—all for money!

HYMAN. (*intervening*) There are many like that in the world, Abram. They are very wealthy.

ABRAM. But I am not like that. I have always worked, you know that, Hyman. I have always paid full price of blood and sweat for my bread. I have been honest. I have tried to hurt no man.

HYMAN. (*with the mild dry humor of an old man*) That is why you are poor.

ABRAM. There are many other poor and honest men. There are many.

HYMAN. Yes, there are too many of us, Abram.

ABRAM. What do you mean? You speak in riddles. What I know is: Let the world be good or bad, a man should be a man. That is what I believe. One ought not make others suffer—as Yonkel made you suffer, Moisha.

YONKEL. I suffered, too. (*He has another spell of coughing.*)

ABRAM. (*with contempt*) You suffered!

YONKEL. Yes.

ABRAM. Bah! You *will* suffer. You have still to know what Moisha here felt. I am going to have you arrested.

MOISHA. (*slowly opening his eyes*) No. I think it isn't necessary, Abram.

ABRAM. What? Is there to be no honesty in the world? I say thieves must be punished!

YONKEL. (*eagerly*) I suffered, yes, I did. You don't believe it, Abram! Let me—

ABRAM. (*with fierce contempt*) But I won't listen to you, I tell you! I will hear you in the court. I will hear you tell the judge how you suffered.

MOISHA. (*slowly*) Let him be. He should not have stolen my money. But I have it back.

ABRAM. What do you think, Hyman? Do you think we ought to let such a thief go?

HYMAN. It is hard to tell, Abram. You are so sure, but I am not. What can one do in this world where there is more evil than good? Let him go, maybe.

MENDEL. I heard a speaker on the street say once that the rich are all thieves. But no one punishes them.

ABRAM. (*pounding one fist into the other*) Do not try to confuse me. The thing is simple—it happened in this cellar. I have eyes, I have ears, I have seen and heard how this happened. Yonkel stole the money. It was like sucking the heart's blood from Moisha. It was unnecessary, too. Yonkel was not starving. He took it because of his black lust for money. He is a louse. As soon as he stops coughing, I will take him to the station house! (*He gets up and stamps about fiercely.*)

YONKEL. (*breaking down into sobs*) Don't have me arrested, Abram! Don't have me put into one of those cold, dark prisons where I would die soon.

There is no one with a kind heart in a prison—I would go mad there. Don't let him do it, Moisha dear! I am a Jew, we are all Jews together. I came from the same town in Poland you did, Moisha.

ABRAM. You didn't remember you were Moisha's kinsman before!

YONKEL. I didn't want to take your money, Moisha, no, no, I didn't. I cried as I took it from the hole in your mattress that night. I knew what it meant to you, and how you worked for it. Believe me, Moisha, I cried for you, Moisha!

ABRAM. You make my head go round. You cried, and yet you took it.

HYMAN. Let us hear him out, Abram. Let him tell why he did it.

ABRAM. But I don't understand. Why should he do it if he cried?

HYMAN. Let him explain. People are like that, Abram. You are made of one piece, like a big tree. You don't understand how people can be both good and bad. Let him explain.

YONKEL. Yes, that's how it is, Hyman. Don't let him have me arrested. Let him arrest the thing in me that got up in the night and went to the money. Oh, how it seized on the money, so glad and hot, while I stood by and wept for you, Moisha! And Moisha, when I saw you suffering all this week, I could bear it the least of all of us. . . . I lay here listening to you—I tore my flesh—but what could I do? (*another fit of coughing*) One night, and then another, I got up—I—and tried to give the money back to you somehow. I stood over you in the darkness, and my tears fell on your white face, and I could have kissed you for pity. I heard you groan, and I knew what was making your whole body shake, and burning it like a fever. It was terrible. I took out the money and started to place it where it belonged, but I could not. I could do nothing. It was like watching a friend drown, and having a life preserver in one's hand, and being unable to throw it. What could I do? Does a man always conquer the beast he meets in a forest? And can a man always conquer the beasts inside himself? What could I do? (*He coughs, and* HYMAN *hands him the water.*)

HYMAN. Drink, Yonkel.

YONKEL. Thanks. Yes, so it happened for three nights. You will not believe it, but I could not return the money. And I would go back to my mattress and lie there, and shiver all night with fear. I was afraid—afraid of Money! What was it—this Beast that God had put into the world? It was in many men, eating and eating their happiness, making them cruel to each other. I was afraid of it. I would feel it move around the room, filling the corners and coming toward me, to spring at my throat. I would be afraid to open my eyes, for fear I would see it standing above me with its hot breath. I was afraid I might see its yellow eyes, that change to green, and look upon men. Do you understand, Moisha? Do you understand, Abram?

ABRAM. (*slowly*) I don't know. But talk on, Yonkel. You were always a good talker.

MOISHA. In the old country, I remember, you did not care for money, Yonkel. But here you seem to have become a miser. It is the old Yonkel that is talking now.

YONKEL. No, in Poland I did not care for money—Moisha remembers that. I was a poor young Talmud student there, but happy. I lived on a radish a day, I slept on the hard benches of the synagogue, I cared for nothing but to live with my soul and to study the sacred books. In the quiet of the room where I sat, I would hear angels' wings moving like music. A joy was in me, for I was alone in a place where there was only God. The world never touched me. Poland is a terrible land for the Jews, but they helped each other, they were friends. I never starved, I was taken care of, they understood my passion. And I would not have cared if I starved—I lived above Life and Death then. It is hard for me to believe it now. I am different now. See how thin and unhappy I am now. But I have money. I have learned to care for money. How did it happen? I remember how it began. I remember when I came here, how friendless I was. It was all different here from Poland. What good did my Talmud study do me, what good was it that I heard angels' wings? I went into a shop where they paid me a few dollars a week. I bent over a machine and fed it my strength and my thoughts, my blood and my desires. And it turned out pants. And it turned out cloaks. I slaved and I slaved—and nothing came of it. There were slack times, and strikes, and days when I was sick. I went to work in a grocery store after that. And I slaved and was sick there, too. Nothing came of it all. I was always poor. And no one cared for me when I had no money. The boss laid us off, or let us walk out on strike, and no one cared. I was sick, and no one cared if I died or lived. I had no money! Something said to me, something in this land—get money! It is not enough to study the Talmud, to work, to be a man. You must have money! And a great fear seized on me, the Beast entered me, and I suddenly grew afraid of being poor! I gave up God, for the Beast was jealous. And I tried to make money, for it is stronger than God. With it I could despise and stand above the world, as I stood above it without money in Poland, with only my soul. Yes, I felt the fear! Men are shot down for want of money. Men are crucified for want of money. Men who have no money live in cellars like this, and are lonely for their children. Don't you awake in the night, sweating cold, Abram, and wonder how long your job will last, what your old age will be like, who would care for your children if you should die? Thoughts such as these? Doesn't the fear of poverty ever come on you, Moisha, and you, Hyman, and you, Abram?

HYMAN. Yes, it does.

MENDEL. Yes.

MOISHA. Yes, often.

ABRAM. Yes, and on me, too. . . . I understand what you are saying, Yonkel. It is true. Money is a terrible thing. But may I ask you something?

YONKEL. Yes.

ABRAM. I can understand how a poor man would get to fear poverty so much he would do anything to escape it. I have felt that myself. But I have beat it down, because I have felt—well, if there are so many poor in the world, I can be poor with them, too. But I can understand your feelings, too, Yonkel. What I cannot understand is this—how could you have stolen money from Moisha? If you took it from a rich man or a worthless man, or if you cheated some one, as these millionaires do, it might not have been so bad. But to take it from Moisha!

YONKEL. I know, I know, Abram. Don't you see that is what has made me suffer? I knew what a terrible thing it was to take Moisha's money from him. I knew it more than all of you. I never knew it more than at that moment in the night when I took it. It was like a madness on me, but I could not stop it. And yet in that moment, I was sanest, too. Like a flash of lightning I saw myself for the first time in many years, and I saw what the desire for money had made of the old Yonkel. I started by thinking I would make money my slave, and I saw in that moment I had become its slave. There is a story in one of the old Hebrew books that explains. It is about a little village to which there came every night a great, terrible snake and ate one of the children. This went on for many years, and the people prayed to God but got no help. Then a very learned rabbi there, taking pity on the people said, "Since God does not help us, we will use other ways." And he went out into the forest to fight the snake, and he stayed there seven years, battling the snake, night and day. He used every means, but they seemed to fail. At last he thought, "There is only one way left." So he chose that way, and changed himself into a snake, too, with flat head and poison dripping from his mouth. And for another year he fought the snake that had eaten the children, and finally he conquered it. But when he returned to the village to tell them of his victory, the people fled before him. And he wept when he remembered that he was no longer a man, but was a snake, whose delight is to poison and to kill all that it sees. Do you understand? . . . And now I will ask you something, Abram.

ABRAM. Yes, Yonkel.

YONKEL. You were angry before, and called me a louse. I do not blame you. (*with a fierce cry of passion*) But I ask you, Abram, who made the louse? Who put it into the world to live on the blood of men? Who gave it that appetite and body?

ABRAM. It must have been God.

YONKEL. Then who but God is to blame for its ways? Is the louse to blame? . . . No. And then am I to blame, for what I have become? Is not the thing that made me so to blame? Is not Money to blame, Money the real God of the world? Oh, my fellow Jews, you who are so meek and suffering, you who understand, I tell you I am my own worst enemy. Money has made me so. I am sick, but I live in this cellar, because I wish more money. I want a quiet mind, with the thoughts that move through all the universe and are free and joyful. But I have let this mind be killed by the one hungry thought—the thought of money. I loved Moisha—here, I pitied him and wished him good fortune and a way out of his misery. But you saw what I did to him—for a little money. Oh, I am sick, I am sick with the disease of money! If I could find where it is in my breast, if I could find this cancer in my soul, I would take a terrible knife and stab it out! But would that cure it? No, for the whole world is sick with it, the whole world is its own worst enemy! I could sell or give away the little goods I peddle, I could throw my money in the river, and tomorrow I would feel free. But the next day I would be seeing men strain and sweat and hurt each other for money. And the fever would come on me again, too, and I would say: It is necessary to have money to live. It is necessary to have much money to stand above the world. And it is true—it is necessary! But it is also necessary to be a man, and to think thoughts that fly to God and are beautiful. It is necessary to be kind, and it is also necessary to make money! What does it all mean? Do you see how sick I am with it all? I am a thief, an enemy to my brothers—

(*A heavy footstep is heard coming down the stairs.* YONKEL *stops and they all look toward the door.*)

MOISHA. (*frightened*) Some one is coming. Who can it be?

MENDEL. (*Goes to door and opens it.)* It is a policeman, Moisha!

(*The* POLICEMAN *enters and stands at the door, looking about suspiciously.*)

POLICEMAN. (*in a big, indignant voice*) For Gawd's sake!

MOISHA. *(scared)* Abram, you know English! Speak to him!

POLICEMAN. What the hell's going on here? What are you Yits up to anyway?

ABRAM. (*meekly, in singsong, broken Ghetto English*) It's nothing the matter.

POLICEMAN. Why, a feller just come up to me on my beat and told me there was a lot of Yits down here fighting like cats and dogs.

ABRAM. (*with the same rising, singsong accent*) Fighting? We should be fighting? No, sahr, we was only talking between ourselves, Mister?

POLICEMAN. You must've made a lot of noise with your mouths then! What'che talkin' about at this hour of the night anyway?

ABRAM. (*shrugging his shoulders*) Oh, I don't know—abaht money?

POLICEMAN. (*bursting into laughter*) Money? Money? That's good. Haw, haw, haw! that's a pippin. A lot of Yits talking at three A.M. in the mornin'—about money! That's rich! Haw, haw, haw! Money!

ABRAM. (*meekly*) Yes, sahr?

POLICEMAN. (*tolerantly, wiping the tears of laughter from his eyes*) Well, fellow citizens, blow out the candle, and don't argue no more about money. Leave it for tomorrow's peddlin', see? Go to bed now, an' happy dreams! (*He goes out.* ABRAM *locks the door after him, stands there a moment, then blows out the candle.*)

ABRAM. (*in Yiddish, in which he has no accent*) He said we should go to sleep. He says we have talked enough. (*They all lie down except* YONKEL, *who sits up and looks around him.*)

MOISHA. (kindly) Sleep, Yonkel, you too!

YONKEL. (*Gives a little sigh and lies down.*) Yes, Moisha.

(*There is a silence as the men shift about their mattresses, each occupied with his thoughts. Then the low, young, tender voice of Mendel speaks in the darkness.*)

MENDEL. I am younger than all of you, and I have not been a Talmud student like Yonkel, but have always worked. But once, I remember, I heard a man standing on the street corner here on the East Side, and he was saying that one day there would be no money, no rich and no poor, only everyone working together like brothers and sisters.

MOISHA. (*interested*) Yes? Who was the man said that, Mendel?

MENDEL. A Jew. A workingman like ourselves.

ABRAM. (*lifting himself on his elbow*) But Mendel, did he say—(*And the curtain drops as they enter a new discussion on the endless problem of the world's misery and Money!*)

CURTAIN

Part Two

From "Towards Proletarian Art"

The Liberator, February 1921

It seems not merely coincidental that this was the last article published under the name Irwin Granich. Here the essayist's voice is firmly in the tenement one final time. Throughout the piece, the author uses the plural pronoun "we," not in reference to radical writers as a collective, but to the two selves battling within him. The essay may be read as an account of Mike Gold's identity struggle and declaration of its outcome. As he defined proletarianism, he defined himself.

~

The Apocalypse

IN BLOOD, in tears, in chaos and wild, thunderous clouds of fear the old economic order is dying. We are not appalled or startled by that giant apocalypse before us. We know the horror that is passing away with this long winter of the world. We know, too, the bright forms that stir at the heart of all this confusion, and that shall rise out of the debris and cover the ruins of capitalism with beauty. We are prepared for the economic revolution of the world, but what shakes us with terror and doubt is the cultural upheaval that must come. We rebel instinctively against that change. We have been bred in the old capitalist planet, and its stuff is in our very bones. Its ideals, mutilated and poor, were yet the precious stays of our lives. Its art, its science, its philosophy and metaphysics are deeper in us than logic or will. They are deeper than the reach of the knife in our social passion. We cannot consent to the suicide of our souls. We cling to the old culture, and fight for it against ourselves. But it must die. The old ideals must die. But let us not fear. Let us fling all we are into the cauldron of the Revolution. For out of our death shall arise glories, and out of the final corruption of this old civilization we have loved shall spring the new race—the Supermen.

A Basis in the Maelstrom

It is necessary first to discuss our place in eternity.

I myself have felt almost mad as I staggered back under the blows of infinity. That huge, brooding pale evil all about me—that endless Nothing out of which Something seems to have evolved somehow—that nightmare in man's brain called Eternity—how it has haunted me! Its poison has almost blighted this sweet world I love.

The curse of the thought of eternity is in the brain and heart of every artist and thinker. But they do not let it drive them mad, for they discover what gives them strength and faith to go on seeking its answer. They realize in revelations that the language of eternity is not man's language, and that only through the symbolism of the world around us and manifest in us can we draw near the fierce, deadly flame.

The things of the world are all portals to eternity. We can approach eternity through the humble symbols of Life—through beasts and fields and rivers and skies, through the common goodness and passion of men. Yet what is Life, then? What is that which my body holds like a vessel filled with fire? What is that which grows, which changes, which manifests itself, which moves in clod and bird and ocean and mountain, and binds them so invisibly in some mystic league of purpose? I have contemplated all things great and small with this question on my lips. And seeking a synthesis for Life, and thus for eternity, I early found that the striving, dumb universe had strained to its fullest expressiveness in the being of man.

Man was Life become vocal and sensitive. Man was Life become dramatic and complete. He gained and he lost; he knew values, he knew joys and sorrows, and not mere pleasures and pains. He was bad, glad, sad, mad; he was color and form; he contained everything I had not found in the white, meaningless face of pure Eternity. Eternity became interesting only in him. He had desires; he engendered climaxes. He moved me to the soul with his pathos and aspirations. He was significant to me; he made me think and love. Life's meaning was to be found only in the great or mean days between each man's birth and death, and in the mystery and terror hovering over every human head.

Seeking God we find Man, ever and ever. Seeking answers we find men and women.

In the Depths

I can feel beforehand the rebellion and contempt with which many true and passionate artists laboring in all humility will greet claims for a defined art. It is not a mere aristocratic scorn for the world and its mass-yearnings that is at the root of the artists' sneer at "propaganda." It is a deeper, more universal feeling than that. It is the consciousness that in art Life is speaking out its heart at last, and that to censor the poor brute-murmurings would be sacrilege. Whatever they are, they are significant and precious, and to stifle the meanest of Life's moods taking form in the artist would be death. Artists are bitter lovers of Life, and in beauty or horror she is ever dear to them. I wish to speak no word against their holy passion, therefore, and I regard with reverence the scarred and tortured figures of the artist-saints of time, battling against their demons, bearing each a ponderous cross, receiving solemnly in decadence, insanity, filth and fear the special revelation Life has given them.

I respect the suffering and creations of all artists. They are deeper to me than theories artists have clothed their naked passions in. I would oppose no contrary futile dogmas. I would show only, if I can, what manner of vision Life has vouchsafed me, what word has descended on me in the midst of this dark pit of experience, what form my days and nights have taken, as they proceed in strange nebular whirling toward the achievement of new worlds of art.

I was born in a tenement. That tall, somber mass, holding its freight of obscure human destinies, is the pattern in which my being has been cast. It was in a tenement that I first heard the sad music of humanity rise to the stars. The sky above the airshafts was all my sky; and the voices of the tenement neighbors in the airshaft were the voices of all my world. There, in suffering youth, I feverishly sought God and found Man. In the tenement Man was revealed to me, Man, who is Life speaking. I saw him, not as he has been pictured by the elder poets, groveling or sinful or romantic or falsely god-like, but one sunk in a welter of humble, realistic cares; responsible, instinctive, long-suffering and loyal; sad and beaten yet reaching out beautifully and irresistibly like a natural force for the mystic food and freedom that are Man's.

All that I know of Life I learned in the tenement. I saw love there in an old mother who wept for her sons. I saw courage there in a sick worker who went to the factory every morning. I saw beauty in little children playing in the dim hallways, and despair and hope and hate incarnated in the simple figures of those who lived there with me. The tenement is in my blood. When I think it is the tenement thinking. When I hope it is the tenement hoping. I am not an individual; I am all that the tenement group poured into me during those early years of my spiritual travail.

Why should we artists born in tenements go beyond them for our expression? Can we go beyond them? "Life burns in both camps," in the tenements and in the palaces, but can we understand that which is not our very own? We, who are sprung from the workers, can we so easily forget the milk that nourished us, and the hearts that gave us growth? Need we apologize or be ashamed if we express in art that manifestation of Life which is so exclusively ours, the life of the toilers? What is art? Art is the tenement pouring out its soul through us, its most sensitive and articulate sons and daughters. What is Life? Life for us has been the tenement that bore and molded us through years of meaningful pain.

"The Password to Thought—to Culture"

The Liberator, February 1922

The long illness of Charles Granich, who was bedridden for six years before his death in 1912 at the age of fifty-one, was the great emotional weight Irwin Granich carried in his early life. Gold rarely spoke of it until his final years, when he began to sift the tragedy directly, first in a series of newspaper columns in 1959, then dictating into a tape recorder in 1966, when his eyesight was failing from diabetes. "My father had been the soul of our home," he lamented. "It was hard to accept this stranger as my father, this struggling invalid with the shrunken face and gloomy eyes. What justice could there be in a universe that punished so?"

In "The Password to Thought—to Culture," David Brandt's exodus from his tenement is the equivalent of Irwin Granich's desired escape from the domestic burden of supporting his family as a teenager. As anyone who has read the ending of Jews Without Money *might assume, David's wanderings in the East Side streets will lead him eventually to Union Square and to a political awakening similar to the one experienced by that book's central figure, the Irwin Granich alter ego known in the novel as "Mikey Gold."*

~

I

The factory of Shinster and Neuheim, Makers of the Hytone Brand Ladies' Cloaks and Suits, rushed along busily in its usual channels that sweet May afternoon; the machines racing and roaring; the workers gripped by their tasks; the whole dark loft filled with a furious mechanical life, hot and throbbing as the pulse of an aeroplane.

Outside the sunlight lay in bright patterns on the dusty streets and buildings, illuminating for two or three hours more the city crowds moving to and fro on their ever-mysterious errands. But the factory was filling with darkness, and the hundred silent figures at the sewing machines bent even lower to their work, as if there were some mighty matter for study before them, needing a sterner and tenser notice as the day deepened into twilight.

The pressers, at their boards at one end of the long loft, thumped with their irons, and surrounded themselves with hissing steam like a fog. The motors roared and screamed, and one of the basters, a little Italian girl, sang in a high voice a sad, beautiful love song of her native province in Italy. It ran through the confusion of the loft like a trickle of silver, but now and again its fragile beauty was drowned by the larger, prosaic voice of Mr. Neuheim, the junior partner, as he bustled about and shouted commands to one or another of his workers.

"Chaim, come here and take this bundle to Abe's machine!" he would shout in Yiddish, and a very old, white-bearded Jew came patiently and slowly, and took the huge bundle of cloaks on his brittle shoulders, and delivered them to the operator.

"Hurry up on this Flachsman job, boys!" Mr. Neuheim would say, rubbing his hands, as he stood behind one of the operators, and a few of them in the vicinity would frown slightly and murmur some inaudible answer from between closed lips.

Mr. Neuheim, a short, flabby man with a bald head and reddish moustache that was turning white, was the practical tailor of the firm and stayed in the factory and looked after production. His partner had been a salesman when they joined their poverty and ambition not many years ago, and there looked after the selling and business end now. Mr. Neuheim liked this arrangement, for he had sat at the bench for years, and still liked the smell of steam and the feel of cloth, the putting together of "garments." Best of all, he liked to run things, to manage, to bustle, and to have other tailors under him, dependent on his word.

He trudged about the factory all day like a minor Napoleon, and wherever he went there was a tightening of nerves, an increased activity of fingers, and a sullenness as if his every word were an insult. He was a good manager, and kept things moving. His very presence was like a lash lightly flicked at the backs of the workers. They did not like him, but they responded when they felt him near.

Mr. Neuheim trotted about more strenuously than usual on this afternoon. There was a big order to be delivered the next morning, and he was making sure that it would be on time. He sped from his basters to his pressers, from his pressers to his operators, a black, unlighted cigar in his mouth, a flush of worry on his gross, round face.

"Where are those fifty suits in the 36 size of the Flachsman lot?" he suddenly demanded of the white-bearded factory porter.

"I brought them to David an hour ago, Mr. Neuheim," Chaim said, looking at him with meek eyes.

"Good. Then they'll be sure to get off tonight," said the Boss, scowling like a busy general. "Good."

He thought a moment, and then hurried on his short legs through the piles of unfinished clothing till he came to the door that led from the factory to the shipping room. There was a glass panel in the upper part of the door, and Mr. Neuheim stopped and looked through it before entering.

What he saw made him take the cigar out of his mouth, swear, and then open the door with a violent kick that almost tore it from its hinges.

"My God!" he cried fervently, "what is this, anyways?"

His shipping clerk, David Brandt, a Jewish youth of about twenty-three, was seated on the table near the open window, staring dreamily at the grey masses of building opposite, that now were flashing with a thousand fires in the sun. He was hugging his knees, and beside him on the table lay an open green covered book that he had evidently put aside for a moment.

David Brandt was a well-built youth, with good shoulders and chest, a body that would have been handsome had he not carried it like a sloven; tense brown eyes, and a lean face with hungry, high Slavic features. He was shabbily dressed, almost downright dirty in his carelessness of shirt and clothes, and he stood up hastily as the Boss spoke and ran his fingers nervously through a shock of wild black hair.

Mr. Neuheim strode over to him, picked up the hook, and read the title.

"Ruskin's Sea-same and Lilies!" he pronounced contemptuously. "My God, boy, is this what we're payin' you good money for? What are you *here* for anyway, to work or to stuff yourself with fairy tales? Tell me!" he demanded.

"To work," David answered reluctantly, his eyes fixed on the floor.

"Then work, in God's name, work! This ain't a public library, ye know, or a city college for young shipping clerks to come to for a free education! What sort of a book is this, anyway? he asked staring again at the title. "What's a sea-same, anyway?"

"It's a sort of password," David stammered, a crimson wave of blood creeping over his dark face.

"A password to what?" the Boss demanded, looking at him sternly, with the air of a judge determined upon the whole truth and nothing but the truth. "Is it something like the Free Masons?"

David floundered guiltily. "It's used only in a sort of symbolical sense here," he explained. "Sesame was used as a password by Ali Baba in the story, when he wanted to get into the robbers' cave, but here it means the password to thought—to culture."

"To thought—to culture!" Mr. Neuheim mimicked grandiosely, putting an imaginary monocle to his eye, and walking a few mincing steps up and down the room. "And I suppose, Mr. Brandt, while you was learning the password to Thought and to Culture—ahem!"—he put an incredible sneer into these two unfortunate words—"you forgot all about such little things like that Flachsman lot! Look at it, it's still laying around, and Chaim brought it in an hour ago! My God, boy, this can't go on, ye know! I been watching you for the past two months, and I'll tell you frankly, you ain't got your mind on business! I didn't know what it was before, but I see how it's this Thought"—he sneered again—"and this Culture. Cut it out, see? If ye want to read, do it outside the factory, and read something that'll bring you in dividends—good American reading."

"Yes."

"What do ye want with thought and culture, anyway?" the Boss cried, waving his cigar like an orator. "Me and Mr. Shinster was worse off than you once; we started from the bottom; and look where we got to without sea-sames or lilies! You're wasting your good time, boy."

David looked at the plump little Jew, with his glittering bald head, his flabby face, and his perfectly rounded stomach that was like some fleshly monument to years of champagne suppers, auto rides, chorus girl debauches, and all the other splendid rewards of success in the New York garment trade.

"Do you ever read Shakespeare?" Mr. Neuheim said more tolerantly, as he lit his cigar.

"Yes."

"Well, ye know in his Choolyus Caesar, this man Caesar says: Let me have men about me that are fat, and that don't think; that is, don't think outside of business, ye understand. Well, that's my advice to you, my boy, especially if ye want to hold your job and got any ambition. The last feller that held your job was made a salesman on the road after five years, and the same chances are open to you. Now let's see whether you're smart or not. I like you personally, but you gotta change your ways. Now let's see you use common sense after this—not Thought and Culture."

He laughed a broad, gurgling, self-satisfied laugh, and passed into the factory again, where the machines were warring, and the little Italian girl singing, and the pressers were sending up their strange, white fog of steam.

David spat viciously at the door that closed behind him.

II

He worked fiercely all that afternoon, in a state of trembling indignation; his hands shook, and his forehead perspired with the heat of the internal fires that consumed him. He was debating over and over again the problem of thought and culture with Mr. Neuheim, and his eyes would flash as he made some striking and noble point, and withered the fat little Boss with his scorn.

Six o'clock came at last; the factory motors were shut off, and died away with a last lingering scream. The operators and pressers and basters became men and women again. They rose stiffly from their seats, and talked and laughed, and dressed themselves and hurried away from the factory as from a prison.

The rage that sustained David died with the iron-throated wailing of the whistles that floated over the city, unyoking so many thousands of weary shoulders.

A curious haze came upon him then. He walked home weakly, as if in a debilitating dream. He hardly felt the scarlet sky above the roofs, the twilight beginning to fall upon the city like a purple doom, the air rich with spring. Mighty streams were flowing through the factory district, human working masses silent and preoccupied after the day's duties, and David slipped into these broad currents without thought, and followed them automatically.

He lived in a tenement on Forsythe Street, on the East Side, and the tides all flowed in that direction; down Broadway, through Grand Street and Prince Street and other streets running east and west and across the dark, bellowing Bowery. Then they spread again and filtered and poured out into the myriad crisscrossing streets where stand the tenements row after row, like numberless barracks built for the conscripts of labor.

It was a Friday night, the eve of the East Side's Sabbath, and Mrs. Brandt, David's little dark, round-backed mother, was blessing the candles when he entered. She had a white kerchief over her hair, and her brown eyes, deep and eager in her wrinkled face as David's own, shone with a pious joy as she read the pre-Sabbath ritual from an old "Sidar" that had come with her from Russia. She looked at David's clouded face anxiously for a moment, but did not interrupt her prayers to greet him when he came in. David did not greet her either, but limp and nerveless went directly to his room and flung himself upon the bed.

There he lay for a few minutes in the darkness. He heard the sounds of life rising from the many windows on the airshaft; the clatter of dishes and knives, the crying of babies, voices lifted in talk. He heard his mother move about; she had evidently finished her prayers, and was coming to his room. Some strange weakness suddenly assailed him; as she knocked at the door, David began weeping; quietly, reasonlessly, like a lonely child.

"David?" his mother inquired, waiting at the threshold. There was no answer, and she called his name again.

"David!"

David answered this time.

"I'm all right, mommer," he said, his voice muffled by the pillows.

"Supper'll be ready in five or ten minutes," Mrs. Brandt said. "Better come out now and wash yourself. And David. . . ."

"Yes?"

"David darling," she whispered, opening the door a little, "you should not do like you did tonight. You should always go and kiss your papa the first thing when you come home. You don't know how bad it makes him feel when you don't do that. He cries over it, and it makes him sicker. He's very sick now; the doctor said today your popper is worse than he's ever seen him. Be good, David, and go speak to him."

"Yes, mommer," David said wearily.

He washed at the sink, and ate the Friday night supper of stuffed fish, noodle soup, boiled chicken and tea. His mother chattered to him all the while, but David listened in that haze that had come on him at the end of the factory day, and answered her vaguely. When he had finished eating he continued sitting at the supper table, and was only aroused when she again suggested that he go in to see his father.

The elder Brandt was a sad, pale, wasted little Jew who had spent fourteen years in the sweatshops of America, and now, at the age of forty-five, was ready to die.

He had entered the factories a hopeful immigrant, with youthful, rosy cheeks that he had brought from Russia, and a marvelous faith in the miracle of the Promised Land that had come from there, too. The sweatshops had soon robbed him of that youthful bloom, however; then they had eaten slowly, like a beast in a cave gnawing for days at a carcass, his lungs, his stomach, his heart, all his vital organs, one by one.

The doctor came to see him twice a week, and wondered each time how he managed to live on. He lay in the bed, propped up high against the pillows, a *Vorwaerts* clutched in his weary hand. His face, wax-yellow and transparent with disease, was the face of a humble Jewish worker, mild and suffering, but altogether dead now except for the two feverish eyes. He lay exhausted and limp, his whole attitude that of a figure noted down in the books of Death.

David's father was sucked dry, and there was only one spark of life and youth remaining in him—incredibly enough—his faith in the miracles of the Promised Land.

He put down the newspaper and looked up with a timid smile as David entered the room. David came over and kissed him, and he sat on a chair beside his father's bed.

"Well, David, boy, did you have a hard day in the shop today?" the sick man began in a weak voice, fingering his straggly beard and trying to appear cheerful.

"Yes," David answered dully.

"Are you getting on good there?" Mr. Brandt continued, in his poor, hopeful quaver.

"Yes."

"And did you ask the boss yet about that raise he promised you two months ago?"

"No," said David, vacantly, staring with lustreless eyes at the floor.

Mr. Brandt looked apprehensive, as if he had made an error in asking the question. He stroked the feather-bed quilt under which he lay imprisoned, and stole little anxious glances at David's brooding face, as if to implore it for the tiniest bit of attention and pity. Another difficult question hesitated on his lips.

"Davie, dear," he said at last, "why don't you come in to see your popper any more when you get home from work?"

"It's because I'm tired, I guess," David answered.

"No, it ain't that, Davidka. You know it ain't. You used to come in regular and tell me all the news. Do you hate your popper now, David?"

"No, why should I?"

"I don't know. God knows I've done all I could for you; I worked night and day for long years in the shop, thinking only of you, of my little son. I wanted better things for you than what you've got, I couldn't help myself; I was always only a working man. Some men have luck; and they are able to give their children college educations and such things. But I've always been a *shlemozel*; but you must try to get more out of life than I have found."

"Yes."

"David, don't hate me so; you hardly want to speak to me. Look at me."

David turned his eyes toward his father, but he saw him only dimly, and heard in the same dim way the feeble, high voice uttering the familiar lamentations. In the flickering gaslight his father seemed like some ghostly, unreal shadow in a dream.

"David, you hate me because I'm sick and you have to support me along with your mother. I know; I know! Don't think I don't see it all! But it's not my fault, is it, Davie, and I've only been sick a year, and who knows, maybe soon I will be able to take my place in the shop again, and earn my own bread, as I did for so many years before."

"Don't, popper, for God's sake, don't talk about it!" David spoke sharply.

"All right, I won't. All right. Excuse me."

They sat in silence, and then David moved uneasily, as if to go. Mr. Brandt reached over and took his hand in his own moist, trembling one, and held it there.

"Davie," he said, "Davie, dear, tell me why you didn't come tonight. I must know."

"I was tired popper, I told you."

"But why were you tired?"

"I had a fight in the shop."

"A fight? With whom?"

"With the boss—with Mr. Neuheim."

"With the boss? God in heaven, are you crazy? Are you going to lose your job again? What is wrong with you? You have never stuck to one job more than six months. Can't you do like other boys, and stick to a job and make a man of yourself?"

"Let me alone!" David cried in sudden rage, rushing from the room. "For God's sake, let me alone!"

III

With both elbows on the sill, and with his face in his hands, David sat at the airshaft window again during the next half hour. His mind whirled with formless ideas, like the rout of autumn leaves before a wind. His head throbbed, and again a haze had fallen upon him, a stupor painful as that of a man with a great wound.

The airshaft was still clamorous with the hymn of life that filled it night and day. Babies were squalling, women were berating their children, men were talking in rapid Yiddish, there was rattling of plates and knives, and the shrieking of a clothes line pulley like a knife through it all. The airshaft was dark; and overhead, in the little patch of sky, three stars shown down. Pungent spring odors mingled with the smell of rubbish in the courtyard below.

David's mother moved about carefully as she took away the supper dishes. She knew David's moods, and went on tiptoe, and let him sit there until she had cleaned up in the kitchen. He heard vaguely the sound of her labors, and then she came and laid her rough hand, still red and damp from the dish water, on his shoulder.

"What's the matter, Davie?" she asked, tenderly. "What are you worrying about?"

"Nothing."

"Why did you fight with your popper? You know he's sick, and that you mustn't mind what he says. Why did you do it?"

"I don't know."

"You must be nice to him now; he feels it terribly because he's sick, and that you have to support him. Do you worry because you have to support us?"

"I don't know."

"It won't last forever, Davie boy. Something must happen—there must come a change. God can't be so bad as all that. Is that what worries you?"

David's eyes grew melancholy and his head sunk more deeply between his cupped hands.

"Life isn't worth living; that's what's the trouble mommer," he said. "I feel empty and black inside, and I've got nothing to live for."

"That's foolishness," his mother said warmly. "Everyone lives, and most people have even more troubles than us. If there are so many poor, we can be poor, too. What do you think God put us here for anyway? A healthy young boy like you saying he's got nothing to live for! It's a disgrace!"

"Mommer," David said, passionately, "can you tell me why you live? Why do you yourself live? Give me one good reason!"

"Me? Are you asking me this question?" David's mother exclaimed, in a voice in which there was surprise mixed with a certain delight that her usually silent boy was admitting her on an equality to such intimacies.

She wrinkled her brow. It was the first time, probably, in her work-bound, busy life that she had thought on such a theme, and she put her finger on her lip in a characteristic gesture and meditated for a minute.

"Well, Davie," she said slowly, "I will tell you why your popper and I have gone on struggling and living. It is because we loved you, and because we wanted to see you grow up healthy and strong and happy, with a family of your own around you in your old age. That's the real reason."

"But supposing I don't want to grow up," Davie cried. "Supposing you raised a failure in me. Supposing I'm sick of this world. Supposing I die before I raise a family. . . ."

"That's all foolishness. Don't talk that way."

"But supposing. . . ."

"I won't suppose anything."

"Very well," said David. "You live for me. But tell me, mommer, what do people who have no children live for? What does the whole human race live for? Do you know? Who knows anyone that knows?"

Mrs. Brandt thought again. Then she dismissed the whole subject with a wave of her hand.

"Those are just foolish questions, like a child's," she said. "They remind me of the time when you were a little boy, and cried for days because I would not buy you an automobile, or a lion we saw in Central Park, or some such thing. Why should we have to know why we live? We live because we live, Davie dear. You will have to learn that some day, and not from books, either. I don't know what's the matter with those books, anyway; they make you sick, David."

"No, it's life makes me sick—this dirty life!"

"You're a fool! You must stop reading books, and you must stop sitting here every night, like an old graybeard. You must go out more and enjoy yourself."

"I have no friends."

"Make them! What a funny, changeable boy you are! Two or three years ago we could never keep you at home nights, you were so wild. You did nothing but go about till early morning with your friends—and fine friends they were too, poolroom loafers, gamblers, pimps, all the East Side filth. Now you read those books that settlement lady gave you; and I don't know which is worse. Go out; put on your hat and coat and go!"

"Where?"

"Anywhere! The East Side is big, and lots of things are going on! Find them!"

"But I want to read!"

"You won't! I won't let you! I should drop dead if I let you!"

David stared wrathfully at her for a moment, stung into anger by her presumptuous meddling into affairs beyond her world of illiteracy and hope. He was about to speak sharply to her, but changed his mind with a weary shrug of his shoulders. He put on his hat and coat and wandered aimlessly into the East Side night, not in obedience to his mother, but because it was easier than to sit here under the impending flow of her nightly exhortations.

"Smoke and Steel"

The Worker, July 15, 1922

Critics and academics including Jim Hoberman and Alan Wald have viewed Mike Gold as a forerunner of the Beat 1950s and countercultural 1960s. Though Gold drew inspiration from Carl Sandburg and Ernest Hemingway, both with roots in journalism, he was also impressed by the abstract expressionism of Eugene O'Neill and the experimentalism of the Soviet avant-gardists Vsevolod Meyerhold and Vladimir Mayakovsky. In this paean to America's Steel City, written after reporting on the 1922 United Mine Workers strike, Gold blends proletarian realism with futurist-modernist elements to address urgent social questions.

~

I came to Pittsburgh on a warm, wet morning, on my way to the great coal strike. A mist filled the streets of the dirty city of coal and steel. It was not the fine tremulous, poetic mist of Corot; it was smoke, raw smoke belched by high heaven, and the fitting garment for this stark city that is the stoke-hold of America.

Pittsburgh is stark. It is stark and straight as a pistonrod; it drives on. There are no fancy skyscrapers in Pittsburgh, no show streets or shady places. I came out of the station and looked about me. I saw the squat, dirty houses, the railroad trestle, saloons, cheap hotels, trucks rumbling along the stones. Beyond the ragged line of roofs I saw tall smoke-stacks everywhere, pointed like cannon at the stupid, ancient skies. They were pouring out thick, rushing smoke; they were vomiting smoke like monster drunkards dizzy with too much life; they were streaming the black smoke of industry, the smoke of vitality, of production, of life, of creation. The monster mills surround Pittsburgh; they taint her air and her skies; there are days when their smoke eclipses the sun at mid-day for a half hour or more, till the wind has purged the cosmos; the mills are a part of Pittsburgh, and make it dirty and hot with being, make it throb like an engine with fire and action.

I walked about Pittsburgh the next few days, waiting for my chance to get out into the strike regions. Who has ever described in words that cruel, hard city that fascinates one like the eyes of a huge python! I walked about it for two days, and saw the most miserable slums in the world, and the most magnificent palaces. And everywhere were the mills—the mills where steel is made—steel, the skeleton of the modern world, steel that is the life-breath of the modern world. Man was once clay, then he became bronze, then iron; now he is Steel! Railroads, skyscrapers, tractors, machinery—their father is Steel! And Pittsburgh is steel; the giant Pittsburgh is dirty and stinking and horrible, but he produces Steel!

I stood on one of the bridges that cross the Allegheny river near Pittsburgh. Coal barges were going up and down the yellow stream, pushed by old-fashioned stern-wheel steamboats. There were raw, naked hills on either bank, scarred and gouged as though great beasts had had them between their teeth, and with splashes of green spring grass here and there. There were empty coal cars on the sidings near the river—rusty long sheds, warehouses and waste places. Is this the gaunt, grim, smoky city, stripped to the primitive buff and reeking with black sweat like a stoker at his furnace? Who has ever painted it?

Who has ever understood it, among the oleomargarine intellectuals, among the lemonade artists, among the gossipy, old maidy, vapory small-town writers of American tragedy? They come to see Pittsburgh and shudder, and run back to their books and their eternal ruminating on the mysteries of married life. They rush back to read and imitate Dostoevsky, and to brood on the infinite, and to utter sickening, yearning moans for the past. And Pittsburgh is here. And Pittsburgh plows thru, like a battleship in a storm. And Pittsburgh lives. And Pittsburgh creates steel and coal, the life-blood of "Civilization." And strong men work and hope and love and fight and die in Pittsburgh, and women bring babies into the world, strong babies, and there is drunkenness and riot, creation and destruction. But the Young Intellectuals go to Paris to sip absinthe, or to Rome to publish little reviews.

The alarming, amazing city, littered with tin cans and rot. Down the river one saw another bridge, and it was surrounded by a fog of black smoke. Pittsburgh lay beyond one of those raw hills, and it was shooting its smoky breath into the clean face of the solar system. Smoke, smoke—the smoke of creation—of steel! On this bank of the river there was a colony of company houses; deadly grey, dirty and alike in every part like a row of blank-faced idiots sitting in the sun, the bright sun that shone on the unanimous grey roofs and made them glow like cubes and squares of ice. The men who made steel lived in those houses. And on the other bank were the steel mills—a colony of strange low buildings squatting somehow like an envenomed octopus with a thousand outreaching thick tentacles, sullen and filled with a fierce angry life. I counted forty smokestacks in the fourth of a square mile where these buildings were placed. They were tall smokestacks that poured forth smoke continuously—the black, green, yellow, robin-blue, white, and gray smoke of the different processes by which steel is made. Hammers and heavy forging machines were clanking and pounding; the smoke rushed from the forty smokestacks; wild satanic fires burst and leaped and glared thru the hundreds of dirty windows of the mills; I could see men stripped to the waist moving about; Pittsburgh was making Steel—Steel!

When I went down to the coal fields I rode for two hours along the Monongahela river, and saw a hundred times this sight of steel being created by man. The river was lined with blast furnaces and rolling mills; it was like moving along the trenches of a great battle, it was the spectacle of America's power, that power that has enabled her to conquer the world. The material life of the world centers about coal and steel; the lives of the world's millions now hang on the fate of the world's coal and steel; and it was Pittsburgh that battered down Essen and ended the war; it was Pittsburgh and the world it has built that killed Rupert Brooke and John Reed and Karl Liebknecht; it was Pittsburgh that created Carl Sandburg and Eugene O'Neill, Dada Futurism, Bolshevism, Capitalism, Gary and Lenin. Pittsburgh is the material and spiritual capital of the twentieth-century world. Here it was now—working at its terrible flaming forges, making steel. [. . .]

"But oh, how monstrous!" I heard the gentle small-town spirit of the past murmur in my ear. "Oh, the horror of these leagues of buildings bursting with flame! Oh, the insane mathematics of it all, the rationality, the inhuman, sleepless lust of these endless machines! Men are fed into these mills as into a giant's maw, and the great jaws eat them, crunch them with cannibal glee, devour their human flesh and bones and dreams! Nothing human can stand against the cold fury and power of these monsters, and the tyrants who own them. Soon the machines will rise from the feast here, and slavering with lust, will hunt thru the other regions of the quiet, simple world. All men will be made the food and slaves of the machines. All dreams, laughter, love and human beauty will go into the furnaces, to be burned into Steel. The human world, this hopeful, varied, beautiful world of man that has struggled out of the primeval slime, will be killed, as the living trees that stand in the smoke of the coke ovens are killed utterly and turned to dismal ash. The machines will enslave the world. The world will become a vast roaring mill inhabited by millions of slaves, slaves obsessed like bees with the madness of work, knowing nothing but Steel. The great cosmic mill will grind away century after century, turning out steel, steel, steel. No one will know why after centuries—no one will question—no one will read and write, draw, paint, love, laugh, fight, adventure any longer. Steel, steel, steel!"

But a big-chested, hairy old man next to me in the train, a white-haired steel worker, was talking to me in a soft Irish brogue as he smoked his pipe. He told me of the little garden he was planting, and how the warm weather had brought the tips of the early vegetables thru the mould. And he spoke of his son, a "fine big feller," who was taking a course in electrical engineering at the Technical Institute. And he jested about his wife, who had been quarrelling with him for forty years because he changed from winter underwear to summer too soon. And he told me how he had worked in the mills since he was a boy, and how the puddlers stand over the cauldrons and stir the metal, and how the steel is made into pigs, and how it is run thru the rollers. And he talked about the Great Steel Strike, and how he had just about got ready to get his gun out to go after the State Cossacks, when it ended, and how there would be another big strike coming, and by God, how he'd be there with it again.

He was old and strong and human and unafraid. He was organized labor. There was a greater power than the machines. It would go up against the beast and conquer it—humanize it. It was the labor movement, and no one in America not knowing the labor movement can look upon the mills of Pittsburgh and believe in life. No one can understand one without the other. Yes, the power of labor is greater than the power of governments and machines. Labor is stronger even than steel. There is no room for despair—Labor has not yet learned from books how to despair. Labor will redeem Pittsburgh someday—make it beautiful as a strong man wrestling with fate. Labor will build up a new culture in which the making of coal and steel will be part of the creative life of man. Labor is the hope of the world.

“The Strange Funeral in Braddock”

The Liberator, June 1924

Gold’s friend and fellow journalist Art Shields called this elegiac verse “the most tragically beautiful poem that has come out of the United States class struggle.” Shields thought it important that the story it told was an actual event Gold had learned about from an aunt who lived in the Pittsburgh steel district: Jan Clepak, a young Bohemian immigrant, was killed when a cauldron of boiling metal burst above him in a Donora, Pennsylvania, mill. The ironworker’s body was submerged in an avalanche of molten lead. Later the hardened block of metal was donated to Clepak’s wife and family, who watched in a state of shock as the three-thousand-pound coffin was lowered into the grave from a company-owned truck. “ ‘The Strange Funeral in Braddock’ is not just a recital of grim facts,” Shields observed; “it is permeated with the grief of Jan Clepak’s bride and the fury of Jan Clepak’s fellow workers.” Composer Elie Siegmeister set this poem to a musical score for voice and piano in 1933.

~

Listen to the mournful drums of a strange funeral.
Listen to the story of a strange American funeral.

In the town of Braddock, Pennsylvania,
Where steel mills live like foul dragons burning, devouring
  man and earth and sky,
It is spring. Now the spring has wandered in, a frightened
  child in the land of the steel ogres,

And Jan Clepak, the great grinning Bohemian on his way to work at six in the morning,
Sees buttons of bright grass on the hills across the river, and plum trees hung with wild, white blossoms,
And as he sweats half-naked at his puddling trough, a fiend by the lake of brimstone,
The plumb trees soften his heart,
The green grass memories return and soften his heart,
And he forgets to be hard as steel, and remembers only his wife's breasts, his baby's little laughters, and the way men sing when they are drunk and happy,
He remembers cows and sheep, and the grinning peasants, and the villages and fields of sunny Bohemia.

Listen to the mournful drums of a strange funeral.
Listen to the story of a strange American funeral.

Wake up, wake up! Jan Clepak, the furnaces are roaring like tigers,
The flames are flinging themselves at the high roof, like mad yellow tigers at their cage.
Wake up! it is ten o'clock, and the next batch of mad, flowing steel is to be poured into your puddling trough,
Wake up! wake up! for a flawed lever is cracking in one of those fiendish cauldrons,
Wake up! and wake up! for now the lever has cracked, and the steel is raging and running down the floor like an escaped madman,
Wake up! O, the dream is ended, and the steel has swallowed you forever, Jan Clepak!

Listen to the mournful drums of a strange funeral.
Listen to the story of a strange American funeral.

Now three tons of hard steel hold at their heart, the bones, Flesh, nerves, the muscles, brains and heart of Jan Clepak,
They hold the memories of green grass and sheep, the plum trees, the baby-laughter, and the sunny Bohemian villages.

And the directors of the steel mill present the great coffin of
steel and man-memories to the widow of Jan Clepak,
And on a great truck it is borne now to the great trench in
the graveyard,
And Jan Clepak's widow and two friends ride in a carriage
behind the block of steel that holds Jan Clepak,
And they weep behind the carriage blinds, and mourn the
soft man who was killed by hard steel.

Listen to the mournful drums of a strange funeral.
Listen to the story of a strange American funeral.

Now three thinkers are thinking strange thoughts in the
graveyard.
"O, I'll get drunk and stay drunk forever, I'll never marry
woman, or father laughing children,
I'll forget everything, I'll be nothing from now on,
Life is a dirty joke, like Jan's funeral!"
One of the friends is thinking in the sweet-smelling
graveyard,
As a derrick lowers the three tons of steel that held Jan Clepak.

(LISTEN TO THE DRUMS OF THE STRANGE
AMERICAN FUNERAL!)

"I'll wash clothes, I'll scrub floors, I'll be a fifty-cent whore,
but my children will never work in the steel mill!"
Jan Clepak's wife is thinking as earth is shovelled over the
great steel coffin,
In the spring sunlight, in the soft April air.

(LISTEN TO THE DRUMS OF THE STRANGE
AMERICAN FUNERAL!)

"I'll make myself hard as steel, harder,
I'll come some day and make bullets out of Jan's body, and
shoot them into a tyrant's heart!"
The other friend is thinking, the listener,
He who listened to the mournful drums of the strange funeral,

Who listened to the story of the strange American funeral,
And turned as mad as a fiendish cauldron with cracked
lever.

LISTEN TO THE MOURNFUL DRUMS OF A STRANGE
FUNERAL.
LISTEN TO THE STORY OF A STRANGE AMERICAN
FUNERAL.

Foreword from *120 Million* (1929)

120 Million, *Gold's highly experimental second book of short fiction and poetry, showed the author's development as reflected in an aesthetic shift from simple, stark realism to a modernist outlook influenced by his first visit to the Soviet Union in 1924–25. The foreword, reprinted below, explains the theory behind the book's use of proletarian chants and recitations.*

The book's title is taken from the final chant. It refers to the size of the US population, the millions who are figuratively cataloged by a proletarian poet on a cross-country journey, a people who worship a "Money God" and make war on each other, a people "whose heart is a Ford car, / Whose brain is a cheap Hollywood Movie, . . . / Whose victims die of hunger."

The sketches of proletarian American life in this book were written mostly from my 19th to 26th year, and are arranged in the order of composition.

Melancholy runs through them, lifting to militant courage in the last part of the book. I have outgrown the melancholy, but feel it was perhaps inevitable in the progress of a proletarian writer.

Youth is not always brave; often it is bewildered. Poverty crushes us in youth; we can see no escape, we are isolated and suicidal. Our revolt then is individual and subjective; we write with lyric pain out of loneliness.

But the adolescent fog clears, giving way to the bold outlines of reality. One learns that others, too, are caught in the cosmic trap of poverty; and that out of despair, melancholy, and helpless rage of millions, a world movement has been born, to abolish poverty.

Mass is strength, mass is clarity and courage. From ego-poet to mass-poet is the usual path of the proletarian writer.

The old Christian socialist literature was written by members of the upper class. It portrayed the worker with the pity, condescension and prayer of a charity lady or slummer.

The worker was rarely portrayed as a human being, but as some strange brute savage living in the subcellars of life.

When a Robert Burns appeared, or a Maxim Gorky or Jack London, he was eyed with wonder, as if a truck horse should suddenly sing opera.

The situation has changed. No one can patronize the workers any longer. Their advance guard are not victims, but fearless soldiers in the world war against poverty.

They ask for nothing they cannot take.

Thousands of writers have appeared to express the new proletariat; a literary generation bred in factories, mines and slums of every land, writing boldly and dynamically of the life they know.

No more slumming or missionary pity.

Proletarian literature now dominates many lands. It is the main current in Soviet Russia, it is one of two mainstreams in Japanese thought. It is strong in China and India, and strong in Germany and Middle Europe.

One finds it bursting into the parlors of British and French literature. There is a great gale of it in Latin-America. Symptoms appear even in our bourgeois United States, last fort of capitalism.

Note that nearly all young proletarian writers today are communists. My own visit to Soviet Russia, and contact with its new life and art, gave me the sense of direction I had needed. Soviet Russia cured me of sentimentality, and gave me courage to persist in a land where the proletarian writer has no friends.

The workers' chants and recitations in the back of this book were inspired by things learned in Soviet Russia. The poets there have socialized the aristocratic art of poetry. Their theory is that poetry should be useful. It should organize the emotion of the revolution, as political leaders organized the intellect.

Poetry is used in Soviet Russia as a means of welding the masses into solidarity. It is chanted at mass meetings, it furnishes new rituals. The Soviet poets have restored poetry to its primitive Homeric utilities.

I have written the first mass recitation in this country, I believe, and some of the first workers' chants. I hope others will write them, too. They are needed. The Social Revolution in this country is a wheat kernel fighting through stony soil. It is a beginning. My book is a beginning, too. I dedicate it to my comrades, the few, brave, scattered proletarian writers of America. Let us persist.

"Coal Breaker"

Chapter 1 of 120 Million, *"Coal Breaker," might today be called flash fiction. All told, the stories give evidence that Gold was one of the first to adapt the futurism of Mayakovsky and Meyerhold to American settings, and to do so in works of prose fiction as well as drama and poetry.*

Always between the sky and their earth the miners saw the unhallowed, grim, irregular mass of the coal-breaker, a tall structure black with dust, ugly as a giant toad. It dominated the whole valley.

There were green trees in that valley, meadows and flowers for the light to kindle in the summer days. The spring brought a soft flush there, much as in other parts of the world. There were stars and moon at night, the sun by day.

There was beauty, but it lived furtively under a shadow. A great somber coal-mine was in that valley. It had dragged its black, slimy trail across the clear brightness of nature. A town of dirty, sad houses was heaped about like stacks of filth on the grass of the valley level. Huge hills of slag stood about the mine's mouth, mounds of darkness from which spurted jets of diabolical flame.

The men of all the races lived in the houses of the town. They shuffled in the morning through the muddy streets toward the mine-pit, and returned in the dusk with their emptied dinner pails, their faces black as sinister masks, their bodies dripping sweat, and stooped in weary curves.

Saturday nights there was one brief candle of romance lit in this dark reality of toil. The miners drew their pay then, and spent some of it on liquor. They danced, they sang, they fought and grew sentimental, they remembered for a moment their human heritage of play.

I was in Miduvski's general store on a night such as this. The place was dimly lit by lamps, and Miduvski, a big, bald-headed shrewd speculator, stood plotting behind his counter. There were a few odd customers lounging about. Nothing happened for an hour or so; then some of the miners came trooping in.

There were about eight of them, and a few boys who worked in the coal-breaker trailed admiringly in the rear. The miners were dressed in overalls and black caps with tiny lamps fastened on them, and these lamps seemed like the horns of a group of wild-faced devils. The men were of all races, most of them short and squarely built. Their white teeth flashed out of the gloom of their faces as they laughed uproariously, for they were all a little drunk.

"Set-em up, Miduvski!" shouted one, a stout, powerful man with a merry black face and little Chinese eyes. "The kid here is treating!"

He dragged forward a youngster who was no more than ten years old, and who was dressed in ragged overalls too long for him, and a miner's cap that came over his ears. The boy had high cheekbones and coal dust darkened his straight nose and sandy hair of a young Slav.

"The little Hunyak is goin' to treat!" roared the stout miner again. "This is his first week in the breaker, and he's celebratin'. Ainchyer, kid?"

"Yeh!" the boy said, laughing mirthlessly and staring at them all with big, dazed eyes. "I'm a man now!"

At this there was a general outbreak of laughter, and one of the men clapped the boy approvingly on the shoulder. Miduvski filled the glasses with whisky, which they gulped down with great smacking of lips and long "Ah-h-hs!"

"Give the kid a hooker too!" shouted a tall reckless Irishman, pounding on the counter. "He's one of us now, by gorry!"

"Yes, yes!" cried the other men, and the storekeeper poured another glass of the red, fiery stuff, which the boy swallowed mechanically.

"Yah!" shouted the man admiringly, "That's the idea!"

They watched the boy take out his pay envelope and extract a dollar bill which he laid on the counter.

"Game to the core!" the Irishman said, slapping the boy on the back again. "Let's have another now! My treat!"

The boy leaned against the counter, and looked about him foolishly. "I ain't goin' to be a miner all my life," he announced, with a superior air. "I'm goin' to be a doctor!"

"Hooray for Jansy!" the men shouted, reaching out for the newly-filled glasses. The boy drank with them again, with a careless pride on his young face. But the next moment, the wide store with its shadows of lamplight, its dark, deep corners and laden shelves, grew dim and whirling to his eyes. He felt like rushing out into the fragrant country night, to fling himself down on the cool grass somewhere, and to breathe pure air. A miner offered him a chew of tobacco, and the boy thought it necessary to stuff the vile brown plug in his mouth, and to munch it busily. But he was sick to the pit of his stomach.

A small boy had crept shyly into the place, and was looking at the scene with fear. He came over finally and timidly plucked the young worker by the sleeve.

"Jansy," he said, "Mommer's lookin' for ye everywhere, and she says she'll give ye an awful lickin' if ye don't come right home. She's waitin' fer yer pay!"

The breaker-boy pushed his young brother away with a silly smile. "Beat it!" he said haughtily, though reeling and sick with the tobacco and rotgut whisky. "I'm a man now. Just tell Mommer I'm a man now!"

The smaller boy drew back in fright, and stood staring at his brother from the doorway, doubtful as to what to do.

"Hooray for Jansy!" the men shouted in glee, lifting the boy on their shoulders. "Game to the core!"

"We'll have to get him a girl tonight!" the Irishman cried waving his glass of whisky recklessly. "He's a real man now, the little Polak, workin', drinkin', chewin', and whorin'!"

The boy grinned wearily. Outside in the night could be seen the monstrous form of the breaker in whose black bowels gangs of children slaved in fierce silence ten hours each day, sorting the slag from the coal with raw fingers. The coal-breaker dominated the town, it blotted out the night and stars from human eyes. Its dust darkened all the houses and rested heavily on the weeds struggling about the mine's mouth, and in that valley even childhood was fouled and withered by the black, black dust of the breaker.

"Faster, America, Faster!"
A Movie in Ten Reels

New Masses, November 1926, reprinted in *120 Million*, 1929

Some of Gold's short fiction deserves to be considered alongside more famous modernist experiments made by filmmaker Sergei Eisenstein and novelist John Dos Passos, both of whom broke with classic realism by deploying techniques of imagist montage. Here Gold paints American decadence as a private freight train rushing to Hollywood; violent, profligate, licentious and cruel, blindly advancing toward catastrophe and arrogantly wasting life. V. F. Calverton's review of 120 Million *in* The Nation *found Gold's avant-garde fiction crude and violent, but "challenging in its very crudity."*

~

MORNING ON THE RANCH

The private train never stopped. It was like war. It smashed the peace of the dark American fields. Frogs leaped into the marsh pools as the monster passed. Birds waked and screamed. Trees bent before the storm. The blow struck the still farm houses, and they trembled in every rafter.

Fever. No more quiet. The moon reeled. The Virgin night was raped from dreams. Speed! The private train never stopped. There were two luxury cars and a locomotive.

A MYSTERIOUS STRANGER WANDERS IN

The private train never stopped. Its whistle and bell banged and boasted: The world is mine! They clanged: Get out of the way! The Big Boss is coming! The private train spat golden sparks into the humble face of Night. It was destined for Hollywood. Erwin Schmidt, the German-American movie millionaire had chartered it for his youngest star and some friends. The boilers bellowed. The rails shrieked like dying women. Loafers at small country towns were grazed by a thunderbolt of flying steel and steam. They saw a shower of golden windows. Cities and towns roared by. Mountains raced up and down, seesawed. The private train never stopped. It had the right of way from Atlantic to Pacific. It owned the American horizon. (America is a private train crashing over the slippery rails of History. Faster, faster, America!) The private train never stopped.

THE RANCHER'S DAUGHTER LOVED GUM DROPS

In a huge, wonderful armchair Mr. Schmidt leaned back and smiled. He was forty-five years old, and bald, pink, shining and perfect. He was very tolerant. He was sure. He pressed a button and the world entered with a tray, and brought him what he wished. He was a sophisticated Menckenite and connoisseur.

My dear, he said in a fatherly voice, to the raw little flapper opposite him, let me ask George to fill your glass again.

Oh, thank you, Mr. Schmidt, she stammered nervously, licking her dry lips and smiling.

My dear child, he cooed, you mustn't call me Mr. Schmidt! Mr. Schmidt indeed! So formal, aren't you? All my little girls call me Pops. Just Pops.

Yes, Pops.

That's better, Angel Face.

George, the tall Negro in white, entered with low, dramatic, oriental bowings and ceremony. He poured, with perfect art, wine into two thin glasses. He dimmed the lights in the Czarist stateroom being whirled 80 miles an hour through the ancient, humble night.

My, my, Dot, now you're a real star. Yes, at seventeen your name will be blazing in electric lights on the theaters of every city in the world. Isn't that wonderful? Yesterday a mere stenographer, tomorrow a world figure, like Gloria Swanson or Valentino, no less. Don't it thrill you, my little Cinderella?

Oh, it certainly does, Mr.—Pops.

She had baby blue eyes, soft as a mongrel's. Blond, wavy bob. Pink and white enamel face, beautiful as a flat magazine cover done by a Hearst artist. Just out of high school, and bewildered. Her little heart was beating. Her little brain was puzzled. What did Pops want?

KISS ME, MY FOOL!

In the next car, a long room decorated in gilt like the Czar's palace, a male press agent, three female movie actresses, a female scenario writer, two male movie executives, and a male British novelist were drinking and dancing to the radio. None of them needed monkey glands.

Gladys La Svelte tossed off a bumper of champagne, bit the neck of the stately British author, and wanted to pull the engine cord.

Henry, a short Negro in white, uttered, with oriental bowings and humility: Please, ma'am, that cord is for emergencies only.

Let's pull it anyway. I want the train to go faster. I want speed—speed—speed.

Please, ma'am—

Speed. Faster, faster! Tell the engineer, faster, faster!

Yes, ma'am.

She didn't pull it. The radio brought the history of science to a grand climax. It transmitted *Yes Sir, She's My Baby* from Chicago. The jazz band at the Hotel Karnac was ya-hooing like mad.

It positively gets into one's blood, said the British novelist naively. What a country, what a country! Faster, faster, he chortled.

He thought of his marvellous Hollywood contract, and bit the neck of Gladys La Svelte to show his joy. He unbent. This was a riotous surprise to everyone, and they whacked him with colored toy balloons.

MEANWHILE OVER THE
SLUMBERING CITY
THE DAWN'S ROSES
FELL SOFTLY LIKE
PEARLS

The fireman was shovelling coal into the fiery furnace. He was a haggard, young American roughneck. He had been in three wrecks, and in one of them a piece of iron entered his skull.

She's going good now, ain't she? he yelled belligerently, his hard face set, as he wiped his smutty brow with a hunk of cotton waste.

Too good, said the old engineer with a sour sneer. He was disillusioned with speed; he had driven express trains for forty years. But Mr. Schmidt had promised him fifty dollars at the end of his run.

Whaddye mean, too good? Ain't I givin yuh all the steam yuh need? yelled the fireman.

The engineer couldn't hear and didn't answer. He was worrying. The fireman repeated the question belligerently. His nerves were on edge. His girl had thrown him down and had married a salesman. The fireman had been on an awful bootleg jag for three days. He was a hard, bitter drinker since that last wreck, when he was knocked on the head. But the engineer was worrying.

I must watch out. There's always a jam near Des Moines. Jim Moore got wrecked there only last month, with a clear track, too. And these specials ball up the schedule. I must watch out. Jim was wrecked. He took the hill, whistling, and there was Number 4 staring him right in the face. I must watch out.

Faster, faster, yelled the fireman. You got all the steam she can stand, ain't yuh? He was mad with rage for some reason, and slammed the coal like a furious devil into the firebox. Faster, faster, you old bastard.

The engineer was startled. Was it me you called that? he shouted, staring down with stern eyes.

Yeh you, the fireman roared, shaking his shovel at the engineer. You, you, you. His hair streamed in the gale, and the black and yellow glare of the furnace illuminated him with the fires of hell.

I LOVE YOU! MAY I,
MISS SMITH? I KNOW
I'M JUST A POOR
COWBOY, BUT—

In the narrow pantry, George and Henry, the Negroes in white, drooped wearily like heartsick mothers at a bedside.

Ain't they awful?

Yop, plumb coo-coo.

I wish I could get some sleep.

No sleep on this trip, Big Boy.

Honest, it ain't worth even the big tips. I hate to serve them.

Last time for me, I'll tell the world.

There's that bell again. Hope the old ofay busts a blood vessel or something.

Slip a white powder in his gin.

Wish I had the nerve.

Then suddenly oriental, George purringly poured for Mr. Schmidt the finest wine money could buy, into the finest glasses money could buy.

Just turn those other lights out, too, said the magnate. They hurt my eyes.

Yes, sir. Yes, sir.

The private train never stopped.

AS IN BABYLON OF ELD

They were Hollywooding in the next car. They were wasting life. They screamed, wrestled, frazzled, mushed, rubbed, gooed and ate huge chicken and bacon sandwiches. An executive and an actress stole off into a stateroom. The others petted, laughed, screamed, gobbled. They smeared mustard on each other. A dress was torn. The floor was cluttered with napkins, salad dressing, corks and cigarette butts. The radio yammered. The night flew by. Through the windows all the dark farmhouses, trees, rivers, flashed by like a cheap movie. The dark, old American fields roared with a mighty voice. There was a protest against this new thing. But the private train never stopped.

Haw, haw, let's serenade Dot and Pops.

No, let's tell the engineer to go faster, shrieked Gladys.

Someone stuck his head out of the window. Fast enough for me. Fast as a Keystone comedy.

Aw, come on, let's serenade Dot and Pops. He's our host aint he? Gotta show our 'preciation, ain't we?

MY WONDER GIRL!

The fireman slammed open the firebox door. He bellowed with delight when the tiger-blast struck his sweaty face. His muscles bulged. His chest gleamed. He danced like a clumsy bull. He climbed up the cab.

The old engineer screamed. He hit the old engineer over the skull with his shovel. The engineer died. The fireman danced.

Faster, faster, the fireman screamed, flinging his giant arms to the gale. Faster when I tell yuh to go faster. I'm boss here now. I'm a millionaire. I'm King of the World!

The private train never stopped. It leaped ahead as if a giant had kicked it forward.

TWO SHOTS RANG
OUT!

Mr. Schmidt was slightly sweating.

I could get any girl I wanted in the world. But I want only you, my bonny daisy.

Oh, Pops, you do say such pretty things. You talk like a poet.

Little rabbit, you're first beginning to know me. People think I'm a cold, dull business man, but I have an artist's soul. That is really the secret of my success. I'll make a great artist out of you before I'm through with you. If it costs me a cool million.

Oh, Pops! You make me so happy.

Kiss me, Dottie.

I'm so young, she lisped coyly, I don't know about these things. Isn't it wrong, Pops?

MEANWHILE A LONE
RIDER—

Henry and George were badly frightened. They stuck their heads out of the pantry window. The wind smote them like an uppercut from Jack Dempsey's fist.

Gawd, she'll jump the track at this rate, sure. I never saw a train act this way.

I guess it's all right, George. I guess so. Old Gordon's driving her, and he knows what he's doing. I guess so.

It don't feel right, I tell yuh. No. Too fast, too fast!

Old Gordon's running her. Guess so. Guess so. It's all right, George. Guess so. Guess so.

A LITTLE CHILD SHALL LEAD THEM

The gaudy mob poured in to serenade Pops. But the stateroom door was locked against them. They pounded on the door with bottles and yelled Hey! Hey! They rocked on their feet. The private train was shimmying like mad. It never stopped. A few were sick. Gladys La Svelte vomited on the Czarist floor. Everyone laughed like a zoo. Britain supported America and held her head down.

Gladys grew histrionic. She wept like Jesus. He's double-crossed me, she screamed, and broke away. She kicked at the door crazily. I know what's going on in there. He's thrown me over for that little Kewpie doll, the old cradle-snatcher. But I'll show him. I'll tell the newspapers he's crazy for young girls. I'll break him. I'll sue him. He dragged me down.

The others laughed like a zoo. They rocked and shimmied with the train. Aw, forget it, Gladys. Come on and sing, Gladys. Be a sport. He's our host, ain't he? The British novelist used his monocle haughtily, and thought of his contract. Gladys was vulgar. But there was laughter of coyotes and peacocks. Everyone burst into song. Hail, hail, the gang's all here, so what the hell do—

Henry and George rushed in with immense eyes and pork-pale faces.

Too fast—too fast, they stammered—

Laughter like a zoo. They bladdered the Negroes with toy balloons.

Then—OUT!

Life exploded like a bomb.

Then—POW!

The world shot from a cannon in flame. Coney Island fireworks. Crucifix pain.

Tidal wave, earthquake, last lonely screams of little children eaten by a giant. Snap and crack. Fade out. Then quiet. A bird sang in the sudden sweet gloom. There was a smell of roasted flesh.

CAME THE DAWN

The great monster lay on its side, tons of steel writhing like a snake. Huge steam clouds hissed from the dragon's wounds. The old countryside was cool, dark and still. Yes, a bird sang.

Mr. Schmidt's pampered guts lay neglected in the ballast. The last white stars shone in the sky. Gladys was grinning with some bloody joke. She was red and nude. The British novelist was undignified; he had no arms. Negro George was long, flat and patient. The night was very dark and sweet. Little Dot hugged the grass by the track. The fireman's wild head had rolled away. There was the smell of flesh. A bird sang. The press agent's belly was like an open mouth.

Faster, faster. A pale farmer came running from the dark. He had a sickle in his hand. A pale worker in overalls came up, with a hammer. They soberly began the rescue work. Dawn grew. The red morning star appeared.

~

America is a private train rushing to Hollywood.

~

Faster, faster, America!

“The Girl by the River”

Late in his life Gold expressed regret that he had never written a simple love poem. Perhaps this tragic imagist recitation was as close as he got. (Originally published in 120 Million.*)*

~

1.

New York is like a Negro fighter quiet after a knock-out blow,
And quiet, like a tired work-horse, the Night stands in its
stall, moon-drowsing by the river.
No one loves me, nobody loves me, a young girl is moaning
by the river,
As she stumbles like a drunkard through the black docks
and wrings her hands by the dark river,
Alone with the stars, the locked warehouses, an old
watchman and the river,
Spattering the peace with her blood, with her young
hopeless passion by the river,
No one loves me! wringing her pale work hands by the dark
river.

2.

O moonlight boat ride up the Hudson River when May
Carty found her young taxi driver,

When he spoke soft love to her in the dark woods near the
dance hall by the river,
When so beautiful and just, the man-flesh cleaved to
woman-flesh, as in the world's beginning, by a river.
O Georgie, Georgie! she cried, the jazz-notes moan through
the trees like a flight of birds lost on a river!
O Georgie, Georgie! I'm so lonesome in the shoe factory
and not having no real friend but the river!
I could die for love, I could die in this grass with the wild
wet smell and my sweet daddy over me, by the river,
O Georgie, Georgie! don't ever leave me; but he left her, and
she bears his child by the river,
And she wanders the night docks and moans and wrings
her hands by the dark river.

3.

We need to be loved, we droop like yellow dogs without
love,
When no one loves us we plunge for peace into the dark
river,
Old watchman, leave the property you are guarding and
speak a word of love to the girl by the river.
Warehouses, smelling of spice and leather, open your locked
doors and give her rest from the river.
Skyscrapers, stoop to her; Stars, tell her the world is a silver
union of rivers,
Tug-boats, send her a brave yellow flare from the boilers as
you chug down the river,
Bosses who drove her, foremen who hated her, be kind now,
she walks by the river,
Pimps who sought to seduce her, she has come to the river
at last,
Landladies, wheels, strong bankers, O factory whistles, O
congressmen, O river,
O America, O you who used her, forget your money-lust
now, she dreams of the river!

She is mad! she is lost! she will drown herself for want of
love, in the river!
The young factory girl who moans by the dark river.

4.

I begged her to wait for dawn.
O my darling, my darling! Revolution will rise from the east
on the dark river,
Bringing peace to workers, and peace to women, and no
more dark river.
This is sure, this is sweet, this is stronger than strong
bankers and the river.
There will be love for all, and in factories and subways, love.
It will float over the skyscrapers, and chug in the tough tug-
boats down the dark river.
Wait, wait! the workers are marching over the mountains
and swimming the stormy river,
The bosses cannot stop them, the old watchman cannot
guard the locked doors by the river,
Wait, wait! but she would not listen, she would not
understand,
She screamed and wrung her hands and plunged into the
dark river.
She did not believe my words, that there would be a time of
revolution and love,
A time of love's children conceived in woods near a dance
hall by a river,
A time of workers' joy in boats down a gay golden river,
A time of no more moaning for factory girls by Life's loud,
huge, red river.

"Lynchers in Frockcoats"

New Masses, September 1927

Having met Bartolomeo Vanzetti during the original Plymouth cordage workers' strike in 1916, Gold felt a personal connection that would underlie a deep commitment to the Sacco-Vanzetti legal fight from its beginnings. By the time of the 1927 execution, he'd been in touch with the case perhaps longer than any other radical writer. The terse appraisal he gave in New Masses *under the title "Lynchers in Frockcoats" was therefore unique not only in its precisely targeted outrage but also in its keen discernment of the xenophobia and bigotry of a "respectable" Boston gentility that Gold had once experienced firsthand and abandoned in disgust over a decade earlier at Harvard.*

~

It is August 14th, eight days before the new devil's hour set for the murder of Sacco and Vanzetti. I am writing this in the war zone, in the psychopathic respectable city that is crucifying two immigrant workers, in Boston, Massachusetts.

All of us here fighting for the two Italians are without hope. We feel that they will burn. Respectable Boston is possessed with the lust to kill. The frockcoat mob is howling for blood—it is in the lynching mood.

If the two Italian workers do not die it will not be the fault of cultured Boston. The pressure of the workers of the world will have accomplished the miracle. But I repeat, the handful of friends working desperately here are without hope. The legal procedure in this case is nothing but a bitter joke. The blood lust alone is real.

You can't understand this case unless you are in Boston now. You must mingle with the crowds at the newspaper bulletin boards on Washington street, hear sleek clerks and ex-Harvard football players and State street stockbrokers mutter rancorously: "These Anarchists must die! We don't want this kind of people running America!"

They whisper, they fidget, they quiver with nervousness and fear, they jump like cats every time a pin drops. The city has lost its head. The atmosphere is like the war days, when George Creel's skilled literary liars were scaring everyone with the news that the Kaiser's airplanes were about to bomb Chicago, New York and San Francisco.

Those who sympathize with Sacco and Vanzetti in the street crowds keep their mouths shut. They are as unpopular as a Northern friend of the Negroes would be at a Southern lynching bee.

Most of the well-dressed, well-mannered Boston bourgeoisie are frank in saying Governor Fuller should not have granted a reprieve. They openly accuse him of being too soft.

The city is under martial law. The entire State militia has been brought into Boston and is quartered on the alert in the armories. The police are on 24-hour watch, equipped with machine guns, tear-gas bombs, and armored cars. No meetings are allowed on the Sacco-Vanzetti case. If you wear a beard, or have dark foreign hair or eyes, or in any way act like a man who has not had a Harvard education or Mayflower ancestors, you are picked up on the streets for suspicion.

You must not look like a New Yorker. Two New York women, Helen Black and Ann Washington Craton, were arrested and questioned at a police station for the crime of looking like New Yorkers. You must not need a shave. Six Italians in an automobile who had come for the demonstration on August 10th were arrested and held on a bombing charge because two of them needed a shave.

Detectives dog you everywhere; yes, those stupid, criminal, blank detective faces haunt you everywhere, in restaurants, in drug stores while you are having an ice cream soda, in cigar stores, even in toilets. At night you can rise like Shelley from your dreams and stare below into the moonlit street and see a knot of evil, legal detective faces, watching you lest you go sleep-walking.

It is highly dangerous to be out in the streets after midnight. A group of us after a hard day's work at the headquarters, went searching for a restaurant at 12:30, and were followed, not by four or five of the detectives, but by a whole patrol wagon load of them.

I was one of those who picketed the State House on August 10th, the first date set for the murder of Sacco and Vanzetti. Forty of us marched up and down the concrete walk between the elm trees near the Common, gaped at by a vast curious mob of Bostonians and police and detectives, and from the capitol's ornate balconies, by the official flunkeys of Governor Fuller.

Our picket line was a good cross-section of the sentiment that has been aroused in America and the rest of the world. There were Jewish needle trade workers and Communists from New York. There were five young Finnish working girls from Worcester, Massachusetts, two of them under the age of fifteen. There was John Dos Passos, the splendid young novelist, and Dorothy Parker, a gay, sophisticated writer of light verse and satirical plays with a flavor of social conscience. There was a group of young Communist workers from Chicago and New York. There were iron workers, sailors, jewelry workers, barbers, bakers, educators, agitators and waiters. There was finally a little fiery Anglo-Saxon aged 62, who made a speech in court affirming that he was opposed to anarchism, was a Harvard graduate, and wanted justice for the two doomed men, for all of which he was fined $20.

Dorothy Parker and I were arrested by the same brace of iron-handed policemen. As they hauled us off on the long walk to the police station, a crowd followed after us—a well-dressed Boston mob, of the type that lynched Lovejoy during the Abolition days.

Some of these respectables booed us, and several of them hooted and howled: "Hang them! Hang the Anarchists!"

That is the mood of respectable Boston at this hour. A friend of mine who is a veteran newspaperman in this city says he has never seen respectable Boston in as tense a mood as now.

"If this were the South they would not wait for Governor Fuller but would storm the jail and lynch Sacco and Vanzetti," my friend said.

But Governor Fuller is in the lynching mood, though he feels constrained to decorate it with Puritan legalities. And President Lowell of Harvard is in that mood, and all those who have conspired one way or another to execute the two Italians.

They will kill Sacco and Vanzetti legally. They are determined on revenge. For decades they have seen wave after wave of lusty immigrants sweep in over their dying culture. For years these idealists who religiously read Emerson and live on textile mill dividends have had to fight rebel immigrants on strike.

New England is dying culturally and industrially. The proud old libertarian tradition of the Abolition days has degenerated into a kind of spiritual incest and shabby mediocre pride of family. The inefficiency of the blueblood factory owners has pushed the textile industry South, where there is plenty of cheap, unorganized and unrebellious native labor.

So these ghosts, these decadents, these haughty mediocre impotent New Englanders have flamed up into a last orgy of revenge. They have the subconscious superstition that the death of Sacco and Vanzetti can restore their dying culture and industry. At last they have a scapegoat. At last they can express the decades of polite frosty despair.

They are as passionate against these Italian workers as white Southerners toward the Negro. They know that New England is rotten from stem to stern, and that the slightest match may prove the brand to start a general revolt in the industrial and political field. They will not be moved from their lust for a blood sacrifice—these faded aristocrats. They are too insane with fear and hatred of the new America.

All I can see now to save Sacco and Vanzetti is a world strike. Nothing less stupendous can shake the provincial Chinese wall of this region. Boston is not conducting a murder case, or even the usual American frame-up—it is in the throes of a lynching bee, led by well-spoken Harvard graduates in frockcoats.

"John Reed and the Real Thing"

New Masses, November 1927

Gold wrote several hagiographic articles about John Reed—the Harvard graduate who rallied striking silk workers in Paterson, New Jersey, by teaching them college fight songs and staging a workers' pageant in Madison Square Garden before going off to fight for (and ultimately die for) the ideals of the Russian Revolution. Reed was exceptional, Gold claimed, because he identified completely with the working class.

Gold never hid his intention to eventually write a biography of Reed. When this piece was published, he was attempting to convince Reed's widow, Louise Bryant, to give him access to her former husband's letters, manuscripts, and personal effects. Bryant personally despised Gold and never let him anywhere near Reed's papers. This slightly abridged version is taken from Sillen's 1954 anthology.

~

John Reed was a cowboy out of the west, six feet high, steady eyes, boyish face; a brave, gay, open-handed young giant; you meet thousands of him on the road, in lumber camps, on the ranges, in fo'c'sls, in the mines.

I used to see Jack Reed swimming at Provincetown with George Cram Cook, that other Socialist and great-hearted adventurer now dead too. I went out a mile with them in a catboat, and they raced back through a choppy sea, arm over arm, shouting bawdy taunts at each other, whooping with delight. Then we all went to Jack's house and ate a big jolly supper.

He loved every kind of physical and mental life; the world flowed through him freely. He lived like an Elizabethan. Because of this, friends like Walter Lippmann would say with affectionate contempt that Jack Reed was a romanticist. They said he never studied politics or economics, and rushed in where wise men feared to tread. But Walter Lippmann, the Socialist, supported the war, and now supports Al Smith for President. He is wrong on everything. And Jack Reed wrote the most vivid book on the Bolshevik Revolution that has yet appeared in any language. After ten years it is as sound and fresh as at first. It was written white-hot, almost at the scene of the event. It is the greatest piece of reporting in history. It is a deathless book that sells by the million.

The Revolution is the romance of tens of millions of men and women in the world today. This is something many American intellectuals never understand about Jack Reed. If he had remained romantic about the underworld, or about meaningless adventure-wandering, or about women or poem-making, they would have continued admiring him. But Jack Reed fell in love with the Revolution, and gave it all his generous heart's blood. This the pale, rootless intellectuals could never understand. When he died they said he had wasted his life. It is they who lead wasted, futile lives in their meek offices, academic sanctums, and bootleg parlors.

Jack Reed lived the fullest and grandest life of any young man in our America. History is already saying this in Soviet Russia. It will say it a century from now in the textbooks of America.

At first he wrote short boyish sketches. He liked roughnecks and he gave himself to queer, far places, he loafed about cities and the underworld. His eyes were keen, his blood boiled with animal joy. The exuberant words leaped in his prose, they swam like laughing athletes, he wrote with broad humor, he exaggerated the bright suns and moons of nature, he splashed the colors on his canvas like a young god. His early stories remind me of Dickens, of Tolstoy, and of Stephen Crane—a strange mixture, but an epic one.

He burst into American writing like a young genius. Everyone followed his work eagerly, waiting for the inevitable masterpiece. At the outbreak of war Jack Reed was the best paid and most brilliant war correspondent in America. He had written some of the best short stories. Everyone waited for the masterpiece. When it came, "they" were all voting for Al Smith, and drinking bootleg with Mencken. "They" had not the great spirit which recognizes masterpieces.

Jack Reed's life was not wasted; he did write his masterpiece, *Ten Days That Shook The World*. But the "intellectuals" haven't yet recognized this. [. . .]

The revolutionary intellectual is an activist thinker. This is what makes him so different from the careful men with perpetual slight colds who write for the *New Republic* and the *Nation*. Jack Reed needed for his activism a magazine like the *Masses*, and helped create it. I was working as a night porter for the Adams Express Company in New York when I began reading the *Masses*. It was the beginning of my education. It educated a whole generation of youth in America, many of whom did not survive the spiritual holocaust of the war. Those who did survive remember Jack Reed, and his courage flows in their veins. And the revolution will grow in America, and there will be a new youth and Jack Reed will teach them how to live greatly again. This depression, this cowardice, this callousness and spiritual death will not last forever among the youth of America. It cannot. Life is mean only in cycles; it sinks defeated, then it inevitably rises. There will be more Jack Reeds in America, his grandchildren perhaps. This mean decade of ours will pass on.

He had his faults. Most people have. But he was never petty in his faults. You can tell that even by his writing. It is difficult to write that way in America today. It is difficult to admit you enjoy life so hugely; that you are simple and loyal, that you are tender to the friendless and wear your heart on your sleeve. A writer must act as mean and as hardboiled as the rest of modern Americans. Maybe this is a good discipline for writers. Maybe it is the way to the strength that writers need in this age. But I am sure that the best elements of Jack Reed's spirit will be preserved in any revolutionary writers who will appear in this country. They will have the bigness to be humane. They will laugh, but they will not sneer. Jack Reed was a fierce enemy to capitalism, but in all his books you will never find a sneer at humanity. And this is difficult to refrain from, too.

Many of his bourgeois friends were always sure Jack Reed was a kind of playboy in the revolution. The revolution was just another one of his huge jolly adventures, like the one in which he dived off an Atlantic liner leaving New York, and swam back to land on an impulse. Yes, the revolution was an impulse. It would exhaust itself when the fun had gone out of it.

Walter Lippmann, in his article in the *New Republic* on John Reed, smiled affectionately as he recounted how his Harvard classmate, Jack Reed, had confessed to the fact that he hadn't heard of Bergson, the latest Paris fashion among the intellectuals of the period. Walter Lippmann and many others thought this showed Jack had no brains, and that his revolutionary philosophy was just a romanticist's impulse.

But Jack Reed went through the Paterson strike, and the Lawrence strike, and the Bayonne strike, and understood their significance. And he understood the economic basis of the World War, and refused to be a tool of J.P. Morgan, like Walter Lippmann and many other wise men who knew so much about Bergson, and so little about the inevitable treaty at Versailles.

And he had read and thought enough to grasp the full political and economic significance of the Bolshevik Revolution for the world, when it was still a raw, bloody, chaotic embryo, which the "intellectuals" predicted could not last a month.

I was in Soviet Russia two years ago and visited Jack Reed's grave under the Kremlin wall. Under the rough stone, near the mausoleum of Lenin lay the splendid body of our comrade. He had not been a playboy. He had loved the Revolution when she was a haggard outlaw fighting for life against the ravening pack of capitalist nations.

He had lived with the revolution in famine, in civil war, in chaos and stern Cheka self-defense. He had seen hundreds of frozen corpses of Red Guards piled high in a railroad station. He had worked himself to the bone for this Revolution. He had wandered through typhus areas, he had been bitten by a typhus louse, and died. It was not all an impulse. It was the real thing with Jack Reed.

And what he had died for was the real thing—but what the boys whom the *New Republic* intellectuals sent out to die for was not the real thing. Walter Lippmann's war to end war did *not* end war, but was the prelude to a more rapacious capitalist imperialism and a greater imperialist war.

But Jack Reed's revolution was all about me in the Red Square of Moscow, where he lay under the rough stone. Peasants passed coming from the land given them by the revolution to lay their problems before Kalinin, their peasant premier, in Moscow. Workers passed, coming from factories where they were masters, not the slaves. Old men passed, who had learned to read and write by the millions since Jack Reed died for them. Young writers and artists passed, thousands of them growing up to express themselves as freely and grandly as Jack Reed. Women passed, walking with their heads up, the freed victims of ancient bondage. Children passed, no longer drugged by the superstitions of a medieval church. There was a new social system growing up; the Elizabethan and Greek genius that had lived in Jack Reed had flowed into a whole nation; it was spreading with red banners in every land; it was the real thing. It was the romance of the real thing.

"Go Left, Young Writers!"

The June 1928 issue of New Masses, *the first under Gold's editorship, was reviewed in the* Daily Worker *as one would review a novel, play, symphony, or other unified work of art. "The* New Masses *died in April and has been reborn in June—a lusty infant," wrote A. B. Magill under the subtitle "Gold Now Editor; June Issue Is Lively." The article noted the disastrous two-year attempt to run the magazine as "a coalition between liberals and revolutionists" and rejoiced that "the liberals have finally been tossed over the wall" and that under Gold, "the* New Masses *will have more than a nominal connection with the American workingclass." Magill pointed to the editor's "strategic reform" of cutting the price of the journal from twenty-five to fifteen cents, saying that it would make "a world of difference."*

The magazine sold out. As Gold recalled, "We had to increase our printing order by 3,000 copies a month." It gave him great satisfaction, he said, but it wasn't enough. He said he wanted to practice "open diplomacy" with readers from that point forward, reverting frequently to his mantra-like exhortations, "Write as you talk. . . . Heart and mind of the workers." As these excerpts show, Gold's New Masses *editorial desk served as a platform from which to process events in the class war and develop an iconoclastic theory of literature.*

~

Go Left, Young Writers! Literature is one of the products of a civilization like steel or textiles. It is not a child of eternity, but of time. It is always the mirror of its age. It is not any more mystic in its origin than a ham sandwich.

It is easy to understand the lacquer of cynicism, smartness and ritzy sophistication with which popular American writing is now coated.

This is a product of "our" sudden prosperity, the gesture of our immense group of *nouveaux riches.*

The liberals have become disheartened and demoralized under the strain of American prosperity. But is it prosperity? No. The great mass of America is not "prosperous" and it is not being represented in the current politics of literature. The Negroes, immigrants, poor farmers and city proletarians—more than forty million of them—live in the same holes they did ten years ago. Upon their shoulders rests the whole gaudy show-palace.

And when they stir the palace will fall. It was that way in Rome, in royalist France, in tsarist Russia. Let us never be dazzled by appearances. The American orgy has been pitched on the side of the historic social volcano. The volcano is as certain to erupt as Mount Etna.

The best and newest thing a young writer can now do in America is to go leftward. . . . In the past eight months the *New Masses* has been finding its way toward an American literature of the proletariat. A new writer has been appearing; a youth of about twenty-two, a son of working-class parents, who himself works in the lumber camps, coal mines, harvest fields and oil tankers of America. He is sensitive and impatient. He has few theories. He writes that way because it is his life. He knows proletarian life the way professor Baker's students at Harvard know the seventeen different ways of ending a second act.

The America of the working class is undiscovered. It is a lost continent. Bits of it come above the surface in our literature and everyone is amazed. In the past eight months the *New Masses* has been fighting for this new proletarian literature! As editor, let me tell our proletarian authors that another year is certain. We are bankrupt; we were about to suspend; we receive no subsidies; but we will survive. Once more we appeal to our readers and writers: Do not be passive. Write. Your life in mine, mill and farm is of deathless significance in the history of America and the world. It may be literature—it often is. Write. Persist. Struggle. ***January 1929***

"Art, Crap Shooting, Etc."

Never before was there such imperial wealth flowing into a nation. Never before in history was there such a vast, feverish, ambitious middle class spending the wealth. These *nouveaux riches* swarm in the capitals of Europe each summer, they buy the castles, paintings, women and opera singers of Europe.

They have created Florida in a few prosperous years, and "modern" furniture and "modern" sculpture, painting and literature. Spend it fast! One portion of America thinks and slaves and labors. The other portion shoots crap. "Our" prosperity is based on the next roll of a pair of dice. It is the crap-shooting bourgeoisie that are the new "culture" audience. They buy things in the blind frantic mood of a gambler on his lucky day. Was there ever such a stock market? But tomorrow the luck and the "culture" may change. And there will be another world war among the crap shooters. **September 1929**

"Letter from a Clam Digger"

I have been down with my old Tampico malaria. I am convalescing now; am swimming, sunbathing, walking, eating, fishing, here on Staten Island. Nothing important here but the way the bluefish and whitefish are biting, and the nightly pot of clam chowder. You have sent me the *New American Caravan* to review. I can't do it. It is expert writing, but gives one the weary blues. It is solemn and pompous, and if a clam could write, a "liberal" and "modern" bourgeois clam, this is how it would write. This insipid mysticizing over petty and obscure sorrows! I am getting old and simple. I want only plain food and the plain and eternal emotions of earthly struggle. New forms without a new content seem as worthless to me as walnut shells whose meat the little bugs have eaten away. In biology it is need that creates form, it is function that creates form. These alleged "moderns" seem to have no life function. I don't understand them. I suspect they are merely passing the time. But I prefer fishing. ***November 1929***

“The New South”

I attended a session of the National Textile Workers Union last month. There was a solid block of southern workers there—tall, rawboned 100% Americans, many of whom five years ago were Ku Kluxers, and now talked in their native idiom the language of socialism.

Southern labor has waked up. This strong sombre giant, whom the American capitalists thought they would use as the Tsar used the Cossacks, has shaken off the traditional chains. The Knights of Labor never could do it. The American Federation of Labor never really tried. The I.W.W. failed. The Socialists avoided the issue with all the cunning of respectable cowards. Only Communists have dared to enter the old evil South with the message of freedom and equality.

How thrilling to hear these southern delegates speak! Lanky, overalled, dignified, shaping their words carefully. Something like Indians in their stoicism, only their sunken eyes showing the fires within, one after the other rose to give his testimony.

They pledged themselves to a square deal for the Negro workers. “We need them, we can’t have a union without the Negro,” said a lean, overalled young southerner. One Georgian told how in his home-town, up to a year ago, no Negro dared walk the sidewalks if a white man was walking there. “It’s changed now, since the union come,” said the delegate, simply.

The Gastonia strike was a new Bunker Hill in American history, opening the way for Negro equal participation in American life. And the Communists led the fight in Gastonia. Thus Communism now is part of Negro history, of all American history. ***February 1930***

“The Crisis Deepens”

Seven million are out of work in America up to the moment. On March 6 they came out into the streets and asked for work and bread. The cops gave them blackjacks and gas bombs instead. This is the way the police mind functions, and how monarchs commit suicide and republics rot into death.

To watch a regiment of armed, beefy cops slug and maim every pale, defenseless man, woman and child in their path is sickening to a normal observer. But most of our newspapers seemed to like the spectacle. Even liberal journals stood behind the cops, and against the unemployed. The intellectuals have discovered a new taunt to cast into the teeth of the millions who protest against unemployment. These starving workers are accused of suffering from a “martyr complex.” This new-fangled Freudian epithet was once invented by H.L. Mencken in a typical Tory moment, but *The New Republic* had a long editorial on the March 6 police attacks that blamed the workers and called their demonstration a neurotic desire for suffering.

How far is it from such “intellectualism” to the Herbert Hoover gulf of class cruelty? The liberals are finding it hard to make up their minds about unemployment. Liberalism has always been the art of straddling. But with every day some new social catastrophe makes this art more difficult.

By the way, John Brown, Thomas Jefferson and Abraham Lincoln were among those present in Union Square when the clubbing began. They received a severe beating, and were arrested and tried. The Judge said he heartily wished there was a law to hang such Reds. He said, as did a local Judge to some other Union Square victims, “I wish I had you alone in a locked room for half an hour!” Jefferson and his comrades were heard to murmur, “We would also like to be alone with Your Honor.” ***April 1930***

"Renegades and Radicals"

America is as full of ex-radicals as an old mattress is of bugs. At best, they become harmless sex writers and detective story merchants, or cynical, tired newspapermen, and migratory bums and businessmen. At worst, they become the misleaders of labor, cynically clinging to a well-paid racket. Or they can become those literary stool-pigeons on bourgeois newspapers and magazines who make a career out of "exposing" the radical labor movement.

Kropotkin once consoled a comrade who mourned over the baseness of such renegades. The great anarchist declared: "Let them go. We have had the best of them; we have had their youth." ***May 1930***

"Give Us Barrabas!"

Every month hundreds of convicted axe murderers, sex-fiends, kidnappers and other gangsters are released from prison by pardon boards throughout America. But Mooney and Billings are still in jail after thirteen years. There was no mercy shown to Sacco and Vanzetti. There is no mercy waiting for six young Negro and white workers facing the electric chair in Georgia as the result of a textile strike. No mercy for the striking farm workers in that hellhole, the Imperial Valley, who were sentenced to 42 years in jail. Or the Gastonia textile strikers facing a framed-up murder charge.

No, the capitalist can never pardon a wage slave who rises from his knees and asserts his human dignity. He understands and pardons only the gangster criminals, they are of his family, and to be forgiven. Sacco and Vanzetti were rebel workers, therefore his most hateful enemy. It is the third anniversary of their murder. Mass meetings are being held all over America to honor the memory of the "good shoe-maker and poor fish peddler." They will never be forgotten. Nor the manner of their murder. It was no accidental mistake of justice, or the prejudice and greed of some judge or prosecutor. It revealed again the pattern of class justice in America. Labor will lose more tragic battles such as this. But it can never lose the war for a new America where there will finally be justice and hope for the workers and farmers. ***September 1930***

Part Three

"Bananas"

Jews Without Money *(1930) reverses the trajectory of the American narrative of upward mobility, recasting the national myth as a family tragedy. The character Herman Gold, for example, achieves early business success as a salesman of suspender fasteners, but when that livelihood is stolen, he descends into ever deeper poverty and ends his career as pushcart peddler, the very job with which the greenest of Jewish immigrants often began life in the New World.*

In chapter 21, "Bananas," the suffering has been compounded by the sudden and traumatic loss of a child. Nine-year-old Esther, Mikey's younger sister and the family's "little dove," has been run over by a delivery truck while out gathering stovewood on a snowy night. "There are enough pleasant superficial liars writing in America," Mike Gold asserted in the novel's opening pages, "I will write a truthful book about poverty."

1.

Esther was dead. My mother had borne everything in life, but this she could not bear. It frightened one to see how quiet she became. She was no longer active, cheerful, quarrelsome. She sat by the window all day, and read her prayer book. As she mumbled the endless Hebrew prayers, tears flowed silently down her face. She did not speak, but we knew why she was crying. Esther was dead.

For months she was sunk in this stupor. She forgot to cook or sweep. My father and I had to do things. She was afraid, too, that I might be killed by a truck, and would not let me go out peddling the newspapers. She clung fiercely to my little brother and me and devoured us with kisses, and kept us beside her for hours. My father watched her anxiously during her long, gloomy apathies by the window.

"Katie, what is wrong?" he implored. "Katie, of what are you thinking?"

"Nothing," she said drearily. "I am only watching the children at play in the street."

"But you mustn't!" my father cried. "It reminds you of Esther! You will make yourself sick, Katie!"

"Let me be sick," she said. "Let me go out of this world. One loves a child for years, then a truck kills it."

My father shook his head mournfully. What could he say to comfort her? Esther was dead. Words were futile. It is twenty years since Esther was killed, but my mother is still unconsoled. She visits the cemetery once a month and scatters flowers over Esther's grave. She still weeps for her child. It is as if Esther had died yesterday; my mother will never be consoled.

2.

With my mother so helpless, my father had to crawl off his sickbed to hunt for work. But he found nothing. He asked here and there in a faint-hearted way. It did no good. He was sick, discouraged, and could speak no English. He was unskilled at any trade but house painting, and his obsessive fear of climbing on a scaffold shut him out of this work. There was little else he could do. He walked the streets gloomily.

It is hard to say how we lived during the next year. Out of every ten Americans one is a pauper, who applies for help to organized charity. There is another pauper tenth that is too proud for such begging. We were in the latter tenth.

I can't describe how we managed to live. Does the survivor remember everything from the time when the ship founders until he is washed up on the beach? All I know is we went on living.

The neighbors helped us, they brought in portions of their suppers, and paper bags containing sugar, coffee, beans, flour. Jake Wolf the saloon keeper quietly paid our rent for months. Other people were kind. Once Rosie the prostitute placed a crumpled five-dollar bill in my hand.

"Give this to your mother," she said. "Tell her you found it in the street."

I tried to relay this lie to my mother, but broke down under questioning. My mother sighed.

"Give Rosie my heartfelt thanks," she said. "Say we will pay it back someday. But don't tell your poppa; he is too proud."

Big Tim Sullivan the Tammany Hall leader sent us a basket on Thanksgiving Day, stuffed with nuts, candies, cranberries, celery, and a huge, blue-skinned turkey.

"What kind of a holiday is it, this Thanksgiving?" my mother asked.

I, the scholar of the family, told her it was the day the Pilgrims had given thanks to God for America.

"So it's an American holiday," my mother said, "and not for Jews."

The turkey was a fine fat bird, but unfortunately of heathen origin. It was not *kosher*, and therefore forbidden to us. We eyed it with longing, but my father sold the turkey to one of the Irish bartenders in Jake's saloon.

3.

"I must do something! I must find some work! We are starving!" my father would cry, beating his breast with both fists in despair.

The neighbors tried to help us, but they themselves were poor. Some well-meaning neighbor secretly mailed a post card to the Charity society, telling of our plight.

One day a stranger called. He was a slim, fair-haired young Christian with a brisk hurry-up manner and a stylish collar and necktie. He placed his umbrella against the wall, and shuffled through a bunch of index cards. He had a bad cold, and was forever blowing the most startling bugle-calls with his nose.

"Does Herman Gold live here? He asked, sniffling irritably.

"Yes, sir," said my mother.

She was very respectful, for this was evidently one of the brusque young men who came from the Board of Health, or the Public School, or the Christian missions, or the settlement houses. They asked many questions, and one must answer them or go to jail.

"I am from the United Charities," said this young man, "and some one wrote us about you. We will help you if you will answer some questions. How many children have you?"

"Two," said my mother.

"How old?"

"One is six, the other ten."

"Husband sick?"

"Yes, sir."

"Private doctor or free clinic?"

"Private."

"Where do you get the money to pay him?"

"We, we—" My mother began.

The young investigator was making rapid notations on an index card. His eyes swept the room as he talked, as if he were tabulating every pot, pan, dish-cloth and stick of furniture in our home. He interrupted my mother in her long explanation of our relations with Dr. Solow.

"And so your husband is out of work? Is he kind to you? Does he drink? What salary does he receive while working? Does he smoke? Has he tried to find a job recently? Does he ever beat you? How much of his salary does he give you when he is working? What rent do you pay? How much do your groceries cost per week?"

My mother was flustered by this Niagara of questions. She resented the brisk stranger who came into her home and asked personal questions with such an air of authority. But he was an official. She cleared her throat, and was about to give him his answers, when my father stalked in.

He had been resting in the bedroom, and was half-undressed. His face was pale, he trembled with rage. He glared at the young blonde question-asker, and shouted: "Get out of this house, mister! You have no business here. It is true we are poor, but that does not give you the right to insult us."

"I am not insulting you," said the young investigator, blowing his nose and shuffling his index cards nervously, "I ask these questions in about fifty homes a day. It is just the regular form."

My father drew himself up proudly.

"I spit on your regular form," he said. "We don't want any charity; we can live without it, mister."

"Very well," said the young man, gathering up his umbrella, his overcoat, his index cards, and making briskly for the door. "I'll report what you just said." He paused a moment to scratch a few more notes; then, blowing a last bugle-call on his damp nose, scurried down the hall. What he reported on his cards we never knew, but we were spared the indignity of any further visits by Organized Charity. Every one on the East Side hated and feared that cruel machine that helped no one without first systematically degrading him and robbing him of all human status. One's neighbors were kinder. Tammany Hall was kinder. Starvation was kinder. There were thousands of families like ours that would rather have died than be bullied, shamed and finger-printed like criminals by the policemen of Organized Charity.

4.

The neighbors were talking about us. They were worrying. In the tenement each woman knew what was cooking for supper in her neighbor's pot. Each knew the cares, too, that darkened a neighbor's heart.

One night a neighbor called. He kissed the *mezzuzah* over the door, and wiped his feet on the burlap rags. Then he timidly entered our kitchen like an intruder.

"Good evening, Mr. Lipzin," said my mother. "Please sit down."

"Good evening," he stammered, seating himself. "It was raining to-day, and I did not sell many bananas, so I brought you some. Maybe your children like bananas."

He handed my mother a bunch of bananas, and she took them, saying: "Thanks, Mr. Lipzin."

The pot-bellied little peddler shyly fingered his beard. He had come for a purpose, but was too embarrassed to speak. Sweat appeared on his red, fat, honest face, which wind and sun had tanned. He scratched his head, and stared at us in a painful silence. Minutes passed.

"How is your health, Mr. Lipzin?" my mother asked.

"I am stronger, thanks be to God," he said bashfully. "It was only the rheumatism again."

"That is good. And how is your new baby, Mr. Lipzin?"

"God be thanked, she is strong like a tiger," he said.

He fell dumb again. He tapped his knees with his fingers, and his shoulders twitched. He was known as a silent man in the tenement; in the ten years we lived there this was the first time he had called on us.

My father fidgeted uneasily. He was about to say something to break the spell cast by the tongue-tied peddler, when Mr. Lipzin became articulate. "Excuse me, but my wife nagged me into coming here," he stammered. "She is worrying about you. Excuse me, but they say you have been out of work a long time and can find nothing to do, Mr. Gold."

"Yes, Mr. Lipzin, why should one conceal it?" said my father. "Life is dark for us now."

"*Nu*," said the little peddler, as he wiped his forehead, "so that is why my wife nagged me to see you. If there is nothing else, one can at least make a kind of living with bananas. I have peddled them, with God's help, for many years. It is a hard life, but one manages to live.

"Yes," he went on, in a mournful, hesitant sing-song, "for a few dollars one buys a stock of bananas from the wholesalers on Attorney Street. Then one rents a pushcart for ten cents a day from the pushcart stables on Orchard Street. Then one finds a street corner and stands there and the people come and buy the bananas."

"So well?" my father demanded, a hostile glare in his eyes.

The little peddler saw this, and was frightened again into incoherence.

"Excuse me, one makes a living, with God's help," he managed to say.

My father stood up and folded his arms haughtily.

"And you are suggesting, Mr. Lipzin, that I, too, should go out peddling bananas?" he asked.

The peddler sweated like a runner with embarrassment. He stood up and edged toward the door to make his escape.

"No, no, God forbid," he stammered. "Excuse me, it was my wife who nagged me to come here. No, no, Mr. Gold! Good evening to you all; may God be with you!"

He went out, mopping his fiery face with a bandanna. My father stared after him, his arms still folded in that fierce, defiant attitude.

"What a gall! What meddling neighbors we have! To come and tell me that I ought to peddle these accursed bananas! After my fifteen years in America, as if I were a greenhorn! I, who once owned a suspender shop, and was a foreman of house painters! What do you think of such gall, Katie?"

"I don't know," said my mother quietly. "It is not disgraceful to make an honest living by peddling."

"You agree with him?" my father cried.

"No," said my mother, "but Mr. Lipzin is a good man. He came here to help you, and you insulted him."

"So you do agree with him!" my father stormed. He stamped indignantly into the bedroom, where he flung himself on the bed and smoked his pipe viciously. My mother sighed, then she and my brother and I ate some of the bananas.

5.

My proud father. He raved, cursed, worried, he held long passionate conversations with my mother.

"Must I peddle bananas, Katie? I can't do it; the disgrace would kill me!"

"Don't do it," my mother would say gently. "We can live without it."

"But where will I find work?" he would cry. "The city is locked against me! I am a man in a trap!"

"Something will happen. God has not forgotten us," said my mother.

"I will kill myself! I can't stand it! I will take the gas pipe to my nose! I refuse to be a peddler!"

"Hush, the children will hear you," said my mother.

I could hear them thrashing it out at night in the bedroom. They talked about it at the supper table, or sat by the stove in the gloomy winter afternoons, talking, talking. My father was obsessed with the thought of bananas. They became a symbol to him of defeat, of utter hopelessness. And when my mother assured him he need not become a peddler, he would turn on her and argue that it was the one way out. He was in a curious fever of mixed emotions.

Two weeks after Mr. Lipzin's visit he was in the street with a push-cart, peddling the accursed bananas.

He came back the first night, and gave my mother a dollar bill and some silver. His face was gray; he looked older by ten years; a man who had touched bottom. My mother tried to comfort him, but for days he was silent as one who has been crushed by a calamity. Hope died in him; months passed, a year passed; he was still peddling bananas.

I remember meeting him one evening with his pushcart. I had managed to sell all my papers and was coming home in the snow. It was that strange, portentous hour in downtown New York when the workers are pouring homeward in the twilight. I marched among thousands of tired men and women whom the factory whistles had unyoked. They flowed in rivers through the clothing factory districts, then down along the avenues to the East Side.

I met my father near Cooper Union. I recognized him, a hunched, frozen figure in an old overcoat standing by a banana cart. He looked so lonely, the tears came to my eyes. Then he saw me, and his face lit with his sad, beautiful smile—Charlie Chaplin's smile.

"Ach, it's Mikey," he said. "So you have sold your papers! Come and eat a banana."

He offered me one. I refused it. I was eleven years old, but poisoned with a morbid proletarian sense of responsibility. I felt it crucial that my father *sell* his bananas, not give them away. He thought I was shy, and coaxed and joked with me, and made me eat the banana. It smelled of wet straw and snow.

"You haven't sold many bananas to-day, pop," I said anxiously.

He shrugged his shoulders.

"What can I do? No one seems to want them."

It was true. The work crowds pushed home morosely over the pavements. The rusty sky darkened over New York buildings, the tall street lamps were lit, innumerable trucks, streetcars and elevated trains clattered by. Nobody and nothing in the great city stopped for my father's bananas.

"I ought to yell," said my father dolefully. "I ought to make a big noise like other peddlers, but it makes my throat sore. Anyway, I'm ashamed of yelling, it makes me feel like a fool."

I had eaten one of his bananas. My sick conscience told me that I ought to pay for it somehow. I must remain here and help my father.

"I'll yell for you, pop," I volunteered.

"Ach, no," he said, "go home; you have worked enough to-day. Just tell momma I'll be late."

But I yelled and yelled. My father, standing by, spoke occasional words of praise, and said I was a wonderful yeller. Nobody else paid attention. The workers drifted past us wearily, endlessly; a defeated army wrapped in dreams of home. Elevated trains crashed; the Cooper Union clock burned above us; the sky grew black, the wind poured, the slush burned through our shoes. There were thousands of strange, silent figures pouring over the sidewalks in snow. None of them stopped to buy bananas. I yelled and yelled, nobody listened.

My father tried to stop me at last. "*Nu*," he said smiling to console me, "that was wonderful yelling, Mikey. But it's plain we are unlucky to-day! Let's go home."

I was frantic, and almost in tears. I insisted on keeping up my desperate yells. But at last my father persuaded me to leave with him. It was after nightfall. We covered the bananas with an oil cloth and started for the pushcart stable. Down Second Avenue we plodded side-by-side. For many blocks my father was thoughtful. Then he shook his head and sighed:

"So you see how it is, Mikey. Even at banana peddling I am a failure. What can be wrong? The bananas are good, your yelling was good, the prices are good. Yes, it is plain; I am a man without luck."

He paused to light his pipe, while I pushed the cart for him. Then he took the handles again and continued his meditations.

"Look at me," he said. "Twenty years in America, and poorer than when I came. A suspender shop I had, and it was stolen from me by a villain. A house painter foreman I became, and fell off a scaffold. Now bananas I sell, and even at that I am a failure. It is all luck." He sighed and puffed at his pipe.

"Ach, Gott, what a rich country America is! What an easy place to make one's fortune! Look at all the rich Jews! Why has it been so easy for them, so hard for me? I am just a poor little Jew without money."

"Poppa, lots of Jews have no money," I said to comfort him.

"I know it, my son," he said, "but don't be one of them. It's better to be dead in this country than not to have money. Promise me you'll be rich when you grow up, Mikey!"

"Yes, poppa."

"Ach," he said fondly, "this is my one hope now! This is all that makes me happy! I am a greenhorn, but you are an American! You will have it easier than I; you will have luck in America!"

"Yes, poppa," I said, trying to smile with him. But I felt older than he; I could not share his naive optimism; my heart sank as I remembered the past and thought of the future.

"Wilder: Prophet of the Genteel Christ"

The New Republic, October 22, 1930

Just after the 1930 publication of Jews Without Money, *Edmund Wilson, editor of* The New Republic, *asked Gold for an essay reviewing several novels by Thornton Wilder. Apparently the shrewd editor suspected that putting the champion of proletarian realism in contact with Wilder's rather genteel and cerebral novels during a crisis of capitalism would be an interesting experiment. Gold had never read anything by Wilder but agreed to study up and write the review.*

The resulting article scandalized readers and touched off a nationwide "Gold-Wilder controversy" that played out for years. Though outraged reader letters ran strongly against Gold, Wilson largely defended him and credited him for exposing "the insipidity and pointlessness of most literary criticism" while making it "very plain that the economic crisis was to be accompanied by a literary one." This was already a meaningful victory for the Left, one that helped define the 1930s as a literary decade. Wilson went on to assert that "nine-tenths of our writers would be much better off writing propaganda for communism than doing what they are at present: that is, writing propaganda for capitalism under the impression that they are liberals or disinterested minds."

A caveat: more than once during the 1920s and early 1930s Gold resorted to implicitly homophobic slurs when attacking political adversaries.

~

"Here's a group of people losing sleep over a host of notions that the rest of the world has outgrown several centuries ago: one duchess's right to enter a door before another; the word order in a dogma of the Church; the divine right of Kings, especially of Bourbons."

In these words Thornton Wilder describes the people in his first book, *The Cabala*. They are some eccentric old aristocrats in Rome, seen through the eyes of a typical American art "pansy" who is there as a student.

Marcantonio is the sixteen-year-old son of one of the group; he is burned out with sex and idleness, and sexualizes with his sister, and then commits suicide. Another character is a beautiful, mad Princess, who hates her dull Italian husband, falls in love with many Nordics and is regularly rejected by them. Others are a moldy old aristocrat woman who "believes," and a moldy old Cardinal who doesn't, and some other fine worm-eaten authentic specimens of the rare old Italian antique.

Wilder views these people with tender irony. He makes no claim as to their usefulness to the world that feeds them: yet he hints that their palace mustiness is a most important fact in the world of today. He writes with a brooding seriousness of them as if all the gods were watching their little lavender tragedies. The style is a diluted Henry James.

Wilder's second novel was *The Bridge of San Luis Rey*. This famous and vastly popular yarn made a bold leap backward in time. Mr. Wilder, by then, had evidently completed his appraisal of our own age. The scene is laid in Lima, Peru; the time is Friday noon, July 20, 1714. In this volume Wilder perfected the style which is now probably permanent with him; the diluted and veritable Anatole France.

Among the characters of San Luis Rey are: (1) a sweet old duchess who loves her grown daughter to madness, but is not loved in return; (2) a beautiful unfortunate genius of an actress who after much sexualizing turns nun; (3) her tutor, a jolly old rogue, but a true worshipper of literature; (4) two strange brothers who love each other with a passion and delicacy that again brings the homosexual bouquet into a Wilder book, and a few other minor sufferers.

Some of the characters in this novel die in the fall of a Bridge. Our author points out the spiritual lessons imbedded in this Accident; viz: that God is Love.

The third novel is the recent *The Woman of Andros*. This marks a still further masterly retreat into time and space. The scene is one of the lesser Greek Islands, the hour somewhere in B.C.

The fable: a group of young Greeks spend their evenings in alternate sexual bouts and lofty Attic conversations with the last of the Aspasias. One young man falls in love with her sister, who is "pure." His father objects. Fortunately, the Aspasia dies. The father relents. But then the sister dies, too. Wistful futility and sweet soft sadness of Life. Hints of the coming of Christ: "and in the East the stars shone tranquilly down upon the land that was soon to be called Holy and that even then was preparing its precious burden" (Palestine).

Then Mr. Wilder has published some pretty, tinkling, little three-minute playlets. These are on the most erudite and esoteric themes one could ever imagine; all about Angels, and Mozart, and King Louis, and Fairies, and a Girl of the Renaissance, and a whimsical old Actress (1780) and her old Lover; Childe Harold to the Dark Tower Came; Prosperina and the Devil; The Flight into Egypt; a Venetian Prince and a Mermaid; Shelley, Judgment Day, Centaurs, God, The Woman in the Chlamys, Christ; Brigomeide, Leviathan, Ibsen; every waxwork in Wells's Outline, in fact, except Buffalo Bill.

And this, to date, is the garden cultivated by Mr. Thornton Wilder. It is a museum, it is not a world. In this devitalized air move the wan ghosts he has called up, each in "romantic" costume. It is an historic junkshop over which our author presides.

Here one will not find the heroic archaeology of a Walter Scott or Eugene Sue. Those men had social passions, and used the past as a weapon to affect the present and future. Scott was the poet of feudalism. The past was a glorious myth he created to influence the bourgeois anti-feudal present. Eugene Sue was the poet of the proletariat. On every page of history he traced the bitter, neglected facts of the working-class martyrdom. He wove these into an epic melodrama to strengthen the heart and hand of the revolutionary workers, to inspire them with a proud consciousness of their historic mission.

That is how the past should be used; as rich manure, as a springboard, as a battle cry, as a deepening, clarifying and sublimation of the struggles in the too-immediate present. But Mr. Wilder is the poet of the genteel bourgeoisie. They fear any such disturbing lessons out of the past. Their goal is comfort and status quo. Hence, the vapidity of these little readings in history.

Mr. Wilder, in a foreword to his book of little plays, tells himself and us the object of his esthetic striving:

> I hope through many mistakes, to discover that spirit that is not unequal to the elevation of the great religious themes, yet which does not fall into a repellent didacticism. Didacticism is

> an attempt at the coercion of another's free mind, even though one knows that in these matters beyond logic, beauty is the only persuasion. Here the schoolmaster enters again. He sees all that is fairest in the Christian tradition made repugnant to the new generations by reason of the diction in which it is expressed. . . . So that the revival of religion is almost a matter of rhetoric. The work is difficult, perhaps impossible (perhaps all religions die out with the exhaustion of the language), but it at least reminds us that Our Lord asked us in His work to be not only gentle as doves, but as wise as serpents.

Mr. Wilder wishes to restore, he says, through Beauty and Rhetoric, the Spirit of Religion in American Literature. One can respect any writer in America who sets himself a goal higher than the usual racketeering. But what is this religious spirit Mr. Wilder aims to restore? Is it the crude self-torture of the Holy Rollers, or the brimstone howls and fears of the Baptists, or even the mad, titanic sincerities and delusions of a Tolstoy or Dostoyevsky?

No, it is that newly fashionable literary religion that centers around Jesus Christ, the First British Gentleman. It is a pastel, pastiche, dilettante religion, without the true neurotic blood and fire, a daydream of homosexual figures in graceful gowns moving archaically among the lilies. It is Anglo-Catholicism, that last refuge of the American literary snob.

This genteel spirit of the new parlor-Christianity pervades every phrase of Mr. Wilder's rhetoric. What gentle theatrical sighs! what lovely, well composed deaths and martyrdoms! what languishings and flutterings of God's sinning doves! what little jewels of Sunday-school wisdom, distributed modestly here and there through the softly flowing narrative like delicate pearls, diamonds and rubies on the costume of a meek, wronged Princess gracefully drowning herself for love (if my image is clear).

Wilder has concocted a synthesis of all the chambermaid literature, Sunday-school tracts and boulevard piety there ever were. He has added a dash of the prep-school teacher's erudition, then embalmed all this in the speciously glamorous style of the late Anatole France. He talks much of art, of himself as Artist, of style. He is a very conscious craftsman. But his is the most irritating and pretentious style pattern I have read in years. It has the slick, smug finality of the lesser Latins; that shallow clarity and tight little good taste that remind one of nothing so much as the conversation and practice of a veteran *cocotte*.

Mr. Wilder strains to be spiritual; but who could reveal any real agonies and exaltations of spirit in this neat, tailor-made rhetoric? It is a great lie. It is Death. Its serenity is that of the corpse. Prick it, and it will bleed violet ink and *aperitif.* It is false to the great stormy music of Anglo-Saxon speech. Shakespeare is crude and disorderly beside Mr. Wilder. Neither Milton, Fielding, Burns, Blake, Byron, Chaucer nor Hardy could ever receive a passing mark in Mr. Wilder's classroom of style.

And this is the style with which to express America? Is this the speech of a pioneer continent? Will this discreet French drawing room hold all the blood, horror and hope of the world's new empire? Is this the language of the intoxicated Emerson? Or the clean, rugged Thoreau, or vast Whitman? Where are the modern streets of New York, Chicago and New Orleans in these little novels? Where are the cotton mills, the murder of Ella May and her songs? Where are the child slaves of the beet fields? Where are the stockbroker suicides, the labor racketeers or passion and death of the coal miners? Where are Babbitt, Jimmy Higgins and Anita Loos's Blonde? Is Mr. Wilder a Swede or a Greek, or is he an American? No stranger would know from these books he has written.

But is it right to demand this "nativism" of him? Yes, for Mr. Wilder has offered himself as a spiritual teacher; therefore one may say: Father, what are your lessons? How will your teaching help the "spirit" trapped in American capitalism? But Wilder takes refuge in the rootless cosmopolitanism which marks every *emigre* trying to flee the problems of his community. Internationalism is a totally different spirit. It begins at home. Mr. Wilder speaks much of the "human heart" and its eternal problems. It is with these, he would have us believe, that he concerns himself; and they are the same in any time and geography, he says. Another banal evasion. For the human heart, as he probes it in Greece, Peru, Italy and other remote places, is only the "heart" of a small futile group with whom few Americans have the faintest kinship.

For to repeat, Mr. Wilder remains the poet of a small sophisticated class that has recently arisen in America—our genteel bourgeoisie. His style is their style; it is the new fashion. Their women have taken to wearing his Greek chlamys and faintly indulge themselves in his smart Victorian pieties. Their men are at ease in his Paris and Rome.

America won the War. The world's wealth flowed into it like a red Mississippi. The newest and greatest of all leisure classes was created. Luxury hotels, golf, old furniture and Vanity Fair sophistication were some of their expressions.

Thorstein Veblen foretold all this in 1899, in an epoch-making book that every American critic ought to study like a Bible. In *The Theory of the Leisure Class* he painted the hopeless course of most American culture for the next three decades. The grim, ironic prophet has been justified. Thornton Wilder is the perfect flower of the new prosperity. He has all the virtues Veblen said this leisure class would demand; the air of good breeding, the decorum, priestliness, glossy high finish as against intrinsic qualities, conspicuous inutility, caste feeling, love of the archaic, etc. . . .

All this is needed to help the parvenu class forget its lowly origins in American industrialism. It yields them a short-cut to the aristocratic emotions. It disguises the barbaric sources of their income, the billions wrung from American workers and foreign peasants and coolies. It lets them feel spiritually worthy of that income.

Babbitt made them ashamed of being crude American climbers. Mr. Wilder, "gentle as the dove and wise as the serpent," is a more constructive teacher. Taking them patiently by the hand, he leads them into castles, palaces and far-off Greek islands, where they may study the human heart when it is nourished by blue blood. This Emily Post of culture will never reproach them; or remind them of Pittsburgh or the breadlines. He is always in perfect taste; he is the personal friend of Gene Tunney.

"For there is a land of the living and a land of the dead, and the bridge is love, the only survival, the only meaning." And nobody works in a Ford plant, and nobody starves looking for work, and there is nothing but Love in God's ancient Peru, Italy, Greece, if not in God's capitalist America 1930!

Let Mr. Wilder write a book about modern America. We predict it will reveal all his fundamental silliness and superficiality, now hidden under a Greek chlamys.

"Proletarian Realism"

New Masses, September 1930

In previous American literature, middle-class authors had been like passengers on the sightseeing bus that rolls down the East Side streets in chapter 4 of Jews Without Money. *A gang of ghetto kids chases the frightened tourists, calling them liars, yelling "Go back uptown!" and pelting the "frightened sightseers" with rocks and garbage. "What right had these stuck-up foreigners to come and look at us? What right had the man with the megaphone to tell them lies about us?" As an authoritative voice in the movement for working-class culture, Gold famously addressed this problem. In his editorial "Notes of the Month" less than a year after the stock market crash, he called for a new literary realism that would without exception be created either by the poor themselves or by artists who had lived sympathetically among them.*

~

I believe I was the first writer in America to herald the advent of a world proletarian literature as a concomitant to the rise of the world proletariat. This was in an article published in *The Liberator* in 1921, called, "Towards Proletarian Art." Mine was a rather mystic and intuitive approach; nothing had yet been published in English on this theme; the idea was not yet in the air, as it is today; I was feeling my way.

But the little path has since become a highroad. Despite the bourgeois ultra-leftism of Trotsky in his *Literature and Revolution*, where he predicts there will not be time enough to develop a proletarian literature, this greatest and most universal of literary schools is now sweeping across the world. [. . .]

Thousands of books and articles on the theories of proletarian literature have been published in Soviet Russia, in Germany, Japan, China, France, England, and other countries. There is not a language in the world today in which a vigorous bold youth is not experimenting with the materials of proletarian literature. It is a world phenomenon; and it grows, changes, criticizes itself, expands without the blessing of all the official mandarins and play-actor iconoclasts and psalm-singing Humanists of the moribund bourgeois culture. It does not need them any longer; it will soon boot them into their final resting places in the museum.

No, the bourgeois intellectuals tell us, there can be no such thing as a proletarian literature. We answer briefly: There is. Then they say, it is mediocre; where is your Shakespeare? And we answer: Wait ten years more. He is on his way. We gave you a Lenin; we will give you a proletarian Shakespeare, too; if that is so important.

To us the culture of the world's millions is more important; the soil must be prepared; we know our tree is sound; we are sure of the fruit: we promise you a hundred Shakespeares.

We have only one magazine in America, the *New Masses,* dedicated to proletarian literature. And there is no publishing house of standing and intelligent direction to help clarify the issues. Nearest is the International Publishers perhaps, but this house devotes itself solely to a rather academic approach to economics and makes little attempt to influence either the popular mind or our intellectuals. It is as stodgy and unenterprising, in a Communist way, as the Yale University Press, and similar organizations.

If there were a live publishing house here, such as the *Cenit* of Madrid, for instance, it could issue a series of translations of proletarian novels, poetry, criticism that might astound some of our intellectuals. There would be a clarification, too, for some of our own adherents.

For proletarian literature is a living thing. It is not based on a set of fixed dogmas, anymore than is Communism or the science of biology.

Churches are built on dogma. The Catholic Church is the classic illustration of how the rule of dogma operates. Here is a great mass political and business movement that hypnotizes its victims with a set of weird formulas of magic which must not be tested or examined but must be swallowed with faith.

In Marxism or any other science there is no dogma; there are laws which have been discovered running through the phenomena of nature. These laws must not be taken on faith. They are the result of experiment and statistics, and they are meant to be tested daily. If they fail to work, they can be discarded; they are constantly being discarded.

The law of class struggle is a Marxian discovery that has been tested, and that works, and that gives one a major clue to the movements of man in the mass.

In proletarian literature, there are several laws which seem to be demonstrable. One of them is that all culture is the reflection of a specific class society. Another is, that bourgeois culture is in process of decay, just as bourgeois society is in a swift decline. The class that will inherit the world will be the proletariat, and every indication points inevitably to the law that this proletarian society will, like its predecessors, create its own culture.

This we can be sure of; upon this we all agree. Proletarian literature will reflect the struggle of the workers in their fight for the world. It portrays the life of the workers; not as do the vulgar French populists and American jazzmaniacs, but with a clear revolutionary point; otherwise it is meaningless, merely a new *frisson.*

Within this new world of proletarian literature, there are many living forms. It is dogmatic folly to seize upon any single literature form and erect it into a pattern for all proletarian literature.

The Russian Futurists tried to do this; they held the stage for a while, but are rapidly being supplanted.

My belief is that a new form is evolving, which one might name "Proletarian Realism." Here are some of its elements, as I see them:

1.

Because the Workers are skilled machinists, sailors, farmers and weavers, the proletarian writer must describe their work with technical precision. The Workers will scorn any vague fumbling poetry, much as they would scorn a sloppy workman. Hemingway and others have had the intuition to incorporate this proletarian element into their work, but have used it for the *frisson*, the way some actors try to imitate gangsters of men. These writers build a machine, it functions, but it produces nothing; it has not been planned to produce anything; it is only an adult toy.

2.

Proletarian realism deals with the *real conflicts* of men and women who work for a living. It has nothing to do with the sickly mental states of the idle Bohemians, their subtleties, their sentimentalities, their fine-spun affairs. The worst example and the best of what we do not want to do is the spectacle of Proust, master-masturbator of the bourgeois literature. We know the suffering of hungry, persecuted and heroic millions is enough of a theme for anyone, without inventing these precious silly little agonies.

3.

Proletarian realism is never pointless. It does not believe in literature for its own sake, but in literature that is useful, has a social function. Every major writer has always done this in the past; but it is necessary to fight the battle constantly, for there are more intellectuals than ever who are trying to make literature a plaything. Every poem, every novel and drama, must have a social theme, or it is merely confectionery.

4.

As few words as possible. We are not interested in the verbal acrobats—this is only another form for bourgeois idleness. The Workers live too close to reality to care about these literary show-offs, these verbalist heroes.

5.

To have the courage of the proletarian experience. This was the chief point of my "mystic" essay in 1921; let us proletarians write with the courage of our own experience. I mean, if one is a tanner and writer, let one dare to write the drama of a tannery; or of a clothing shop, or of a ditch-digger's life, or of a hobo. Let the bourgeois writers tell us about their spiritual drunkards and super-refined Parisian emigres; or about their spiritual marriages and divorces, etc., that is their world; we must write about our own mud-puddle; it will prove infinitely more important. This is being done by the proletarian realism.

6.

Swift action, clear form, the direct line, cinema in words; this seems to be one of the principles of proletarian realism. It knows exactly what it believes and where it is going; this makes for its beautiful youthful clarity.

7.

Away with drabness, the bourgeois notion that the Worker's life is sordid, the slummer's disgust and feeling of futility. There *is* horror and drabness in the Worker's life; and we will portray it; but we know this is not the last word; we know that this manure heap is the hope of the future: we know that not pessimism, but revolutionary elan will sweep this mess out of the world forever.

8.

Away with all lies about human nature. We are scientists; we know what a man thinks and feels. Everyone is a mixture of motives; we do not have to lie about our hero in order to win our case. It is this honesty alone, frank as an unspoiled child's, that makes proletarian realism superior to the older literary schools.

9.

No straining or melodrama or other effects; life itself is the supreme melodrama. Feel this intensely, and everything becomes poetry—the new poetry of materials, of the so-called "common man," the Worker molding his real world.

From "Why I Am a Communist"

New Masses, September 1932

There is still some uncertainty about whose oratory inspired Gold's conversion to socialism on a pivotal day in April 1914. In interviews Gold gave in the 1930s, he claimed that the Union Square speaker was Elizabeth Gurley Flynn, the fiery communist-feminist "rebel girl" who had risen to prominence in strikes led by the Industrial Workers of the World (IWW). But some biographical studies give credence to the claim made here that the speaker was Emma Goldman, whose anarchist views later became anathema to the Communist Party.

In either case, the speaker's words may not have been the most crucial factor in Gold's political awakening. Within the many versions of his origin story, one element remained consistent: "I have always been grateful to that cop and that club. For one thing, he introduced me to literature and the revolution."

In 1914 there was an unemployment crisis in America, and I was one of its victims. I was 18 years old, a factory worker and shipping clerk with five years experience, and the chief support of a fatherless family. Unemployment was no academic matter to me, but the blackest and most personal tragedy.

Well, the hungry workers were raising hell in New York. There were demonstrations, marches, and raids on fashionable Fifth Avenue churches by the unemployed. The anarchists were then still a brilliant and fearless revolutionary group in America, and they led the fight in New York.

I blundered into a big Union Square meeting, where Alexander Berkman, Emma Goldman, Leonard Abbott and other anarchists spoke. The cops, as usual, pointed [sic] the anarchist denunciations of capitalism by smashing into the meeting, cracking the skulls and ribs of everyone present. I saw a woman knocked down by a beefy cop's club. She screamed, and instinctively I ran across the square to help her. I was knocked down myself, booted, and managed to escape the hospital only by sheer luck.

I have always been grateful to that cop and his club. For one thing, he introduced me to literature and revolution. I had not read a single book in five years; nothing except the sporting page of newspapers. I hadn't thought much about anything except baseball, jobs, food, sleep and Sundays at Coney Island. I was a prize-fight fanatic and amateur boxer. Now I grew so bitter because of that cop that I went around to the anarchist Ferrer School and discovered books—I discovered history, poetry, science, and the class struggle.

Nobody who has not gone through this proletarian experience can ever understand the fever that seized me in the next year. I read myself almost blind each night after work. My mind woke up like a suppressed volcano. I can never discharge this personal debt to the revolutionary movement—it gave me a mind.

And I think I can understand what the Soviet state means today to millions of grateful Russian workers and peasants—it has given them a mind.

I was an anarchist for several years. The poetry, the strong passions and naive ideology of that movement appealed to a literary adolescent. I found a job as night porter at the Adams Express Company depot on West 47th Street. I wrestled big trunks and half-ton cases from seven at night until seven the next morning. I sweated, but in my mind I lived in the idealistic world of Shelley, Blake, Walt Whitman, Kropotkin. I was a revolutionist, but it never occurred to me to do anything about it. Nothing, really, was demanded of me.

It was the I.W.W. who made me conscious of the proletarian basis of the revolution. I left New York, had some road experiences, and was present in several Wobbly strikes. The history of this heroic organization has still to be written. It is decadent now, but among the finest veteran leaders of American Communism are those who went through the I.W.W. experience—Bill Haywood, William Z. Foster, Bill Dunne, Earl Browder, Harrison George, and others. (But of course nobody ought feel grateful for this to the bourgeois Civil Liberties liberals who now run the poor old Wobblies.)

The War came; the Russian Revolution; I was against the War, I was 100 per cent with the Bolsheviks. It seemed marvellous then, beyond any words, and it still is as marvellous, that the workers' state had come down from the clouds of Shelley's dream and established itself on the earth.

We formed a Red Guard of about a thousand youth in New York, which Hugo Gellert and I joined, to go to Russia and fight for the cause. Our captain went to Washington to interview the State Department, but they told him that if we wanted to fight we had better enlist for France. This, of course, didn't satisfy a bunch of young Red Guards.

And now I will end the autobiography by saying that the Russian Revolution forced me to read Lenin. I read his pamphlet, *State and Revolution*, and for the first time really seemed to understand the necessary historical steps by which the world could be changed from a filthy capitalist jungle into an earthly paradise of socialism.

[. . .] I have wanted for fifteen years one supreme thing. I have wanted it more than love, health, fame or security. It is world socialism that I want—for I know this alone can banish the miseries of the world I now live in. It will free the factory slaves, the farm drudges, it will set women free, and restore the Negro race to its human rights. I know that the world will be beautiful soon in the sunlight of proletarian brotherhood; meanwhile, the struggle. And I want socialism so much that I accept this fierce, crude struggle as my fate in time; I accept its disciplines and necessities; I become as practical and realistic as possible for me; I want victory.

Whoever really desires the victory of socialism is forced today into only one party—the Communist. Whatever strengthens the Communist Party brings socialism nearer. The liberal and opportunist roads seem smoother and fairer, but they lead nowhere. The Communist road is rough, dangerous and often confusing, but it happens to be the only road that leads into the new world.

"Examples of Workers' Correspondence"

Daily Worker, January 20, 1934

Under the headline "What a World!" (the name of his regular column before it became "Change the World!"), Gold titled several columns simply "Examples of Workers' Correspondence." Appearing without commentary were verbatim excerpts, organized into Whitmanesque stanzas, from the letters he regularly received from working-class readers. With these columns, Gold theorized not solely what made literature but who made it, striving to convince the common people that they were artists: "Write," he told them, "Your life in a mine, mill and farm is of deathless significance in the history of the world. Tell us about it in the same language you use in writing a letter. It may be literature—it often is."

~

Hood River, Oregon

The orchardists have made an agreement
Not to gather 25 per cent of the Bosc pears
Now thousands of tons rot on the trees
And it makes me mad to see it
Now, hungry kids could eat up all this good fruit
Mother Nature is big-hearted and free
It is capitalism that makes the famines
I tell you, we must have a Workers' America.

Uniontown, Pa.

Last winter I sent my kids to school barefoot
There was snow on the ground but the school gave them milk
This is our life, though our men were working
We women begged for food at the relief
And our kids picked coal on the slate dumps
Four were killed, do you remember, on the Buffington dump
So now women we cannot afford to lose this strike
Come on out on the picket lines, our men and children need us.

Herkimer, N.Y.

An Italian worker's little boy
Caught a blood poisoning in his hand
The parents being on charity relief
Asked W. Cress, the welfare director
To get them a doctor for the beloved boy.
But the officer waved the mother away.
The boy is O.K., he said, and needs no doctor.
The mother went home, the little boy died in a week.
Workers, why are we so patient?

"Songs for the Masses"

Daily Worker, January 2, 1936

Beginning in the early 1930s, music was seen as a necessary element of the communist program, but initial production of leftist songs was sporadic, in part because there was no set theory about the form such music should take or how it was to be created. Though Gold had no formal musical training, he was interested in this problem and knew good "people's music" when he heard it. From his Daily Worker *platform he endorsed songs that were both "realistic in form and agit-prop in character" for the purpose of awakening class consciousness in the masses.*

As critic Jim Hoberman understood, "No one was more ardent than Gold in opposing the highbrow proletarian music of Hanns Eisler, Marc Blitzstein, and Charles Seeger. Rather, he advanced the notion that Appalachian folk songs and Black spirituals were the authentic songs of working people."

Folk historian Richard Reuss argued that Gold's endorsement of the Auvilles, a southern folksinging couple, "marks the single most identifiable watershed in the American left's acceptance of traditional songs and lyrics composed in the folk idiom." In Reuss's view, twentieth-century American folk music bears to a significant degree Mike Gold's philosophical imprint. In this column Gold takes issue with the elitist standards of Charles Seeger (then using the pseudonym Carl Sands), shaping an argument that eventually won over the trained musicologist and father of Pete Seeger.

~

Music is of great importance to a people's movement. Songs have a positive value that can almost be calculated in watts and volts of mass-energy and mass-morale. Who will say that the song "John Brown's Body," sung by the first nothern troops that marched against the slave-owners, had no little part in winning the Civil War?

It is a sign of the health of our movement that it is writing and singing many songs. We haven't yet developed a Joe Hill, that epic proletarian martyr who wrote "Pie in the Sky" and other classics loved by the American workers. Nor have we as yet, at the other extreme, a Hanns Eisler of our own, some musician steeped in the best of bourgeois culture, who has successfully translated the historic riches of world music into our own treasury.

But we have groups working throughout the country, consisting of trained musicians from the middle class conservatories, and of workingmen like Joe Hill, who sing spontaneously out of their life experience.

Out of this ferment a great music will surely come. Only the other night I attended a concert in New York given by the cultural committee of the International Workers Order. A fine band of some 60 pieces played Beethoven's Fifth Symphony and the exotic Caucasian Sketches of Ippolito-Ivanov. A well-trained symphony orchestra played Schubert's Unfinished Symphony and Ballet Music from Rubinstein.

They were amateurs, but their work was serious, loving, disciplined. What is more significant, all were workers in factories and offices. Among them were found needle-trades workers, clerks, carpenters, plumbers, stenographers, storekeepers, etc.

Negroes and women were amongst them, something you will never find in the professional symphonies, which even in music have set up racial and sex discriminations.

It was a beautiful evening, and the audience, made up of the same social group as the players, was more inspiring to me than any of those stale, deadly mobs one finds in Carnegie Hall.

To have great poets, said Walt Whitman, you must have great audiences, too. Music will enter into its glorious heritage in America only when it has become the property of the people, as it was on this I.W.O. evening. And geniuses will surely flower in such a rich soil.

~

The Auvilles

In New York a leadership on the musical front has been set up by the Workers' Music League, a group of trained professionals, some of them with national reputations in the bourgeois world, the best of the younger generation of American musicians.

They have done a great deal of useful and noteworthy work. It is all a new world of experiment, and they have been daring and thorough.

Yet like all pioneers, our comrades, the composers of the Workers' Music League and the Pierre Degeyter club, have been apt to fall into sectarianism (at least I, although not a trained musician, think so).

Certainly, a review published on this page some months ago, by Carl Sands, one of the chief theoreticians of this important group of pioneers, smelled to me of sectarianism.

Comrade Sands had some mighty harsh things to say about the songs of Ray and Lida Auville, among other comments. Now I happen to have heard Ray and Lida sing before a workers' gathering in Cleveland. They are a couple of southern mountaineers who for years had toured the country with their two kids and and old Ford, making a living out of singing mountain ballads.

Ray Auville fiddles; no, he doesn't play the violin, he fiddles with gusto and native style, as rousingly as any old moustached veteran of the Great Smokies in Tennessee. And his wife, lovely, soft-eyed Lida, she plays the guitar, and they sing together.

About two years ago this mountaineer couple ran smack into the working class revolution. Ever since they have devoted their talents to writing and singing songs of and for the American workers and farmers.

It is the real thing, folk song in the making, workers' music coming right out of the soil. I wrote about them in this column some time ago, and reprinted some of their songs.

But Comrade Sands called their work a "hybrid mixture of jazz and balladry" and bore down on it with all the heavy thunder of professional estheticism. He also took occasion to condemn the work of Jacob Schaefer, conductor of the Freiheit chorus, who, to my mind, is the father of proletarian music in this country.

~

What Do the Masses Sing?

Really, Comrade Sands, I think you have missed the point. It is sectarian and utopian to use Arnold Schoenberg or Stravinsky as a yardstick by which to measure working class music.

What songs do the masses of Americans now sing? They sing "Old Black Joe" and the semi-jazz things concocted by Tin Pan Alley. In the South they sing the old ballads. This is the reality; and to leap from that into Schoenberg seems to me a desertion of the masses.

Not to see what a step forward it is to find two native musicians of the American people turning to revolutionary themes, converting the tradition to working class uses, is to be blind to progress.

Some highly sophisticated painter may dislike the comic strips, but if he criticized our Little Lefty as not being as good as Picasso or even Daumier, we should have to laugh at him as a man who had never wandered out of his studio.

Or would you judge workers' correspondence by the standard of James Joyce or Walter Pater? No, a folk art rarely comes from the studios; it makes its own style and has its own inner laws of growth. It may shock you, but I think the Composers' Collective has something to learn from Ray and Lida Auville, as well as to give them. They write catchy tunes that any American worker can sing and like, and the words of their songs make the revolution as intimate and simple as "Old Black Joe." Is this so little?

"They Hated Jane Addams"

A sampling of memorable Daily Worker *columns from the early 1930s, initially collected by Robert Forsythe in his 1936 anthology of Gold's journalism,* Change the World! *(International Publishers).*

~

"The doors of heaven did not swing open for Jane Addams when she passed on," I heard Bishop White of New Jersey shout in a radio sermon the other day. "Jane Addams was a pacifist, and untrue to her country! God does not love such people, and neither does any real red-blooded American. The life of this woman was a menace to the safety of the American family!

"There are Christians who say like Jane Addams that they do not believe in war. I do not believe in war myself, but I do believe in preparedness. It is the Christian duty of the church to uphold the flag of our country. People like Jane Addams would leave our beloved land open to the attacks of the foreigners. They are traitors to God and the flag!"

And on and on it went, the sermon. The Bishop (of what church I could not find out) had a bellowing, vehement voice that choked at times with a sort of arterio-sclerotic passion. He felt very strongly on the subject of Jane Addams and pacifism. Preaching in the name of God who is said to be love, he expressed a coarse hate of this noble woman.

So this was a Christian bishop speaking! His voice reminded one of Hitler, as did the pathological brutality of his hatred. So there are Nazi bishops in America! And they hate people like Jane Addams, just as much as Hitler hates Albert Einstein!

I wish some of the liberals who are so complacent about American "democracy," and who lull themselves to sleep every day with the Coué formula, "Oh, no, there can never be fascism in this country!" could have heard this American bishop's fascist sermon.

In all the words of mourning that were spoken at the passing of Jane Addams, one strain could be heard: 'This woman was a saint, and everyone loved her."

Yes, Jane Addams was one of the finest flowers of all that is good in American civilization. She was beloved by thousands, and she deserved their love. But it is a liberal folly to ignore the fact that there are just as many thousands who hated her.

She was hated by the bloodthirsty generals and parsons against whose war plans she preached; she refused to support the World War, and many a jingo hates her since that time. She was hated by many of the slum riff-raff of Chicago; all the pimps and machine politicians whom she exposed. She was hated by the sweatshop bosses and the racketeering landlords against whose profits she fought.

She fought against race oppression, too, and was hated for it by the fascist dregs of Chicago. Yes, Jane Addams had many enemies; and their hatred is as good a monument to the ethical beauty of her life as is the love of her friends.

Jane Addams was a settlement house liberal. She was worlds away from being a Communist; but let the lesson sink deep into the heart of her liberal friends: the fascist business men and their gangsters hated her as much as they do any Communists.

Jane Addams was the mother of the settlement house idea in this country. This movement had a certain historic influence at one time. It was an expression of the troubled conscience of liberal members of the upper class, younger sons who had come to understand that their father's wealth was wrung from the misery of the poor.

In Russia a similar group had created the Narodniki movement, their slogan being, "Let us go to the people." Tolstoy, for whom Jane Addams had a great devotion, was an example of the landowner with a bad conscience. The settlement house was a polite version of the Tolstoyan-Narodniki idea in America. These sons and daughters of the well-to-do went in groups to live in the slums. They set up communal houses in different neighborhoods, and invited the children of the workers to come for lessons in good manners, hygiene, athletics, cultural study and the like.

Many of these settlement house residents joined in the early fight for the trade unions. They fought for children's playgrounds and other neighborhood needs. They agitated for social legislation, fought political corruption. Some of them used their observation of the slum life to write fine sociology and fiction.

Ernest Poole's *The Harbor* and Arthur Bullard's *Comrade Yetta* and *A Man's World* (darn good examples of the "proletarian fiction" of an earlier time which some of our young writers might study), were produced by settlement house residents. Judge Ben Lindsey, Robert Morss Lovett, Robert Herrick and others came through the settlement house. Many of these men and women went through an intellectual evolution such as is pictured in the works of Poole and Bullard, and became leaders of the Socialist Party.

They were the first middle-class allies of the workers' movement in this country, pioneers of a historic transformation that has now achieved a mass character.

The settlement house laid much of the groundwork for this necessary united front and Jane Addams was its chief pioneer.

"For a New World Fair"

The officials of New York are all in a dither. It seems that a world's fair is being planned for our noisy, overcrowded, neurotic city in 1939–40.

This is years away. We may all be bombed out of existence by then; haven't the city fathers heard the big guns on the horizon, presaging a new world war?

Or maybe we'll all have starved to death meanwhile in the capitalist famine. Don't the officials know people are starving in New York, or do they eat so regularly they can't even imagine such a thing?

Anyway, the stuffed shirts are all in a twitter of optimism, oratory and plans for the big fair in 1940. A site has been chosen on Flushing Bay, and the swamps will soon be filled in. Millions of dollars will be poured into that swamp. It will mean prosperity, is the given reason; just as the Max Baer–Joe Louis million-dollar gate was said by the grave and learned economists of capitalism to have been a signal for the return of the American boom.

I like fairs, I like Coney Island, parades, circuses, any kind of a good show. But I like the truth a whole lot better, and I can sense in advance that our New York fair, if we are still alive to put it through, will be one of the typical gaudy lies of a capitalist world.

These fairs are supposed to be a concentrated picture of the state of civilization, a sample of its scientific and artistic glories.

The Chicago fair, as you may remember, had a model Ford plant shown in action, and a gallery of fine paintings, and scads of modern inventions, and lagoons like Venice. It also had a midway that concentrated a hundred Coney Island freak shows and circuses.

But there wasn't a single realistic reproduction of a typical Southern lynching shown at the fair, to illustrate American justice and mercy and the race question.

There was a great deal of dazzling modern architecture, but not a single drab, rotten, bug-crawling tenement house, such as those in which many millions of good Americans must live.

There was no attempt to show how coal miners must sweat in terrific underground heat and gas, for a lousy wage. There were exhibits of paintings, but not a single farm mortgage in a beautiful frame, or the photograph of a poor farmer and his family being kicked off their own homestead by a prosperous banking shark from the city.

I could make many suggestions as to exhibits for the New York fair.

I should like to see a reproduction of the municipal flophouse, for example, with hundreds of sick and hungry men groaning in the dark, and scratching after bugs all night.

A sweatshop at work would make a nice inspiring scene, too. Pale men and women humped over machines, and driving themselves furiously to earn seven or eight dollars a week, slaving from dawn to dark to keep their families alive.

Or a Home Relief station, with broken-spirited unemployed being third-degreed by some haughty snip of a college girl, their private lives pried into as though they were criminals. This would make a beautiful sample of America and New York today.

Or why not, also, for comedy relief, have the reproduction of a Tammany club, and show how democracy works in New York one hundred and fifty years after the revolution to make America safe for democracy? Those Tammany mugs are splendid actors, Mr. Mayor, and would put on a good show that should teach every child how elections are really won, and what a great thing it is to be a citizen with a two-dollar vote.

But why indulge in foolish hopes that even a tiny slice of truth will be found at this new World's Fair? Mademoiselle La Truth is the most unpopular person you can ever find in every capitalist land. The stuffed shirts of capitalism hate her; they call her an agitator, a kill-joy, trouble-maker, a pessimist, a Bolshevik. They arrest her on sight; they send gangs of vigilantes after her; they defame her in the newspapers and colleges and churches; they slap her into jails and concentration camps, and throw away the key.

If she comes near the World's Fair, a hundred trained dicks will be there to spot her, and to haul her off to the can, before she can make trouble.

But can't we persuade our mayor, formerly a valiant liberal, to let her slip in for just a moment? Can't we effect some sort of "liberal" compromise? We know that too much truth at the fair would hurt business and discourage free spending, but why not have in some dark, forgotten corner just one or two truthful exhibits? If even for the aesthetic effect of contrast, if only for the record.

American boys in a military training camp, being taught how to shove their bayonets into the flesh and bone of an enemy soldier (Japanese? British? Soviet Russian? Mexican? or maybe only a striking coal miner?)

Or a group of New York kids who've never had a square meal in their lives. A fourth of the school kids are chronically undernourished, a commission of doctors reported recently. We could have a fine delicatessen store window, such as those one sees uptown, and the kids standing in front of it, mournfully.

It would be a very touching sight. Pathos, and all that, Mr. Mayor. A contrast to all the gargantuan optimism that will swell the fair. Contrast is the very basis of good art, Mr. Mayor, and the fair "will be a work of art," your officials promise us, if not of truth.

“In a Home Relief Station”

The line is long and extends from the staircase at the end of the school courtyard to the door at the entrance. There must be at least two hundred people in the line at a time. And more come in. Every minute new ones come in. They pour through the door at the entrance where there are four big cops and a special dick with a badge on his coat lapel. Inside there are two more big cops. They seem to pick the biggest cops in the precinct for the job. You never can tell what may happen here. There are two lines like that. Two hundred workers at least in each line. Backed up against the tiled wall. Single file. Four hundred people. Waiting. Waiting for hours. Waiting until everything aches with waiting. Feet and back and shoulders. Waiting and standing up for hours. No benches. Or just one. The bench that holds four at a time in front of the interviewer’s table. That’s where you hand in your application slip. That’s where they check up on you. Four at a time. It takes hours. And you stand and wait. Wait. Until everything aches. Feet and back and shoulders.

That’s why you can never tell what may happen. That’s why every ten minutes the police car comes driving around to the Home Relief Bureau. That’s why there are so many cops. In case all these poor and jobless and hungry people got tired of waiting? In case they got tired and desperate standing up against the walls for hours, while the thin long line creeps forward a bare inch, an imperceptible shove at a time? In case they used those hands, tough and hard as iron with countless years of labor, now hanging at their sides to take over the management of this relief station? What then? They would destroy this line. There wouldn’t be any standing for hours then. They’d give themselves the relief they need because each knows the need of the other. That’s why you never can tell what may happen. That's why there are so many cops and every ten minutes the police car comes driving around.

It happened once before here. They lost their temper once. They got tired of standing and answering stupid questions. They were hungry and they wanted relief. It began with a woman, a big brawny Swedish woman. Four hours she had been standing in line. If you've never been on a line in the Home Relief Bureau you don't know what it is. You don't know the feeling you get standing there, hour after hour, like an animal, like a dog waiting to be fed. Nobody talks. Nobody says anything. You just stand. Somebody asks a question. What do they ask you? How much relief do you get? Somebody tells you how tough he's been having it. How long he's been out of work. How they're going to be put out if something isn't done soon.

The city has set up these Home Relief Bureaus. They had to set them up. Everybody knows that. They had to set them up. But they made it as difficult as possible to get relief. It is given grudgingly, and wound around with yards and yards of red tape. And they herd you like dogs there. Beggars ain't choosers. Workers ain't human. They don't deserve better. Courtesy? Why, you ought to be glad they don't let you die in the streets. You ought to be glad they don't let you freeze to death in the winter. You ought to go down on your knees and thank the big shot that his heart is big and his liver is red and his pocket is full. Thank him for the check that can't support one person decently, no less a family of four. Thank him for the rent that pays for two rooms in which five people are crowded. This is relief.

This is what the big brawny Swedish woman got tired of. Suddenly, she walked out of line, just walked right out, and plunked herself down in the chair of the interviewer. In the interviewer's chair! The staff of the Home Relief Bureau must have had a fit. Imagine, having the nerve to sit down in a chair! But she sat there, the big woman, folding her hands deliberately across her broad breast and waited. For a moment the big fat cop, the ugly one, just stood and stared at her. Then he asked her to get back in line. She refused. She said she was sick and tired of standing up there. She had children to attend to. She had a home to take care of. Hadn't she worked and slaved long enough? Did she have to come crawling on her hands and knees to get a piece of bread from the city? Was it her fault her husband was out of work? She wanted to be taken care of. She refused to stand any longer in that line that moved forward an inch at a time. If they were short-handed why didn't they hire more people? They took the people's money through taxes, why didn't they use it to help the people instead of grafting it?

The cop said: "You gotta get up or get out." But he forgot something. He forgot that four hundred people standing on line there felt just as the big brawny Swedish woman felt. He forgot that her words were the words of all, her thoughts were the thoughts of all. He thought he was dealing with one woman, but he was facing four hundred people who had suffered as she had and felt as she did.

She refused to leave the chair. The cop moved over to grab her arm. And then it happened. It looked as though he had grabbed the arm of four hundred people so quickly did those two long lines move. It looked as though there was only one voice shouting, "Let me alone!" so quickly did the four hundred workers move.

And before it was over, they had not one police car sirening through the streets, but half a dozen. It looked as though they had called out all the cops in the city. But nobody was arrested, except a member of the Unemployment Council in the district whom the cops had been trying to grab for some time. He wasn't even there. But many times he had been in the line, talking, explaining the need for organizing. The cops picked him up but it was like arresting a thunderstorm. It was something that was in the minds of those four hundred people and in the minds of millions of other workers scattered throughout the land. It was the thoughts which poured out of the mouth of the big brawny woman who walked out of the line and plunked down in the interviewer's chair.

This is only a slight instance. A brief little episode in the class struggle. But it flares up in the great battles of the workers in great strikes. It will flare up in the great struggles coming. This time it was only about a chair. An interviewer's chair. The papers called it a "riot." Someday it will be not for a chair in a Home Relief Bureau but for a government. And there will not be four hundred, but millions.

“Just Like Lindbergh’s Baby”

In Flemington, N. J., Bruno Hauptmann is being tried for the murder of the child of Colonel Lindbergh.

Justice is being tested, as the newspapers say, in that small Jersey farm town. The air is full of righteous indignation. The newspapers, the news-reels, the magazines, the radio, are suddenly attacked with a veritable vertigo of justice. Everybody has become the apostle, the warrior and the defender of justice.

But there is another crime which no newspaper has reported. A child was murdered in Jacksonville, Florida, a three-year-old child, and no editor has gone running to the copy desk with a flaming editorial calling for the death of the murderer.

It was not a spectacular crime. There was no ransom of fifty-thousand dollars demanded. There were no wealthy celebrated parents weeping in the spotlight. There were no hordes of reporters scribbling down the mother’s tearful words. There were no diagrams of the scene of the murder. No photos of the instruments which killed him. No close-up of the killer’s shifty eyes. No evidence and no indictment. No detectives and no go-betweens.

The crime was committed in open daylight. The murderer was known. The justice of the peace was in on it. The police shrugged their shoulders.

Eddie Lewis, three years old, was killed, murdered, and the murderer was never brought to trial.

Eddie Lewis was killed the morning of December 13, 1934. He was three years old. His parents were poor Negro workers of Orange Park, Florida. They were unknown people, who had never done spectacular deeds, flown oceans or married colonels. All their life long they had toiled obscurely for the benefit and comfort of others. They rode in Jim

Crow cars in Orange Park. They had a difficult time meeting the rent each month. They never knew when the jobs they had would end. They never knew what tomorrow held for them—what hungers, or miseries.

Mrs. Lewis worked six days a week caring for the child of a wealthy white man. She was free to tend to her own child, three-year-old Eddie, only one day a week, Wednesday. The rest of the time Eddie had to take care of his own three years without his mother's help.

On Monday evening Eddie got sick. Tuesday evening he was much worse, feverish, and trembling. But his mother had to leave him to take care of the wealthy white man's child.

Wednesday morning he could barely lift his head. There was only one doctor in Orange Park and he was away. The parents, the grandparents and the relatives did not know what to do. There was a hospital in Jacksonville. But they were too poor to have a car. There was no way of getting the sick child to the hospital.

The hours went by. Finally, at one-thirty that afternoon, a white man to whom the grandfather appealed took Eddie to Jacksonville in his car. They drove to a Negro doctor. He blamed the mother for neglecting the child, for not giving him medical attention sooner, charged her two dollars, and handed her a note saying that he had examined the boy and found him suffering from appendicitis.

By this time Eddie's eyes were shut, he breathed faintly, there seemed no life left in him at all.

Everybody got back into the car and began to drive to the Duval County Hospital. On the way they stopped at St. Luke's Hospital. They carried the quiet, dying body of the boy wrapped in an old blanket. But the attendant refused to admit Eddie into St. Luke's Hospital. It did not matter that the boy was dying. The mother's pleas meant nothing. St. Luke's Hospital cures only the whites. They do not take Negroes, not even dying Negro children.

They drove on, to the Duval County Hospital. There the boy was carried into a ward and the doctor's note was read. But then the attendants discovered that little Eddie Lewis came from Clay County. Clay County was outside the hospital's limits. They took care of only Duval County. Orange Park, where Eddie Lewis came from, was just two miles outside the Duval County line. But the two miles were fatal. Duval County refused to help dying Eddie Lewis. He could not be treated in Duval County Hospital—it was two miles this side of the Clay County line.

For two hours they pleaded, and then drove away. Now one could hardly hear the breath from the little boy. He was as still and as cold as one dead.

They came at last to Brewster, a Jim Crow hospital in Jacksonville. Here they refused to examine Eddie, or give him a bed, until the white man had sworn to them that all the hospital bills would be paid. When they were assured that their money was safe, the doctor examined the boy. Now he disagreed with the diagnosis of the Negro doctor. The small body lay there quietly, coldly in the bed. It was too late. The new diagnosis was not appendicitis—but death. Little Eddie Lewis never awoke to know that at last he had been permitted to enter a hospital. He never learned why he died. He was murdered.

After he was dead, after the white race-hatred of the boss class had killed him, after he was slain by the hospitals, there was no trial in Jacksonville. Neither in Clay County nor in Duval County. There were no reporters sent down by the metropolitan press to write the story of the murder of Eddie Lewis. Was Duval County Hospital charged with his death? Then one should indict, not the hospital authorities alone, but the whole class who were accomplices in the murder of Eddie Lewis. The white bourbons, the plantation owners, the factory owners of the South. These are the ones who are responsible for the murder of Eddie Lewis. They killed him. They murdered Eddie Lewis as surely as though they had smothered him in a dark woods, or slain him in a secret house off some unfrequented road.

Today they are trying Bruno Hauptmann for the murder of a rich man's son. But some day Eddie Lewis' murder will also be avenged. Some day the criminals will be brought to trial for the murders and crimes they have committed against millions of obscure and unknown workers.

On that day, when the murderers, the class which rules America, will stand trial, Eddie Lewis will wear the authority of a judge. He will sit high with those others who will be there to judge and pass out sentence on the criminals. He will sit and preside with Sacco and Vanzetti, with Harry Simms, with Claude Neal, with the host of others unknown and nameless who have been murdered by the ruling class. And among their voices, the voice of Eddie Lewis will not be least.

Battle Hymn

The Experimental Theatre

Federal Theatre Works Progress Administration, 1936

Battle Hymn, *a play about the life of John Brown, was scripted by Gold with editing help from Michael Blankfort. The ambitious three-act drama was produced during the Federal Theatre Project's initial New York season of 1936. The play blends socialist realism with agitprop elements to both represent Brown's life and assert similarities between the abolitionist past and the Depression-era present. Theater historian Morgan Himelstein observed that* Battle Hymn *"implied that the agitational activity of John Brown was a predecessor of the current work of the Communist Party and that the Civil War was a forerunner of the coming proletarian revolution." In a* New York Times *assessment of the play's premier, reviewer Lewis Nichols praised the "good solid history" of the production. Another reviewer claimed that the play was so enthralling that the audience forgot to walk out during the intermission.*

A fascinating ensemble scene occurs at the home of Gerrit Smith in 1859. Brown reveals his daring plan to Emerson, Garrison, Sanborn, and Thoreau. Less famous participants in the scene include Mr. Hickey, a New Englander who stood with Brown in the Kansas border wars, and August Bondi, a Jewish American proletarian who seems to speak for Mike Gold. Though the encounter is fictional, it draws aptly on social history to sum up the logic of revolutionary activism.

~

Act Three, Scene 1

DESCRIPTION OF CHARACTERS

AUGUST BONDI, 35. A clear-thinking realist who has worked with hand and brain many of his years.

JOHN BROWN, 54. The old tiger. Tall, gaunt, keen, alert. A farmer who has turned warrior. A fundamentalist like Moses on the mountain.

RALPH WALDO EMERSON, a cold-natured man of letters but lighting warm over Brown's fight. In his 56th year.

WILLIAM LLOYD GARRISON, 54. The great man of the *Liberator* who is somewhat tired of the great fight.

MR. HICKEY, 55. A transplanted Yankee.

DAVID THOREAU, the saint of the Woods, but a man of great stature, 42.

FRANKLIN SANBORN, 24, a hot, passionate youngster.

GERRIT SMITH, 62, an old friend of Brown's.

The home of GERRIT SMITH, *Peterboro, N. Y.*

Present are GERRIT SMITH, *a wealthy Abolitionist, a mild-mannered, stoutish man about sixty;* RALPH WALDO EMERSON, *his long, lined face gentle with an inner light. He is in his late fifties. There is* THOREAU, *brown-bearded, thin and short, gentle, retiring and uncomfortable;* WILLIAM LLOYD GARRISON, *fifty-four, a well-preserved, well-set man;* FRANK SANBORN, *a young man about twenty-five, idealistic and passionate. The room is heavy with fine paneling, books, etc. At the Left is a costly oval table on which there are teacups, dishes and books. It is late afternoon. As the Curtain rises,* THOREAU *is at the window up R, looking out.*

GARRISON *is pacing the floor impatiently, the* OTHERS *are sitting at the table L.*

There is a KNOCK at the R. door.

SMITH. Come in.

MARIA. (*a woman servant*) Mr. Smith, there's a gentleman with some friends.

SMITH. Have them come in, immediately. (*The men in the room rise. Enter* BROWN, GREEN, BONDI, OWEN *and* HICKEY.) Welcome.

BROWN. Mr. Smith, I hope we are not too late. We missed the earlier train from Westport. These are my lieutenants: my son Owen, Mr. Bondi, Mr. Green, and Mr. Hickey.

SMITH. And this is Mr. Emerson, Mr. William Lloyd Garrison. Mr. Thoreau I believe you met.

BROWN. Yes.

SMITH. And Sanborn you know.

BROWN. I am honored. (*The men exchange greetings and handshakes.*)

SMITH. Shall we sit down, gentlemen?

EMERSON. Are you from these parts, Mr. Hickey?

HICKEY. No, I'm from the same part of New England as you, sir. I'm mighty proud to meet some book-writers. I cain't say I ever read anything but the almanac and The New York Tribune, but I've heard of you. Well, what do you think of what we did in Kansas, Mr. Emerson? (*The men sit around the table. Bondi and the other Brown men stand in the up stage of the table.*)

EMERSON. It was worth many libraries.

HICKEY. Glad to hear you say it, friend.

SMITH. (*to Servant*) Bring some tea in, please. (*Maria exits R.*)

SANBORN. Did you have any trouble with spies, Captain Brown?

BROWN. I believe we were followed.

SMITH. (*worried*) Here?

BROWN. Of that I am not sure.

GARRISON. Shall we go to the business at hand?

BROWN. If you please.

SMITH. Will you kindly explain your project?

BROWN. I will, but forgive me for being short. I have a good deal to do. To be brief, therefore, what I am asking is that you raise another thousand dollars for the cost of my expedition.

GARRISON. I understand that.

BROWN. Naturally, it isn't practical to raise this money at public meetings. That is why I have to make private appeals to leading Abolitionists.

SMITH. Naturally.

GARRISON. Now just where do you intend to operate in your slave running?

BROWN. Before answering I would like permission to ask first whether you gentlemen are with me?

THOREAU. With all my heart!

EMERSON. For every slave you free, I'll thank God.

SANBORN. (*passionately*) Are we with you? What a question. I'm yours to command.

BROWN. Mr. Smith?

SMITH. (*mildly hurt*) I've given you many hundreds of dollars. I don't think you have to ask me that question.

BROWN. Mr. Garrison?

GARRISON. (*brusquely*) Of course I'm with you, Brown, but I want to know more details.

BROWN. That's my reason for asking to speak to you today. Listen, gentlemen. My whole life I've hated slavery. The last four years of my life I have given to fighting it as it must be fought,—with blood. I have lost two sons in the fight. My family is broken. We have been hounded like mad dogs. We don't know, any longer, what one single night of peace is. But I have concluded that there is a greater blow to strike against slavery than any we have struck before. I propose to take the fight into the South—to set-up a center of rebellion in Virginia.

GARRISON. In the South?

SMITH. Virginia?

GARRISON. That's madness.

EMERSON. You can't mean that.

SANBORN. (*harshly*) Let him finish.

THOREAU. How will you do it?

BROWN. (*takes out a map*) Around Harper's Ferry the blacks outnumber the whites three to one. There are mountains on the Maryland side right across the bridge. And in Harper's Ferry there is a Federal arsenal practically unguarded. I plan to take it in a surprise attack.

SMITH. (*incredulous*) What did you say?

BROWN. (*calmly*) I plan to take the arsenal in a surprise attack.

GARRISON. (*rises; paces angrily*) This is the most preposterous plan I ever heard of.

EMERSON. You're mad, Brown.

SMITH. But a Federal arsenal—that's treason! I'd never have given a cent if I had known—

EMERSON. Come—you're testing us.

BROWN. I don't test men this way. Yes, I plan to use the guns and ammunition I capture to establish a slave republic in the Maryland mountains.

SANBORN. How many men do you have?

BROWN. I expect with your help to get one hundred.

GARRISON. A hundred? You can't do that! A hundred men! You're talking nonsense.

BROWN. You forget the slaves, Mr. Garrison. They will flock to us—just as soon as the word goes forth. Perhaps in five years they will have all come to us. Yes, gentlemen—this is the deed America needs. Perhaps this is the only way to end slavery.

GARRISON. I can't listen to this outrageous plan anymore. It's the most incredible—(*crosses up C.*)

SMITH. Brown, you're my friend, but I tell you it's impossible.

BROWN. What are you talking about, gentlemen? I can't fail. You don't know how easy it can be done.

GARRISON. Well—I want to be frank with you—

SMITH. Ssh! (*Maria has entered carrying a tray with a teapot and cups.*) Just set it down here, Maria.

MARIA. Shall I pour?

SMITH. Never mind. I'll do it. Just set it down and leave us, please. (*She does so on table. As she is about to leave*) By the way, take a look and see if there are any strangers loitering around. And if anybody comes to call, I'm indisposed.

MARIA. Yes, Mr. Smith (*She exits R.*)

GARRISON. (*continuing*) Of all the crackpot plans—the arsenal in a surprise attack! You can't do that.

BROWN. I say it can be done!

SMITH. It's too dangerous.

BROWN. Slavery must be made dangerous for the slave-holder.

EMERSON. Gentlemen, let's examine this calmly, please.

GARRISON. Does anyone else know this plan?

BROWN. I am going to tell Frederick Douglass—and my men.

SMITH. Does anyone else know it now?

BROWN. Yes—one other—a military man, who has had experience in guerrilla warfare—Captain Hugh Fordes.

GARRISON. Hugh Fordes! Listen, I know that man. He's a buccaneer, a professional adventurer. How do you know you can trust him?

BROWN. I don't know that, but I'm willing to take the chance. I need his help.

EMERSON. Do you realize the powerful forces you are up against?

BROWN. (*rises*) I do, sir. We are attacking the Government of the United States.

THOREAU. (*bitterly*) And why not?

GARRISON. (*scornfully, sitting down R.*) Brown, you say the slaves will rise and join your mountain republic. How do you know?

BROWN. They'll come. How will the slave-owners be able to stop the rumor of our deed? They'll flock to us like bees to a hive.

BONDI. May I speak, Captain?

BROWN. Yes, do, Mr. Bondi.

BONDI. (*comes down C.*) I merely want to place on record that on this part of the plan I have disagreed with Captain Brown. I believe that a long time must be spent in agitation and preparation of the slaves before they'll be willing to join us. As yet they don't know who we are, and what we are doing.

BROWN. They'll find out as soon as the first gun is fired.

SANBORN. Captain Brown is right.

BONDI. The task would be heartbreaking and dangerous. Without it, I'm not sure they'll follow us. I wanted to tell you this, gentlemen, because I want you to know also that, even if they don't follow us, this deed will rock the slave system; it will be a mightier agitation than ever your *Liberator*, Mr. Garrison; it will be an act on which people of both North and South will be forced to take sides.

EMERSON. It's a bold experiment.

BONDI. Many such bold experiments will have to be made before slavery is destroyed. Each will cost life, but that is the cost of freedom. As an American Abolitionist, and as a wage-worker, my place is beside Captain Brown.

BROWN. Thank you, Mr. Bondi.

THOREAU. (*abruptly*) Anything is better than human slavery.

SMITH. (*despondently*) Mr. Garrison?

GARRISON. (*rises*) I am utterly opposed.

BROWN. How would you end slavery?

GARRISON. Let the erring sisters depart. Let the South secede. We don't have to share their guilt. Practice non-resistance. In twenty years slavery will die of itself.

BROWN. (*wryly*) I don't remember you practicing non-resistance when that mob in Boston dragged you from Cambridge to the Commons.

GARRISON. Gentlemen, I must leave now. I've a lecture at eight. But let me speak frankly. Your plan, captain Brown, is a program of murder.

THOREAU. (*accepting it as an inevitable fact*) Murder, yes.

BROWN. Pray, don't call my deeds murder. I'm doing only what I believe.

GARRISON. If you do this crazy deed, the Abolitionist cause which is gaining every year thousands of new converts, new publications, new forums, will be set back fifty years. Besides all this, I know Harper's Ferry. It's a death trap for you. You don't stand a chance. You'll be crushed in an hour.

SANBORN. You're wrong. You're wrong.

BROWN. Mr. Garrison, pray continue with your writing and your lecturing. I shall go on to do what I believe. I would prefer a life of peace, but I will not endure slavery. If I must kill to end it, I will kill, and the sin be on my soul.

GARRISON. I didn't mean to offend you.

BROWN. No man can offend me. God alone knows what is in my heart on this subject of killing. I have thought the matter through. Mr. Smith, what is your decision? I beg you to help me. Without your money—my project may be postponed for too long a time.

SMITH. If there was only a way I could stop you. If I could only show you how wrong you are.

BROWN. I have to leave shortly. Don't attempt to persuade me, please. It'll lead to nothing. Some of my men are already waiting in a farmhouse near Harper's Ferry. (*pause*) America needs a great deed, gentlemen. God is with us; who can be against us? (*silence*) I await your answer. (*Pause. He exits R. Green follows him out. The others start. Garrison catches hold of Bondi.*)

(WARN *Curtain.*)

GARRISON. Wait. Can't you talk to him? He's leading you to death. There's bound to be a war!

BONDI. I tell you, gentlemen, I'm interested in the freedom of the slaves, and not the preservation of a corrupt and oppressive peace. (*He follows the others out R.*)

GARRISON. Don't give him money. I warn you all, the political consequences will be extremely serious. This is treason, gentlemen.

THOREAU. (*bursting with bitterness*) Treason? You talk of treason. He brings us human beings, he acts on a higher law than governments, he gives us the word of God, and you talk of treason.

GARRISON. (*hotly*) But we're living in a world of men.

THOREAU. He's living in a world with God. (*silence—uneasy movement*)

EMERSON. I'm a little ashamed of myself that I even question him.

SMITH. There'll be blood. I can see it now, flowing over this land like flood waters.

SANBORN. And there'll be freedom!

SMITH. I can't give him money for this.

EMERSON. (*rises*) Mr. Smith, you'll have my bank draft for two hundred and fifty dollars in the morning. My God, we talk of money. This man is going forth to die.

(EMERSON *starts for the door.* THOREAU *puts his head in his hands, and starts to weep silently as the lights dim, and—*)

Curtain Falls

"What Side Are You On?"

New Masses, October 3, 1939

When the German-Soviet Non-Aggression Pact was announced in August 1939, Western leaders feigned shock and indignation, though it was their own policies that made the pact inevitable.

Since the mid-1930s, the appeasement governments of France and especially Britain had acted deliberately to deflect Hitler's war machine toward a collision with the Soviet Union. Eventually a consensus formed that there was only one way Nazi Germany could be deterred: an airtight mutual-assistance alliance between Britain, France, and the USSR. The Soviets repeatedly proposed this partnership, but it was rejected at every turn. British foreign minister Neville Chamberlain delayed, deceived, and affronted Russian diplomatic efforts, working instead to create the conditions for a war between fascism and communism that could annihilate the latter.

The Soviets, with ample evidence that London and Paris meant to isolate them, were left with little choice. The Non-Aggression Pact bought valuable preparation time for the long-expected Nazi attack on the USSR that came two years later. Gold's first New Masses *article about the pact was published five weeks after the agreement was announced and a month after the German invasion of Poland, a period when the Soviets were being broadly accused of "the greatest double cross in history." Though the Soviet Union bore the brunt of the war, suffering more than eight million deaths in combat against Hitler's armies, the 1939 pact was nevertheless cited during the McCarthy years and after as evidence of communist perfidy. The republication here of "What Side Are You On?" adds balance to the historical record.*

~

Mike Gold poses the question that clears all the issues in the whirling events of today. The salesmen of Munich start selling each other.

If this were a war to crush fascism, I know that millions of Americans would hasten to assist the anti-fascists. But though the organic sympathies of this country are with England and France, that long, horse face of the evil old prohibitionist, Chamberlain, intervenes to sour and slow down the warmer emotions.

It is almost impossible to believe in the honest intentions of the Tory architect who achieved the masterpiece of Munich. His elderly voice cracked with the same calculated pathos when he spoke of "peace" as it does now when he vows to end "Hitlerism." It was as thick with unctuous hypocrisy, too, when he pretended to grieve over his own murder of Spain as it does now in lamenting over Poland.

As I understand it, the next diplomatic victory Chamberlain is intriguing for is to win fascist Italy over to the side of Britain and France. It will take an enormous bribe to buy everybody's sweetheart, Mussolini, and if I were a Frenchman I would shudder in anticipation of the cost. For it will be with large chunks of French property that Chamberlain will undoubtedly tempt the black-shirt hero of Guadalajara, Addis Abbaba, and Albania. The British Tories are no sentimentalists like our American newspaper publishers and commentators. They would even sell out France, a non-British nation. They did not shed any moral tears as they sold out Czechoslovakia, Spain, Austria, Manchuria, and a lot of other non-British peoples and lands in their historic plot to bribe the fascist axis into a war against the Soviet Union.

That plot miscarried, though it has already cost the lives of perhaps a million non-Britishers, including non-British women and children. It may cost many more, but still there will be no Tory tears.

But the new plot with fascist Italy may miscarry. What surprises me is to find that it rouses no moral indignation in the swollen bosoms of the Chamberlain press in America. It awakes only cynical hopes that the deal will go through.

Yet this is supposed to be a war to end Hitlerism. Should it not also be a war to end Mussolinism? True, the trains in Italy run on time, but they are the same trains of fascist aggression and inhuman slaughter as the Nazi trains. If this is the war to end fascism, then how can Mussolini be regarded as a possible partner in it?

One knows the answer. When capitalist governments are fighting their wars, they do not stop to become moral, or to examine the ideology of any possible allies. They play every trick in the dirty game of power politics, for that is the way to win.

It is obvious why so few American journals ever pause to condemn the power politics of the British Empire, while at the same time they can rise to remarkable heights of moral indignation over the strategy of the Soviet Union. This is not another routine hypocrisy, but a natural identification of themselves with one warring system or the other. They find nothing immoral in the objects pursued by the British Empire. The empire, built on the same blood and slavery of millions that Hitler is using to cement his mad dream of a Nazi empire, seems to American conservatives like some eternal truth that one never even unconsciously questions.

Power Politics

But they fear and hate the political objects pursued by a Socialist and anti-imperialist state such as the Soviet Union. Power politics for what end? Power politics for whose benefit? When power politics is ruthlessly pursued for the benefit of British landlords, it seems moral to American landlords and industrialists. When the USSR skillfully uses its immense economic, political, and military power for the benefit of workers and peasants, it is not only immoral but damned dangerous.

In their new lynching bee against the Soviet Union, most of the American press has forgotten to think. It is appalling to see to what a low intellectual ebb most political comment has fallen here; it is almost as if America were at war.

I haven't yet heard one such analyst, a man who is paid to interpret events scientifically, point out what a great new turn the Soviet-German pact has given to world events. It precludes, for example, any revival of the Four-Power alliance that Chamberlain, Hitler, and Mussolini had so often advocated. The Soviet Union will be sitting in on all future peace conferences as an equal.

The pact has also overthrown the famous European balance of power which the British Empire had used for centuries to keep the continent at war, while it grabbed and arbitrated. The pact throws Nazism to the mercy of its worst enemy, the Soviet Union, as Goering so ineptly boasted in his speech. If Germany can fight a major war only with the help of Soviet materials, what does that make the Nazis but the economic prisoners of the Soviets? For needless to say, no such materials in the amounts required by the Nazis will be forthcoming.

The Soviets now have the balance of power in their hands. If they chose to swing to the Allies, they could crush Germany. If they chose to aid Hitler, they could possibly end the French and British empires. Both sides know it. But American commentators don't know what even old George Bernard Shaw could see through the mists of his dotage—that the Soviets will help neither imperialist cause, but will use their mighty power to establish some sort of democratic peace.

The Soviets have made no wars in twenty years. The Soviet system does not need war to solve economic contradictions, as does capitalism, since no such contradictions exist under Socialism. The Soviets have infinitely more to gain by peace than by war; for their system is ascending, while capitalism is hastening deeper into its final crisis, come war or peace. That is the Soviet policy; it has been on the records for twenty years.

It would help the cause of American clarification if a few of our political sharks did some homework, and read a primer or two explaining the Soviet Union. Most of them have fed only on hymnals of hate gotten out by the professional Soviet-baiters, and hence their minds are in as much of a fog over Russia as if it were the Cathay of Sir John Mandeville.

They have no accurate information as to the twenty years of diplomacy and foreign policy of the Soviet Union. And they know nothing about the Socialism that is the basis of the Soviet state, and that determines and inspires its every move. Yes, they should really read up on this thing called Socialism; it will be heard from again in the news.

Jews Overjoyed

Meanwhile, as one who has ever been loyal to his Jewish inheritance, and who has agonized with his kinsmen over the cruelty and horror visited on the Jewish scapegoat by the insane defenders of a decaying capitalism, it has given me joy, a "moral" joy, to see that the Soviets have saved a million Jews from the Nazi and Polish anti-Semites.

The Jews of America had been whipped up to fear and hatred of the Soviets by a Yiddish press that is certainly as venal and reactionary as Hearst. But the truth can never be crushed. It remains, deeply buried, if only in the instinct of self-preservation, for in a real crisis lies do not work. And in the present crisis every normal Jew could not help rejoicing at the deliverance of the Jews of western Ukraine and Byelo Russia.

I have met some who have fathers and brothers in those parts, and they are happy. They don't understand politics, but they are very happy. Most of the Ukrainian-Americans are also happy. They are not Communists, but they knew the Polish landlords, and they know Hitler. Some of the newspaper commentators should take a moment out and ask the simple folk why they are happy. This might also help them find some clue to the policies of those "mysterious" Soviets.

Part Four

"The Second American Renaissance"

As major liberal writers one by one sundered ties with communism circa 1940, they also began a process of denigrating the aesthetic priorities and cultural modus operandi of the decade that had made Mike Gold's voice significant. He saw what was happening to his legacy and spoke about it in an address to the Fourth Congress of American Writers in 1941.

~

A shabby genteel scorn for the people and an equally shabby contempt for life were the predominant strains of the literary Twenties. Joseph Wood Krutch, the *Nation*'s critic, expressed some of the prevailing sentiment in several dreary books, out of which one can pluck as an underlying thesis this line: "We have come, willy-nilly, to see the soul of man as commonplace and its emotions as mean." T. S. Eliot, a young man writing poetry concerned with the emotions of tired and burned out old men, named the period "the wasteland" and characterized its intellectuals as "hollow men." Robert Frost complained that "life went so unterribly" in America, and hence there could be no great literature.

Among the younger participants in the general chorus of gloom and sterility of the Twenties, one might recall Ernest Hemingway, Scott Fitzgerald, John Dos Passos and Edmund Wilson. They and their friends who had come out of the war into a decade of bourgeois prosperity and disillusionment were called the "lost generation" by Gertrude Stein. They were a little proud of that label, and with Archibald MacLeish, who wrote a long, whiny poem of self-pity, "The Hamlet of Archibald MacLeish," each fancied himself a solitary and tragic Hamlet lost in a vulgar world.

But it was Thornton Wilder, I believe, who most adequately represents the Twenties. His novel, *The Bridge of San Luis Rey*, was a best-selling sensation of the publishing season of 1929–30. With his other novels, it offers a good synthetic pastiche of the tastes of the bourgeois decade.

It isn't sporting to slug a corpse, and I am not going to reassault Mr. Wilder at this late date. He remains useful as a landmark, however. He was the perfect flower of the "New Capitalism," that wave of post-war prosperity which dazzled so many liberals and Socialists into believing that Marxism was outmoded, and that the capitalist system could go on expanding indefinitely.

A new parvenu class had risen in America, swollen with quick profit and as anxious as the old mining camp millionaires to acquire culture in a hurry. Thorstein Veblen, in 1899, had described almost exactly in his *Theory of the Leisure Class* the face of this group. Veblen was a grim and sourpuss St. John the Baptist who foretold the coming of the genteel, country club Christ incarnated in Thornton Wilder.

Wilder contained all the virtues Veblen had prophesied a parvenu leisure class would demand: the air of good breeding, the decorum, priestliness, glossy high finish; as against the intrinsic qualities: conspicuous inutility, caste feeling, love of the archaic, etc., etc.

All these virtues were needed to help the parvenu class forget its lowly origins in American industrialism. It yielded them a short-cut to the aristocratic emotions. It disguised the barbaric sources of their incomes, the millions wrung from American workers and foreign coolies. It permitted them to feel spiritually worthy of that income.

But ten years after Thornton Wilder occupied our literary sky, a different sort of star appeared there. The success of John Steinbeck's *Grapes of Wrath* is a sensation too recent to need much description. The novel won the Pulitzer Prize; it was made into a popular movie; the book itself sold almost half a million copies; and the story of the Joads, the family of Oklahoma farmers turned into migratory workers by the bankers and the dust storms, has passed into the American folklore.

Only two other novels in America's literary history have had the same social effect as *The Grapes of Wrath*. They were Upton Sinclair's *The Jungle* and Mrs. Stowe's *Uncle Tom's Cabin*. Less than a year after *Grapes of Wrath*, another novel made a success as phenomenal. This was Richard Wright's *Native Son*.

It is not conceivable that two such novels, based on such proletarian themes as the travail of a family of poor farmers, and the psychology and murder of a Negro boy in the slums of Chicago, could have won the same amazing success ten years earlier in the parvenu epoch.

What had happened in the ten years lying between Wilder and Steinbeck was a revolution of taste, morals, aspirations and social consciousness. American literature and the audience that read it had reached a certain maturity. A people's culture and hundreds of fine novels, plays and poems impregnated with proletarian spirit had battered down the barricades set up by the bourgeois monopolists of literature.

The individual talents of Steinbeck and Wright fused and synthesized what had become a new tradition. In their work can be traced the influence of scores of experiments, of agitprop plays, of critical essays, of southern novels, of plays about migratories, of the new America revealed by hundreds of proletarian writers.

[. . .] So, from 1930 to 1940, our literature set forth on a second discovery of America. As in a famous decade in czarist Russia, the inverted, book-proud intellectuals "went to the people." Whole new areas of American life were opened up—the deep South, the daily life in factories, mills and mines, the struggle of the farmer, the souls of black folk, the problems of the recent immigrant and his children.

Now, at last, American literature came to grips with its own enormous and wonderful continent. Scores of gifted young "depression" authors appeared during each publishing season. There appeared a host of little magazines no longer filled with the usual poetic dewdrops, but proletarian in tone. The older writers were affected, too; many tried to come out of their introspective skins or warm little nests of sophisticated comfort. Some failed, but all were shaken and changed.

A sign of the renaissance was the furious literary controversies that set in. Literature was alive and dangerous, a social factor in the national life such as it had not been since the days of the Civil War. The Federal Arts Projects were created, a veritable revolution in popular culture such as America had never known.

Yes, it was a great and fruitful decade, one that burned much of the shoddy opportunism and adolescent fear and hesitation out of our literature. It taught American authors to be proud of their craft, because through it they could lead the people to great goals. It taught them to act and write like men and citizens, not like mere entertainers or perpetual Harvard boys or mystic outcasts from the national life. No longer was the writer an alien; he had rooted himself in the soil of the American people.

To describe this renaissance in detail is, of course, impossible in a brief paper. Future historians will devote books to it, as we now do to the movement of abolitionist, transcendentalist and socialist writers since the

Civil War. We are too close, anyway, to the renaissance of the Thirties to judge it with sufficient objectivity. What impresses one . . . is its breadth and sweep—its vitality and genius in a dozen directions.

[. . .] Let me, however, before concluding repeat that the proletarian decade of the Thirties was no misunderstanding or accident, no foreign plot, no feeble esthetic cult that a few critics had artificially created and now can as easily destroy. It was a great movement out of the heart of the American people. It can no more be erased from our national history than can the public school system or trade union movement. It is fascistic to want to destroy the trade unions of America. It is just as fascistic to try to destroy this people's culture and literature of the Thirties.

[. . .] The Thirties compares favorably with the Civil War decade, the greatest single chapter in the history of American culture. Its importance lies in its mass character. Therefore, no single Emerson or Walt Whitman stands out, though thousands of potential Emersons and Whitmans were formed. They are still young. Many will be drafted into the army. They will not surrender their souls to the army sergeant or to the literary Fuehrers now on the scene. Democracy still has a future in America,—as it has all over the struggling world. The present war interrupts the democratic renaissance of the Thirties. But that renaissance and its literature will in turn end the system of war and profit.

Let us persist.

"Renegades: A Warning of the End"

From *The Hollow Men*, 1941

Gold's role as an unofficial gatekeeper of the American Communist Party's artistic standards was apparent in The Hollow Men, *a collection of* Daily Worker *columns expanded for publication in 1941. The book's purpose was to expose the literary "renegades" who had abandoned the left in the late 1930s. In Gold's view, these artists, "fashioned in the womb of the middle class," had duplicitously claimed solidarity with oppressed workers only to eventually return to their bourgeois roots.*

The denounced "turncoats" included Sherwood Anderson, John Dos Passos and Lewis Mumford. Gold's analysis of Ernest Hemingway's 1940 novel For Whom the Bell Tolls, *excerpted below, is especially caustic.*

Responses to The Hollow Men *were divided along political lines, but the book certainly ended Gold's friendships with a number of mainstream writers. Hemingway's reaction was representative. On his next visit to New York, the famous author took a taxi to the* Daily Worker *offices, where he left a message: "Tell Mike Gold that Ernest Hemingway says he should go fuck himself."*

~

It takes years to make a Marxist out of a bourgeois intellectual. He was fashioned in the womb of the middle class; his every fiber absorbed its traditional fears, loves, and "eternal" values; to bring all these deeply hidden fears and dogmas to light, is almost the task of a psychoanalyst; and the relatively high percentage of renegades among intellectuals, as contrasted with workers, is only the ultimate demonstration of this truth.

Begin, for example, with the simple dogma named "individualism." It is the core of bourgeois life and thought. The capitalist system of economics is based on individual enterprise and the competition of one against all. But the worker has already been removed from much of this world by the very technique of modern industry. He works in large factories, with thousands of other workers, in a cooperative process. To earn a raise in wages, he finds he must still cooperate with his fellows in a trade union. Out of this difference in the manner of making a living, psychological differences take place between the worker and the middle class.

What the unbridled individualism of capitalism has made out of the middle class can be traced in a hundred different directions. Let us look at but one trait—the lack of human feeling, the absence of love for people, that is such a major strain in modern bourgeois literature.

[. . .] The worst tragedy in bourgeois life is to lose one's money. During the panic hundreds of bankrupt stockbrokers and businessmen committed suicide. They were still in good health, but they feared poverty more than death. One of the most difficult things during the depression decade was to organize the so-called white collar people. There was a profound psychological hurdle in the way. Not only newspapermen, engineers, technicians and other professionals facing sure starvation, but even your lowliest $12-a-week clerks and typists could not bring themselves to acknowledge that they were "workers."

Many were frightened by the very word. Calling oneself a "worker" meant, to the middle-class subconscious, the surrender of the class dream of being a millionaire someday, of giving up one's individual chances in the great capitalist lottery.

This crude desire for wealth is naturally translated into more "spiritual" terms and conflicts in the minds of the bourgeois intellectuals. It becomes an obscure and complex fear of being regimented, coarsened, robbed of freedom, of being told "what to think" by Communist or trade union "dictators," of being reduced to cogs in an organization, after having experienced the large freedom of a bourgeois superman, etc., etc.

So here are two psychological elements that go into the makeup of a renegade: his deep fear of proletarianization, from which he has never freed himself, and his lack of love for people, a trait arising out of the inhuman competitiveness of bourgeois society.

At certain great crises, such bourgeois intellectuals have enough brains to understand that there is a class conflict, and that the workers may even win it. So they hasten to jump on what looks like a bandwagon. But it is really with fear, doubt, and hatred of their new associates. They are never at home. It is opportunism that sends them to the workers, not deeply felt convictions and loves. When the tide turns, and the workers must temporarily retreat, the same opportunism makes them jump off the bandwagon as hastily as they jumped on.

[. . .] Ernest Hemingway is another example of this same historic process.

There is no better story teller in America than Ernest Hemingway. A great artist, but limited, narrow, and mutilated by his class egotism, the very brilliance of Hemingway's talents has only served to illuminate the poverty of his mind.

It is poor because its owner has for years lived the limited life of a rich sportsman and tourist. Hemingway's novels so often express this spectator without responsibilities, who holds a box seat at the crucifixion of humanity, and is a connoisseur of the agony and sweat of others.

You go through the Hemingway country and find it a world of cafés; bullfighters; big game hunting; scotch, more scotch, absinthe; long-limbed, gallant, "aristocratic" women who succumb easily; and expensive pleasure fishing; and expensive traveling hither and yon; and bootleggers; prize fighters—a colorful if sterile world and one completely divorced from the experience of the great majority of mankind.

It is interesting to search through Hemingway's writings for a single portrait of a man at work. There is never such a hero. The bondholder lives by coupon clipping or other abstract financial means. He can be very philanthropic and even as "pure in heart" as a lean, ironic, hard-drinking, Hemingway hero. But he knows nothing about the factories and fields where men must work and where the sources of his income arise.

All these traits account for the strange distortion that affects Hemingway's recent novel of the Spanish Civil War, *For Whom the Bell Tolls*.

The hero, Robert Jordan, is the same lean, ironic, hard-drinking, very, very noble Gary Cooper–Ernest Hemingway hero. He meets the same long-limbed, gallant Hemingway–Greta Garbo girl (this time a Spanish maiden). Against the backdrop of the civil war, they go through the same old gallant, skillfully arranged death. (The Hemingway pattern of love, by the way, is as juvenile as the Hemingway picture of society. Just as money comes from somewhere, by magic, and not from the most fundamental fact of life: which is labor; just so does love never become marriage, and babies, and common domesticity. Just as he has never been able to portray a worker, so has he been unable to draw the figure of a single mother.)

Robert Jordan, former Spanish instructor at an American university, now a volunteer in the International Brigade, had been doing guerrilla work back of the fascist lines. Hemingway's story is concerned with the last four days of his life when Jordan is assigned to blow up a certain bridge in enemy country.

The inner life of this young volunteer, however, is not that of any loyal member of the International Brigade, so far as one can judge from the letters, writings, speeches and other public records of the majority of them.

It is obviously Hemingway's inner life, intimately resembling the philosophy, or lack of philosophy, of the autobiographical heroes in his other books. It is interesting to note, first, that this Hemingway-Jordan cannot work up any real hate of the fascists. He is forever searching for excuses for them; he wants to find the "humanity" in these people.

He is so anxious to be "fair" to them, that he goes to the length of spending more time telling of Republican cruelty than of fascist cruelty.

That there must have been, in a merciless civil war, some typical peasant excesses against landlords, cannot be doubted. But Hemingway is unable to see, what even the aged Miguel Unamuno saw, that peasant terror is sporadic and individual, but fascist terror is organized in cold blood, on a mass scale.

[. . .] But from Hemingway's book, it is obvious that he cannot see the class difference. The war to him is exciting, terrible, dangerous: really a bullfight on a vast scale. If one takes sides in it, it is for this very personal reason:

> He fought now in this war because it had started in a country that he loved and he believed in the Republic and that if it were destroyed life would be unbearable for all those people who believed in it.

But the majority of the Spanish people fought not only for the forms of a republic. They also fought for bread, against feudal taxes, against the great estates. They were fighting against the fascists so fiercely because they hated the landlords, usurers, and bloated hierarchs and generals who had oppressed them for centuries.

Regarding these class lines, or the enormous central fact of hunger in Spain, Hemingway has not a sentence. Not a word. Not a hint. He doesn't know it exists. The war is some sort of vague battle over words, without roots in man's earth. It is like every other war. It is a thrill.

It is an accident, into which Jordan-Hemingway has been accidentally placed, "because he loved Spain." When it is over, Jordan-Hemingway means to lose all further interest in the people.

> People should be left alone and you should interfere with no one. So he believed that, did he? Yes, he believed that. And how about a planned society and the rest of it? That was for the other to do. He had something else to do after this war. What were his politics then? He had none now, he told himself. But do not tell anyone else that, he thought. Don't ever admit that. And what are you going to do afterwards? I am going back and earn my living teaching Spanish as before and I am going to write a true book.

But can the man "who has no politics" and hence no loyalty to democracy or the people write a true book about the Spanish Civil War, which was a political war, made by the people in defense of democracy and their right to bread? Of course not, and Hemingway's novel, despite its narrative genius, is a false picture of the war.

[. . .] One of the tricks of the Hemingway style consists of its short, positive, declarative sentences, each of them a final and authoritative judgment on everything. This rhetorical device never admits modifying clauses, or doubt, or, let us add, the painful processes of thought.

Thus, with the usual swagger, Hemingway-Jordan explains all there is to be known about that little subject, communism. What is communism? It is bigotry, he dogmatizes airily. And what is bigotry? Bigotry is something that happens to you when you have not slept for a long time with a woman. "Maria was very hard on his bigotry." After he slept with this long-limbed, gallant dream-girl, he tells us, his bigotry and his "communism" left him. But drunkenness would have served just as well. A drunkard is as little "bigoted" as an adulterer, he says.

Based on this piffling barroom philosophy, this class persiflage of the rentier, is it any wonder that Hemingway-Jordan, after respecting "Communist discipline, because it is the soundest and sanest for the prosecution of the war," immediately repeats the filthiest slanders that appeared in the Spanish fascist press during the war? He employs and even adorns their slanders of Andre Marty, a man who has lived for twenty-five years the life of a heroic leader of the people, a man who was the brains of a great naval revolt, who was the first communist deputy of France, who spent years in prison for his beliefs, and who has led great strikes. No rich tourist can ever understand the mind or heart of such a man. It must always remain a mystery to him; since, if understood, it might shatter his own smug universe. He is fatally compelled to slander all the ethical and moral values forming such a mind, lest they destroy him. He must slander the Russian technicians and officers he met in Madrid. He must even slander La Pasionaria.

Here again one meets the opportunist strain that corrupts the intellectual under capitalism. If the Spanish Civil War had been won by the people, Hemingway would not have thus slandered the communists, and been so painfully fair to fascists and "enemies of the people." But the people lost. One of the obvious reasons for their losing was that the Soviets could not afford to intervene on a major scale. That was exactly what the British and French statesmen of Munich wanted. It would have opened the war of a united capitalism against the Soviets for which they had been plotting with Hitler and Mussolini. The Soviets evaded the trap. Yet they did risk the security of their own great Socialist land and stretched the diplomatic limits to help the Spanish people. They were the only nation other than Mexico that helped. The French and British ruling class conspired with the fascists. They gave no help. They assisted in the treacherous murder of Spain. But you will not find a harsh word or even a little "slander" against them in Hemingway's book. He is too busy kicking La Pasionaria around, the "gallant" soldier!

[. . .] Hemingway-Jordan tells himself that after the Spanish war, he will return to his old job of teaching Spanish at an American university. It is a sign of how ignorant of social reality Hemingway is that he can make this sound like some sort of cushy peace for a former Lincoln Brigader. There were actually a number of university teachers in the Brigade. But when they came home, they found no such peace. They found boycott, persecution and blacklist. Can one conceive of that furious red-baiter, the president of Brooklyn College, returning his job to David McKelvey

White, a former professor who fought in Spain? Of course not; for to the reactionaries of America, the Spanish veterans are poison. It is a black mark against any young American conscripted in the present "war for democracy" that he has previously fought for democracy in Spain.

For Whom the Bell Tolls is only the story of Hemingway in Spain. It is a minor story. It is not the great story, the new story, the hopeful and epic story of our time, the story of Brooklyn clogdancers, and Bronx machinists, and Iowa farm boys, and California university instructors, and Alabama sharecroppers. They were not military men. They were not supermen or "lean, ironic" adventurers. They were just people. And with little training, and almost no arms, they went out against the professionals of fascism—the Moors, the army generals, the planes of Mussolini and Hitler, all the trained killers of capitalism. They stopped the Goliath dead in his tracks for three years. They actually did this—these rank-and-filers of the American democracy. They will do it again. And when the breaks finally come, they will win. Not only in Spain, but over the world.

Yes, it is the story of democracy itself that Hemingway has missed.

"The Crime of Lynching and Its Utility to the Southern Ruling Class"

Daily Worker, April 15, 1940

Southern poverty, a poverty as degraded as that of the slums of India or China, is the rotten humus in which the institution of lynching thrives. That is something to bear in mind in connection with the attempt to smother the Anti-Lynching bill in Congress.

The Garners and the Martin Dies and the wealthy white class for whom they speak need this mass filth, poverty and violence—they need lynching.

Organizations like the American Civil Liberties Union often issue bulletins in which they cheerfully note that the number of lynchings has dropped in a certain year, and thus progress has been made.

They congratulate themselves too readily. They miss the main point, which is, that the basis of lynching continues in every Southern village and town every day in the year. Lynching is the method by which nine million Negroes in the South are kept in the state of terror where they will work for any wages and not protest. Hence, lynching is useful to the white ruling class, because it also depresses the wages of the white workers.

~

There is a county in Kentucky that has been nicknamed "Bloody Breathitt." For years homicide has been the chief cause of death there; not lynching, but mutual murder among the white mountaineers.

John F. Day, a reporter on the "Herald-Leader" of Lexington, Ky., recently did an unusual thing for an average newspaperman on an average American paper.

Called to the scene of another killing in Breathitt County, and tired of the usual "picturesque feud" angle with which such stories have always been treated, Mr. Day decided to take a chance on truth.

Armed with only a camera, he spent two days among Breathitt's "483 square miles of scraggy mountains and lean, infertile hollows." His subsequent report suggested some of the reasons why life was cheap in "Bloody Breathitt."

"Like a great walnut cleaned of its meat, it lies there a shell—no timber, no coal, no petroleum, no farm land really farmable." Twenty-five years ago, people first moved in numbers to Breathitt, to cut trees for railroad ties. The hills were stripped, the timber business expired, floods washed the topsoil off the farms. "Now one farmer after another has given it up as a bad job, has even deserted land he owns . . ."

Of Breathitt's 21,600 inhabitants, 15,000 are on relief. Only 700 have WPA jobs and that number is about to be cut, because the Government believes battleships and big guns more important than the Americans who man them.

Breathitt had one hospital—it is closing. There will be only two doctors and a young County health officer left to take care of the 21,600—or those among them who can afford to pay. Most cannot pay. Of 625 live births recorded last year only three occurred in the hospital; mountain midwives delivered 531 in the tumble-down mountain shacks.

"People just don't have money for doctors," the reporter was told.

Nor for undertakers. Perhaps one out of ten is buried formally by an undertaker; the other dead are buried by the hands of friends and relatives.

Most Breathitt reliefers live on insufficent Federal surplus commodities; corn grits, flour, lima beans, lard, prunes, raisins, apples in a good month; and little but grapefruit,—"sour oranges," they call them—in bad months.

It is a diet and life on which nothing good can thrive. And the South is covered with such vast slums; in cities, on the hills, along the coastal swamps, hunger, everywhere.

It was a Southern paper that printed this story, one out of so many. Such a story would not have appeared ten years ago. One of the most heartening things in American life has been the awakening of the South to its own vast social problems.

Southern authors have played a great role in this awarness, this revival of conscience. Despite the amazing success of that fustian epic of a decayed gentility, "Gone With the Wind," a success that owed much to the nostalgia all Hoover Republicans have these troubled C.I.O. days for some golden age of slavery, the majority of Southern writers have faced their problems not only bravely but with a new realism.

The obscure reporter John F. Day is an example of this new realism. I have recently read the latest novel by Erskine Caldwell, "Trouble in July," which struck me as another good example. Mr. Caldwell tells the story of a Georgia lynching. It is a theme that has been handled before, of course, but too often the moral indignation of the authors blurred the concrete facts of the event. A lynching has to be understood as coolly as a war, if all lynching, like all war, is to be ended forever. Behind each lynching there are great social, political and economic forces at work. Mr. Caldwell is weak on the larger economic backgound, I believe, but in this novel shows a rare understanding of the smaller political currents that move under a Southern lynch party.

The Sheriff in his story is lazy, good-natured and fat, and has only one worry in life—how to hang on to a job that pays better for less work than farming. A lynching presents him with a hard decision—if he opposes it, he loses the votes of the lynchers. If he doesn't oppose it, he loses the votes of the smaller group that hates lynching, for various reasons.

His political boss always tells him what to do, but in this case there is confusion. It is harvest time, and the chief plantation owner of the district doesn't want his Negro workers scared away by a lynching. The Sheriff generally solves all his political problems by going off fishing for a few days. And he hates fishing. But this time he can't escape—he has to see it through. Caldwell treats these politicians with the rare and grim humor that is his special gift. They are as comical as a Nazi official, or a British official, full of high moral indignation and concern over the rights of neutrals. And they, and the men who do the vile murder of a Negro child, are also products of a barbarous poverty and social backwardness that is the shame of America.

But no Northerner can cast stones at the South on the score of lynching. Richard Wright's great novel is also a story of race hatred and injustice, and the scene is laid in Chicago. And Boston and Philadelphia and New York know segregation, slander and rioting. It is a national crime, and until we solve it, America cannot without hypocrisy point an accusing finger at Hitler, who only does to Jews what we have always done to the Negro people.

"Some Reflections on Richard Wright's Novel, *Native Son*"

Daily Worker, April 17, 1940

At least two readers have written in to dissent from my recent leap over the deep-end in praise of Richard Wright's great novel "Native Son." And now I have been reading the review by Ben Davis in the *Sunday Worker*, and I see that Comrade Ben also has quite a few complaints to make.

The letter writers will not be answered by me, because they are temperamental balls of fire who cannot be reasoned with. Every columnist gets scores of letters that rip, swear, snort and fume. He learns to let them roll off his back, even when the writers end by saying, "Stop my subscription at once." Our *Daily Worker* readers don't stop the paper because of any such trifle as an objectionable book review, but some do have the American need for blasting their favorite newspaper to hell at intervals. Well, it makes for a live newspaper.

These correspondents, however, gave me the feeling they had not carefully and honestly read Wright's novel, but had been deeply prejudiced beforehand by the fact that many bourgeois critics praised it for the wrong reasons.

I think Ben Davis has been affected by the same thing. He repeats the point again and again, "The bourbon enemies of the Negro people will try to seize upon this weakness to further their slanders against the whole Negro people," and it is a fear that runs through his whole review.

It is a legitimate fear, of course. No writer whose first loyalty is to the working class permits himself even for a tiny second to play into the hands of the enemy.

But in Communist politics the workers have always had the habit of self-criticism. This is also a danger, because it is done openly, and the enemy does seize upon it. A great deal of the ammunition used by the Hate-Stalin mobsters in America is culled from the columns of self-criticism in the Soviet press. But this has not induced the Soviets to give up the practice of telling the whole truth. They know that there is more danger in fooling yourself than in worrying as to what the enemy will say.

~

The writers of proletarian fiction have had the same problem to face here as Communists engaged in organizational work.

Shall we indulge in wishful thinking or shall we grapple with the more painful truth?

For a period in our writing, the early period, the leftist and experimental time, there was a great deal of wishful thinking. The stories were cut to pattern; a Communist organizer as pure as young Frank Merriwell, and as one-dimensional, led some big strike and was killed by the cops. He never made mistakes. He was never tired and disheartened at the end of a bad day. He never loved or argued with his wife. He never had a wife. He was not a man at all, but a pious wish.

If you met such a person in real life you would want to escape from him. But our writers were afraid that the enemy might use any admitted weakness, and so we had a sloganized, unnatural and unpopular fiction.

It was unpopular even with our own most loyal Communist readers. They could smell the unreality of all this, and like any vigorous mind they wanted a portrait painted with warts and all.

Today our fiction is mature. Richard Wright's novel is an example, and this maturity is the reason such fiction has broken through the more narrow partisan circles and reached a national audience. It is mature because it does not shirk the enormous difficulties presented by the human material.

~

It is a fallacy to demand of proletarian fiction that its characters shall only represent the finest and most militant elements of the working class.

But this, it seems to me is a mistake in the categories of art. The Soviet writers made a distinction between agitational and propaganda writing. One is meant for the immediate occasion, like a strike poster; the other is the long-range argument, thought out, rounded and complete.

Lenin worked in both the styles; he wrote strike appeals and daily journalism as well as books on philosophy and political economy.

It is equivalent to asking our readers to give up all theoretical work when one demands that our proletarian fictioneers give up all study of complex human nature and write only agitational tracts.

Richard Wright's book is a study in psychology that is worthy to have come from the pen of Dostoyevsky, master of this field. And it seems wrong to me to suggest to the author of such a book that he should have written a simpler agitational novel instead.

There is room, in the great house of labor, for all categories of art from the strike leaflet to Dostoyevsky—not only room, but need.

~

But what many readers mostly fear is that Richard Wright's tragic hero will be taken by many outsiders as a symbol of the Negro people.

Perhaps Bigger will be thus taken by some, who already are prejudiced enough, heaven knows, against all skins darker than the Aryan lily.

But again, should we fear slander or misunderstanding if we have a job to do? Dick Wright set himself down to the job of making America feel the terrible truth behind every execution by the State of a Negro boy who has gone wrong.

The boy is somewhat neurotic and flies into murderous rages. He has been warped badly by the life into which he was born. His is not a pretty story, but it is his story.

And what we have come to understand in proletarian literature is that no one worker's story can ever be the story of all of them—not if they are living characters. Each is an individual. And a writer merely tries to write that individual story as honestly as he can, hoping that it will be another brick in the great total of proletarian literature.

Because it is a collective job, and not one that can be confined in one book or one author.

What is common in all the books is the class values that affect the individual's life—in this case, add the race problem. Wright has tied these forces in with the individual psychology of his Bigger in a masterly and universal manner, I believe.

The book has greatness—and we don't have to fear its minor errors when the total greatness is so overwhelmingly on the side of the poor and oppressed.

"Still More Reflections on Wright's Novel, *Native Son*"

Daily Worker, April 29, 1940

The question to ask about any novel or drama cannot be: "Is It True?" but rather, "Could It Be True?"

Marvelous journalism, like John Reed's "Ten Days That Shook the World" or Ruth McKenney's more recent "Industrial Valley," occupies a place in literature beside that of the best novels or dramas of our time.

But journalism is a different art medium than fiction. It must answer the first question, "Is It True?" or it has failed in its chosen medium.

Journalism is like photography in that it must furnish an exact reproduction of the object. Photographers once went off on a wrong trail and tried to make photographs look like paintings. Today the best of them like Margaret Bourke-White, use their art and imagination, only to deepen and strengthen the reality of their reports. They don't play the old painting tricks, but shoot for exactness, not fuzziness.

The painter chooses painting, instead of photography, because he is at once freed of this esthetic law of fidelity to the strict facts. He can invent, improvise, re-arrange reality, he can telescope it backwards and forwards, as in a giant mural that pictures side by side on one canvas all of a nation's heroes and history for two hundred years.

Painting, like fiction, has only to be emotionally true. It is an attempt to convey the emotion behind the facts. This is mainly done by focusing almost to the point of distortion on the one emotion that is to be conveyed. It is like a big spotlight thrown on an actor which leaves the rest of his environment in temporary darkness. The spotlight is to make you concentrate on him, force you to forget too many other confusing details.

~

I throw out these general remarks because I believe them necessary to any further discussion of Richard Wright's novel, "Native Son."

Many more letters arrived this past week, discussing the book. This is grand. It testifies to the vitality and bigness of "Native Son." Lesser books could not arouse such controversy. Nor could a lesser theme arouse it. One thing we must thank Dick Wright's book for is that it is stirring up a national discussion on the tragic status of Negro America.

~

Any discussion is always in itself a breach in the status quo. How rarely does one read in the white capitalist press any editorial or news-item relating to the great daily injustice that is done the Negro.

He is locked up in segregated ghettoes. He can't get jobs. His intellectuals are not permitted to practice their professions. He can't vote. In the South his life is considered less sacred than a pet dog's. Lynching is made a sadist holiday that deepens the degeneracy of Southern cities and villages. The President of the United States dares not speak out against lynching. The Congress refuses to pass any anti-lynching law.

Fifteen million Americans born here under a constitution that makes every "native son" a full partner in the democracy, are daily robbed, beaten, flouted, cheated, slandered, murdered and generally treated with the same sort of horrible race-hate that Hitler and all his Storm Troopers must yet pay for on the revolutionary guillotine of the German folk. It was Birmingham that taught Berlin.

And it has been going on for more than a hundred years, this national horror whose entire mechanics were taken over by Hitler.

But our American press rarely utters a word about this great evil in our front-yard. The great crime of Negro oppression is taken for granted. It is not a major political issue. They ignore it. They accept it as final. You are called a Communist and breaker of the peace if you bring it up.

They are even honestly surprised that you get indignant about the matter. Devout Nazis express the same naive surprise: Hasn't Hitler brought Germany imperial greatness? Why should anyone bother about a little issue like the Jews? That concerns only Jews.

For hundreds of years, your average Britisher has been just as annoyed and surprised when anyone brought the Hindus or the Irish to his attention. "The Irish are only madmen, the Hindus are disunited, backward heathen," were ever his cheap, smug and self-deluding answer.

So it is plain that to force a discussion of Negro wrongs on America is like forcing a discussion of the Jewish problem in Nazi Germany, or of India in England. It is in itself a step forward, a break in the huge wall of chauvinist complacency. It forces a re-examination of the national conscience. It teaches many who had never known what a volcano of injustice and horror their little comfortable lives had been built on, and perhaps even makes them fearful enough to do something at last.

But only a strong book can effect such a break-through in the criminal conspiracy of silence. Only great art can do it.

~

Which brings us back rather belatedly, to my opening paragraphs. Dick Wright's book could not have accomplished its revolutionary miracle if he had not had his mastery of the art form in which he was working.

There have been quite a number of novels about Negro life: none has had this overwhelming effect. It only was the same subject matter; but victory came only when the matter attained some supreme form.

But where precisely does Wright's esthetic mastery of form lie?

I believe it lies in the exact spot where some of the critics have chosen to direct their fire—in his intensive use of the fictional spotlight.

He has written a psychological melodrama in which, for the sake of unity and movement, he has allowed not a word of extraneous detail to enter.

His spotlight has blacked out the rest of the world, and illuminated with an almost unbearable blaze a Negro slum boy, and his struggle against the nightmare world of whites.

The critics believe that Wright should have included Negro Communists, militant and intellectual Negroes. But that is a completely other story, big enough for another book. It might have drawn attention away from the story Wright started to tell—the story of the Biggers.

Do they exist? Yes, they do. Are the Negro people all fully awakened, militant and self-conscious? No, alas, they are not any more than white Americans. There is only a minority who have begun to think politically and socially; and a smaller minority are Communists. Same as the whites. This is the fact; and this is still the problem. And you don't solve it by some novel that makes it look easy; this is Communist escapism, of which we also have our share.

No, the Biggers must be faced, understood, and answered just as Gorky was not afraid to describe the backwardness of the Russian peasants and workers. That is art; and it is also science and revolution.

And I still cannot understand how any reader misses the heroic character of the Communist lawyer in Wright's book. He is a sufficiently positive hero to offset the negative aspects; and he occupies at least a third of the book.

The Birmingham Public Library has banned Wright's book. Other southern cities have spoken of it harshly. A few southern newspapers have praised it, however; the line follows the general attitude of liberalism or reaction on the Negro question. Every such book is bound to be hated, misused and misunderstood; but its deep lessons have begun and will continue.

"Pappy Gold Meets Woody and Finds It's Catchin'"

Daily Worker, April 21, 1940

In 1938 the Dies Committee (a precursor of HUAC) opened congressional inquiries into alleged disloyalty among cultural figures with socialist and communist ties. Federal Theatre Project director Hallie Flanagan was subpoenaed and interrogated. Leftist folksingers adopted protective pseudonyms (Pete Seeger, for example, started going by "Pete Bowers"). The singer known only as "Woody" in the article below is of course Woodrow Wilson Guthrie.

When this piece appeared in the Daily Worker *in 1940, Guthrie had just written his famous collectivist song "This Land Is Your Land" as a response to Irving Berlin's hyperpatriotic and chauvinistic anthem "God Bless America." Here Gold welcomes "Woody" to New York and champions the Okie singer to the extent of becoming his unofficial promoter.*

~

Met this boy Woody t'other day down a dark holler of a cafeteria. Hoot-owls and countermen wuz screechin' fit to scare the black fur off a gangster's cat. But Woody dunked his doughnuts quiet and brave like he wuz weaned on the Second Avenue L. Nuthin' kin scare that young Okie, not even Martin Dies. New York is jest another home to him.

Cordin' to the opinion of Ole Pappy Gold, people is divided into climbers and comrades. Irving Berlin he's a climber, fr'instance. Born three garbage cans away from where Pappy Gold lost his first tooth on a *begel*, Irving clum and clawed till he grabbed him the Princess of Postal Telegraph stocks.

Now Irving Berlin dassent bring a salami home and enjoy it—the butlers would call an etiket strike. Bet he never dast touch his own kids—the nurses'd quit if a Park Avenoo pappy rough-housed with his own flesh and blood. Irving wears whatever monkey suit the Princess and her crowd tell him is etiket. Goes where they tell'm to go. Laughs only 'cordin to their blue book. Worries and talks only bout his investments, like they. Turns out the songs they want—come a war, a girlie show or an election. Climbed hisself out of the mob, he thought, but look where Irving landed—on the Park Avenoo chain gang.

But Woody—he's free, wide and handsome. Seem he wuz just nachurally born on the comrade side. Never worries that he's Okie red clay as common as the stuff used for Adam or Abe Lincoln. No, sir, et seems to puff up the young-un. He makes songs about et, so's he kin sit on a fence come a purty night and howl at the Park Avenoo coyotes. "I'm common, I'm dirt, I'm the moon and the stars. I'm jes the homely old human race."

Woody makes up songs. Sings his songs to his own guitar before people. Sings songs to himself in the subway. Talks songs in cafeterias. Writes songs in the *Daily Worker*. And all his songs is one comrade song, and Woody laughs more than Irving, I bet.

Also the salami-eating Okies of New York love him like a brother. So do the Okies of Oklahoma and the rest of the U.S.A. where he has roved and sang. Woody's helpin' the salami-eatin', common-dirt people to climb altogether. Irving helped only hisself. In a shipwreck the captain'd shoot you for that. In capitalism they shoot you if you try to help people off their shipwreck. It's hard to understand. They hate and fear the Communist life-preservers and achually prefer dyin'. But Woody keeps on a-singin'. "I'm a common dirt proletaire, jes' inchin' along. I can't give up, cause it ain't in my bones."

Excuse me, Woody, if I got infected by your Okie style, and did this imitation of the real thing. But it is really only a passing Oklahoma cold. Don't you go now and catch a New York pneumonia. It'll have you wearing checked plaid coats. The germs are in the air here and it takes a strong proletarian tourist to resist them.

~

Woody comes right out of the book by John Steinbeck, "The Grapes of Wrath," that has revealed America to itself more than any book since "Uncle Tom's Cabin."

There may be some readers of that book dumb enough to believe it merely a "quaint" story about "picturesque" folk.

But the vast majority of readers see that Steinbeck's Okie is not only an Okie. He is also a symbol of working class America. His voyage out of a Dust Bowl toward a Promised Land where he finds only Californian sheriffs who thug and degrade him is an Odyssey that could be told of miners, seamen, clothing workers, or the ten million unemployed.

"Fortune" magazine recently concluded as the result of one of its surveys that something like a fourth of the American people are permanently dispossessed. They can never get back into farming or industry. Even if there is a "recovery," some temporary fever flush of prosperity, they will remain outside the capitalist economy.

I suppose the Okies are in that fourth, sentenced to death by the laws of a system that functions more badly every day.

But in the "Grapes of Wrath" there are Okies who refuse to die, or have their people die. They begin to see the naked outline of the cruel profit system that has created their misery.

They begin to talk like communists. And Woody, who was raised on the songs of his people, whose head is full of a thousand ballads, who was singing and writing ballads long before he heard of the *Daily Worker*, finds it a natural transition to make the old ballads sing the songs of a new militancy.

Aunt Molly Jackson, singer of the Kentucky miners, made the same transition as easily. So have other folk singers.

This is the answer to the frame up charge of "foreign agent." Aunt Molly Jackson did not need Marx or Stalin to "agitate" her when she was writing her Mining Camp Blues. She had never heard of Marx. But she had lived in a mining camp all her days.

Woody, I am sure, knew no Russian out in Oklahoma when the earth began whirling away on the wind, and the people were left homeless, and he wrote his Dust Bowl Blues.

~

Welcome to the *Daily Worker*, Comrade Woody. It's good to have a young Will Rogers in our midst. There was a bankers' Will Rogers—now we have our proletarian Will Rogers. You belong here, Woody, as much as Ben Davis, the Atlanta Herndon lawyer, or Clarence Hathaway, the machinist of Minnesota, or Beth McHenry, the Irish lass from Kerry by way of San Francisco, or Art Shields, the long Carolinian hill-billy, or Fred Ellis, the Chicago house painter, or even this-heah Suthen Culnel of Second Avenue, who was born about a mile from the office, and was first rolled to his work in a baby carriage. We welcome you to the all-American team!

The clubs and forums of working class New York are having a chance to hear you on your travels around our subway circuit (and I'm told that next Saturday evening you're being honored at a Writers and Artists Spring Frolic). From what they tell me, Woody, you sure sing the "Grapes of Wrath" for them. I guess that's why you feel so much at home—it isn't all night clubs here, is it? There's folks too, Okies and workers among the skyscrapers.

“Woody’s Songs Full of Poverty and Genuine Dirt: Democracy Is like That”

Daily Worker, May 28, 1943

War-related events would temporarily halt Woody Guthrie’s career just as his audience was growing. In the mobilization period that followed Pearl Harbor, he accepted duties in the Merchant Marine. A few days before Guthrie shipped out in August 1943, he realized he owed something to the columnist who had ignited his fame and helped him understand the antifascist purpose his life and music could serve. He wrote a letter to the Daily Worker *stating that he would not be afraid of U-boats as long as there was “a whole world full of people like Mike Gold to keep things going.”*

~

Publication date of Woody Guthrie’s confession story, “Bound for Glory” was more than a month ago. I have been nursing the book since, reading it in bed, chuckling at it in L trains and subways. It is full of American language, it is rich as Piper Hiedsick chaw tobacco. It is red-skinned and native language with the bark still on it.

Just as an example of true American speech this book of autobiography is worth studying. Lincoln’s people talked this way when young Abe was growing up in the Valley of Democracy. Their talk corresponded to their thinking. When Lincoln got big enough to study politics he took to Jeffersonianism like a young duck to its own pond. Democracy came natural to him because it was the way of life among his pioneer kinsfolk.

Woody Guthrie's early life in Oklahoma was almost as poverty-stricken, adventurous and proud as that of Honest Abe's. Yet the comedown of his father as a booming real estate speculator is the modern deviation from the pioneer.

Woody's father became a declassed bourgeois, and his defeatism and sense of failure were the psychological signals of the new time. Lincoln's people always could move on to new and richer soil; but Woody's people merely shifted from a good house to a cheap, dreary and leaky one.

Kid stories are always fascinating; and perhaps the best thing in American literature, which down to the latest Saroyan has generally been adolescent.

But Woody is no streamlined Pollyanna like the tricky Saroyan; he avoids no bitter truths about poverty in childhood. Listen to this little moment:

> I got up and walked out real easy and went out on the porch. Papa got up and walked out behind me. He followed me to a big rocking chair that was out there, and he sat down and called me over to him. He took me in his lap and told me over and over how good all of us kids was, and how mean he had treated us, and that he was going to be good to all of us. This wasn't true. He had always been good to his kids.
>
> This was after the house had burned down, and little Clara had been burned bad and the family broken up for a time. And then Mama got to having fits, and lost control of her muscles and started breaking glasses and furniture because the family was now pauperized and without an income or a house.
>
> Mama had things on her mind. Troubles. She thought about them too much, or didn't fight back. . . . I used to go to sleep at night and have dreams; I dreamed that my mama was like anybody else's. I saw her talking, smiling, and working just like other kids' mamas. But when I woke up it would still be all wrong, all twisted out of shape, helter-skelter, let go, the house not kept, the cooking skipped and the dishes not washed. Oh, Roy and me tried, I guess. We would take spells of working the house over, but I was only nine years old, Roy fifteen. . . .

I hate a hundred times more to describe my own mother in any words such as these. You hate to read about a mother in any such words as these. I know. I understand you. I hope you can understand me, for it must be broke down and said.

We didn't want to send Mama away. It would be better to start off in some other place. So in 1923 we packed up and moved to Oklahoma City. We moved in an old T model truck. Didn't take much stuff along. Just wanted to get away somewhere where we didn't know anybody, and see if that wouldn't make her better. She was better when we got gone. When we moved into an old house on Twenty-Eight Street she felt better. She cooked. It tasted good. She talked. It sure sounded good. She would go for days and days and not have one of her spells. That looked like the front door of heaven for all of us.

~

I have quoted a passage at length, to give you the full flavor of Woody's sincerity. It is heart-breaking truth he tells, the same bitter story that others have told of the East Side or the slums of Puerto Rico, China, India or Ireland. But it strikes one with peculiar poignancy in this brave, fearless language of American pioneers—it hurts one to see how even in our rich country there have been all the deaths and despairs of India or barren Patagonia.

Woody, as many know, has become one of the true voices of American folk song. For years he has travelled the roads with his guitar and made up ballads about American life and sung them everywhere. He has been heard in many hobo jungles, along the western skid roads, in lumber camps and boxcars and at hundreds of working clubs, union halls and Communist gatherings.

Woody was one of the singers who brought much authenticity to the Almanac Singers, and helped that group's astounding success during the years when it was going good.

He is a graduate of the Dust Bowl, and made a strong series of ballads on that folk migration which a phonograph company made into a notable album. Woody was even asked to come and sing at the Rainbow Room but a lady there with a fanciful tea-room imagination wanted him dressed up in a Harlequin costume but he refused to shed his honest dungarees and broke her contract.

Where is Woody heading? I don't know. Where are we all heading who have bet our lives on democracies? Who can say? One thing is certain, though—a people's theatre in America could be built around someone like Woody. The truth in his book is harsh and painful, his songs reek of poverty and genuine dirt and suffering. Democracy is like that; and it is a struggle and a song.

Democracy will win in America and the world; and Woody is one of its truest voices; something that started long ago at Valley Forge, and that needs no Communist International to tell it to make its songs of pain and protest.

"Some Words on the Loss of a Good Comrade and My Brother"

Daily Worker, September 3, 1946

Gold's response to his brother George's death filled three deeply personal "Change the World" columns. The passing of George Granich was probably also a factor in Mike's decision to take his family to France, where they lived with the family of his wife Elizabeth from 1947 to 1950.

~

I must write a few words about my brother George, who died last week, before I can get back to writing anything else.

Families often drift apart because of political or money differences, even though there may be some basis of personal affection.

But my brothers and I were united in the working class movement from our earliest years and it strengthened the family bond.

I was the first to go to work after our father died and worked in some of the vilest East Side sweatshop factories that Uncle Sam ever grew. My first job was in a Bowery factory that made gas mantles. In two months I lost eight pounds. I was 12 years old at the time.

George, my "kid brother," greeted me every night when I came home. He was very blonde then, a towhead, and had the brightest smile and most affectionate nature. I will never forget that little towhead who threw his arms around me and greeted me with such joy each night when I came back from a miserable factory hole.

~

George's turn to work came when he was 14. It was in some run-down cigar factory, where he had to work in another miserable hole like mine under electric light all day.

He was not built for willing toil in the concentration camps of the wage slavery system, however. George escaped as fast as anyone could.

I was the first in my family to be bitten by the radical bug. New York streets were filled then with soapbox agitators of one sort or another. I learned my first Marxism and working class ideas at these street corner colleges.

Soon we were arguing socialism versus capitalism at our supper table every night. George was against it the first few times we argued. He was strictly on the side of big business and the rights of millionaires. But my other brother and I managed to swing him over, despite my poor mother's fears.

Two weeks after he first heard about socialism, I was walking along Second Avenue. It was a slow, warm summer night, and the soapboxers were talking to leisurely crowds.

At one corner I was amazed to find my brother George, 16 years old, making a red-hot speech for the Socialist cause.

A few months later, after reading a lot of Jack London, George left home. He stowed away on a boat bound for Jacksonville, Florida. His companion was a shock-haired, poetic young firebrand, a soapboxer of the ripe age of 18, whose nickname along Second Avenue was "Percy the Rebel."

I will always remember George's note to the family. It came in the mails the next morning after he disappeared, written in red pencil on a YMCA letterhead. "Dear Mom and Brothers—When you read this I will be on a ship bound for the South. I am leaving New York for the following reasons, and I hope Mom will not feel too bad about it—"

Then he listed, in a scholarly and precise order, the six reasons why he was running away. The first reason was that his job had no future; second, the electric light was ruining his eyes; third, he was feeling pale and weak, etc.—but the last reason, No. 6, was simply, "And, please Mamma, I want to see the world before I die."

George saw a lot of America, certainly, in the six or seven years of wandering that followed.

He followed the western harvests for years, working the crops as they matured in California, Oregon, the northwest, the Mexican border regions.

He worked as a cowboy on a cattle ranch one year, I remember, and got hurt trying to ride a tough bronc. He was in jail another time, for riding the box cars, but broke away somehow, because they had locked him up with a crazy guy too full of religion and violence.

George was a member of the IWW then, as every western migratory worker was, if he had self-respect and courage. It was a great organization then, fabulous in its defiance of the brutal killers and exploiters of the profiteer system. The IWW "wobblies" of those days have passed into American folklore, with their songs, their battles, their earthly slang and tragic and noble attitude to the class struggle.

Some of the veterans of that movement degenerated after the first world war. Some became bootleggers; others drifted into cynicism and Coolidge banality and money-making. Some became Soviet-haters and little else; but the best of the "wobblies" came into the newly formed Communist movement, I believe. Of these, George was a charter member of the CP.

~

He had settled down in New York again, had married and became a father. The tall, handsome young athlete who once roved and rambled the country talking Marx was now faced with family responsibility.

I often wondered how he made the adjustment. There was something in George that could never accept being locked up in the usual offices, factories and other bourgeois prisons where a man must eat dirt or starve.

He craved and needed the outdoors. I can remember him saying once, "I've wasted part of my life, just as everyone has, I guess. But Mike, I never felt any day was wasted that I had spent in the open air."

George was a good farmer, and a skilled carpenter, builder and cabinetmaker, as well as a good father and an active and hard-working Communist.

He made his adjustment from free, adventurous migratory to that of a New York family man and worker, because of his love of children, I believe. His children gave George compensation for the loss of personal freedom and the wind and rain and adventure of the broad highway.

It was in New York that he found his vocation, too, as a teacher of arts and crafts to children. Imagination, manual skill and a sweet-tempered affection and respect for humanity, especially children, made George an outstanding teacher.

(To be continued.)

"Further Notes on the Life of a Good Comrade and My Brother"

Daily Worker, September 7, 1946

To continue the remarks on my brother George, who died this August 22nd:

I can't remember at what exact moment my brother found his vocation of children's arts and crafts teacher.

Perhaps it was the year his first child, Michael, was born. George had found a job at the big Jewish orphanage in Pleasantville, N. Y., where he managed the food commissariat. He was given a fair wage, a private house and all the food his family needed. It was a soft and comfortable berth, yet he was chafed by it.

The food was flat and standardized, the education just as insipid and routinized.

George reacted against it all, chiefly because he found himself growing attached to dozens of the kids. He often engaged in fights with some of the drab-minded careerists who ran the big institution, fighting for the right of kids to be complete human beings.

George had to resign from the comfortable job. He and his wife both felt as if everything good in them was dying in that comfortable, sterile, dull institutional world.

They came back to the city with their baby son, broke and jobless, but preferring any struggle to the spiritual suicide of being under a soulless bureaucracy.

~

George worked at different jobs in the following period. He was a taxi driver for more than a year, then a stage carpenter at the new Playwrights Theater for two years, and so forth.

All the time, he was active in different stages of the evolving Communist movement—from its sectarian underground days, then the diseased factional time, into the great unemployment crisis, when the party found its soul and became a national force, the heroic leader and teacher of 20,000,000 hungry Americans.

Pete Cacchione developed in that struggle, and I was touched to see this busy Councilman take time off for the parting services of my brother.

Leaders may come and go, turn phony and smug as Browder, or treacherous as Jay Lovestone; but the people's movement that has a solid core of rank-and-file incorruptibles like my brother George will survive them all.

Pete Cacchione is cast in the same true metal; and I know his thoughts must have gone back to the unemployment struggles of the 1930's as he gazed at George's quiet form.

"We have suffered defeats, humiliations and disappointments in this struggle for a decent society," Pete must have mused. "But it has been worthwhile. No man in our generation has found any higher task than to be a Communist—a leader guiding the people out of this capitalist nightmare of endless war and hatred, of race persecutions, market fever and greed, of graft, climberism, the chaos and the cheapness, the profiteering in misery and blood.

"No, George, you have lived the only life possible to a decent human being in this time. Rest well after your labor. Your monument will rise one day in happy playgrounds and sunlit schools of an America built on fraternity, equality and freedom."

I will never forget the great hunger march to Washington.

There were participating about 2,000 unemployed delegates from all over the nation, and I went along as a reporter. Hoover was the President then. Under military advisement his Washington police prepared a trap for the battered trucks and dusty autos of the hunger marchers.

They were not allowed into the city, but shunted into an unfinished road on a suburban hill. Here thousands of police, armed with guns, teargas bombs and other weapons, set up a guard at both ends of the canyon.

The hunger marchers, consisting of men, women and children were confined on this hillside for two days and nights—without food, sanitary arrangements, or anything.

My brother George had been a route captain on the way from New York—running up and down the line in a scout car, and responsible for a section of the march.

On the Washington hillside he was also busy with a thousand details, and, when the word came to march into Washington, despite the cops, he was in the forefront of the parade.

I stood with a press card in my hat among the cops, and watched them get their tear gas guns and riot guns at the ready. Many of them were half drunk; they had been passing the bottle openly all night. Cursing, sweating with fear and whiskey, shouting barroom provocations, they were ready for slaughter, a fascist horde.

I could see George's face in the first rank. He might have been the first to be murdered, and my heart beat wildly. I knew I was going to lose my head if these brutes got to shooting. But George seemed quiet and steady, as always. He took little half glances around him, as if he were attending to details of his job. Then he lifted his chin and breathed deeply. He was ready to step over the deadline, into the gunfire, come what may. It was his faith that alone counted to him—not any guns of the brutal enemy.

(To be continued.)

"Final Notes on the Life of a Good Comrade, My Brother"

Daily Worker, September 10, 1946

My brother George never lost a certain innocence of heart. He never acquired in 46 years of living any of that dreadful commercial sophistication of today, that talks so glibly about "selling yourself," and how much "money there is" in doing this or that job.

George was no weakling but fully able to take care of himself in danger or difficulty. Neither was he competitive or acquisitive. He was born ahead of his time in commercial America. The fact remains, George didn't fit too easily into our commercial culture, and millions of plain American proletarians are like him.

At various times, he engaged in small enterprises, like building furniture or doing house carpentry on contract. Then there was the children's camp he conducted for over 12 summers, and the after school workshop and playroom he conducted with his wife, Gert.

Some people tried gypping him because he couldn't be hard boiled about money. I remember one eminent young divorced author who left his badly-neglected, neurotic boy of seven under George's care for several years.

The kid was a bedwetter, a thief, a liar and a coward—all of it the fault of his selfish Bohemian parents. George and Gert, his wife, gave the child the love and understanding he needed. It was difficult and at times a disgusting job to handle. I wondered where Gert and George found the faith to go on with this poor kid. And for almost a year they received not a cent for his board, though the father was earning over $100 a week and the mother was working, too.

The neurotic mother finally popped in one night with a strange man and they took the kid without paying a penny or saying a word of thanks. George was broke at the time; he needed the money for his own family. But the incident left him unshaken.

"I expected something like this," he said. "They are just lousy specimens of bourgeois humanity."

"Can't you sue him or something? He must owe a couple of hundred dollars."

"Let him keep it, if he is such a louse. Also, we got interested in fixing up the kid. I think we finally saved him."

George was that way with carpentry, too, or any other work. He enjoyed any work better when he wasn't doing it for money. Money seemed to get in the way of the work. George was always doing "friendship" jobs in carpentry and the like for his friends.

He was, when all is said, an artist. The word has come to have a lot of foolish and frivolous meanings. But the true artist is a grand human figure, as pure a specimen of the Communist future as one finds in the terrible capitalist arena of today.

George found himself in working with children, because of the art in him. Kids fell in love with him the moment they met. I saw it happen with my own boys. He never talked down to a kid. His way of teaching them was simply to make work seem more interesting than chaos and destruction. He taught them how to make things; his hands were always busy, and the kids imitated him.

George had wonderful hands, big, strong and plastic. He could do almost anything with those wonderful tools, it seemed; plumbing, carpentry, painting, growing fine flower and vegetable gardens, anything.

The kids saw his hands always busy making things—carving, whittling, carpentering, metal-working, teaching by example, rather than by exhortation. George's kids all learned to make beautiful and useful things with their hands.

When, in his last sickness, the word got round that George needed blood transfusions, dozens of friends appeared. But the kids wanted to help

George, too. A group of them asked Gert whether they could go to the hospital and help George. She told them blood was never taken from kids for this purpose.

"We know that," said one of the kids, a nine-year-older. "But we figured out that each of us could give a little blood, just a child's portion, and then, all of our blood put together, would be as much as a grown-up's share."

George was a very original crafts teacher, I believe, inventing constantly, and getting his kids to see, dare and experiment. He sometimes sketched and showed a sensitive feeling for form and color, but never had time to develop. In his last few years he would often fool around with clay—he was a natural sculptor, I believe.

Yet more than half of his feelings, ambitions, thoughts and labors were thrown into the "movement." From the time he ran away from home at 16 to become a migratory worker and IWW organizer, George never lost his faith in the "singing tomorrow" of communism.

George's swell comrade wife, Gert, is a German-American girl from Greenpoint. Her grandfather was a Forty-Eighter, one of that great breed of German immigrants who brought Marxism to America. During the Nazi decade, Gert, the German, and George, the Jew, and their children, never found any racial note disturbing their love. For the great ideas of world fraternity, which are the foundation of Marxism and communism, united this family, as they unite millions of others.

Good-bye, beloved brother. You were a good artist and a good man and a good Communist! You perished of cancer, and so are millions of other Americans who could be saved, if humanity ruled here ahead of atom bombs and profiteering. Good-bye, you were gentle and good; and your kind will inherit the earth, write an end to all the pushers, killers and profiteers of capitalism!

“Moe the Barber and the Young Vet”

Daily Worker, 1946

This piece's treatment of American fascism, along with its attention to hate-motivated attacks on New York Jews by "Christian Fronters," is based partly on a personal incident. In 1944 Gold's firstborn son Nicky, eight years old, was beaten up on his way home from school by a gang of Catholic boys who had shouted "Christ-killer! Christ-killer!"

In his next "Change the World" column Gold stated, "Antisemitism is breaking forth in every corner of New York" and implored Daily Worker *readers, "Is it not a symptom and a warning?" The account of the attack on his son referred also to the complacent reactions of public officials who had been downplaying hate crimes, calling them "pranks" and "little accidents."*

Moe the Barber almost sheds a sentimental tear each time some tall young cub in khaki drops into his tonsorial chair, and says:

> Remember me, Moe? I'm Rootie from Fifth Street. Just got back from Germany. Met Hymie Gordon and Blackie at the Anzio Beach. We talked about you, Moe, and the old neighborhood. Gee, it's great to be back! Gimme the works, Keed!

It happens often these postwar days, when every troopship brings regiments of East Side boys who gaze with misted eyes at the Statue of Liberty and the shining gas tanks of home. Moe suppresses his tear and goes to work. He proceeds to sculpture the soldier's head into a cast-iron imitation of Frank Sinatra's hairdo.

And as he snips and shears, Moe remembers this tall young soldier as a cute little snot-nose being dragged to his first haircut; then as a rugged stick-ball player busting windows of the block; then a working youth, a sharpie who swaggered in before big neighborhood dances for a tonsorial treatment.

"In your fighting experience, Rootie, how many Nazis would you estimate scientifically could be licked by an East Side soldier?" Moe inquired of the young veteran.

Rootie pretended to cogitate profoundly, and with mock solemnity replied: "To the best of my scientific experience, Professor Moe, I should estimate it was about one Fifth-Streeter to 10 Nazi bastards. Yes, sir."

"Hoops! you hear that, Mr. Raskin?" Moe yelled triumphantly to the next chair, where his boss, the deaf and nearsighted Mr. Raskin, was shaving the Italian iceman's craggy chin.

"Rootie here, which is the son of that carpenter Mr. Weintraub, that broke his leg in front of the fruit store in 1939, was fighting in Germany, and he says one Jewish boy can lick a dozen Nazis. I told you so, Mr. Raskin!"

"Is this a fact?" the boss responded amiably. It was his usual remark after another's statement, not because he doubted but because he needed time to catch the drift.

"Is this a fact?" Moe mimicked him. "All through the war, he has been denying facts! Rootie, this bullheaded boss of mine has been arguing that one East Sider could only lick three or four Nazis! It has been positively an insult to the neighborhood!

"From my own figures, which I have measured through the average number of defunct Nazis listed in the newspapers when East Side boys was getting medals of bravery and so forth, I figured it out scientifically. The exact amount is 16 Nazis to one Rootie. This is statistics, Mr. Raskin! This is a fact! Put it in your pipe and choke on it like a bunch of green bananas, Mr. Raskin, your highness!"

"Is this a fact?" murmured the employer amiably, as he peered at the iceman's purple chin with near-sighted fascination.

Moe grinned at Rootie. "I insult Mr. Raskin every day, but he never hears. You should work for an employer who is deaf, Rootie. They are a real pleasure."

The young soldier lay wrapped in silent thought. After a spell of artistic hair-sculpture he opened his eyes and said quietly: "But what's the use of bragging, Moe? Sure, I admit I mighta knocked off a couple hundred Nazi bastards or so. But that was because I was with the machine guns. I was also lucky.

"One soldier is brave like another. What is in the heart is what counts. Them Nazis are full of crap. They have to be killed, so we did it to them—we, America, north and south, from New York to San Francisco. I had buddies from everywhere, Moe, so why brag?"

"Here is why," Moe answered gravely, no longer the humble barber. In a flash, like Superman, Batman or Captain Midnight, he was changing from humble mortal into a political sage, the "poor man's Walter Lippmann."

"Let me scientifically explain, Rootie. While you was away fighting the Nazis for Uncle Sam, these Christian Fronters at home was busy fighting your father and mother, your little brothers and sisters.

"It was real war, Rootie. I remember one battle which will go down in history along with Gen. MacArthur and the *Daily News.* It was when two squads of Christian Front commandos beat up an old Jewish grandma on a lonely subway station. What strategy, what guts it took!

"Then they cut a swastika on a schoolboy's face in the Bronx. What courage! They bombarded synagogues and trampled all over the Holy Book. They smeared altars with garbage, they attacked a Jewish graveyard and bravely pulled down the memorial stones.

"Boy, they took New York like Hitler took Berlin. Have you heard of the Battle of Klein's Candy Store? This was in the famous Bronx, also.

"Fifty heroes infiltrated gradually into no-man's land, one asking Mr. Klein for a chocolate bar, another for a pack of Camels, and so on. It was all to confuse the enemy, Mr. Klein. Finally, he was confused and surrounded, so they conquered him and the candy store. Mr. Klein lay in the hospital for months. His store was a total loss.

"See what I mean, Rootie? The Nazis are growing up in New York. That's why I believe we should brag about our soldiers a little. It cheers us up. Our poor old grandmas and lonesome Mr. Kleins will feel more secure if they know what boys like you done in Europe and the Pacific.

"Also, Rootie, we have produced Einsteins, Charlie Chaplins and other great thinkers. What has it got us with the dumb Hitler-lovers? Nothing. All they care about is whether you are able to fight them. The Jews must follow the example of the Irish, a small nation which never got licked by the British because it was always ready to fight. See what I mean, Rootie? People which is persecuted like the Jews and Negroes needs pride. They need courage and even a little bragging."

Rootie seemed stunned by the lecture. But he was only thinking, somberly and deeply.

"Look Moe," he said at last, "while all this was going on—this beating and synagogue stuff—didn't anyone fight back?"

"Rootie," said Moe, his voice full of affection and pity, "the fighting here is different from Germany. Here, when the Christian Fronters are resisted in battle, they flash their police permits. This forbids anyone to fight back. Some of them are even on the police force. Hitler never had a police permit, did he, Rootie?"

"No, he didn't," answered the somber youth.

"Well, cheer up—I done you a haircut job that will make Frankie himself jealous. Look at it in the glass. Nice, hey?

"Cheer up, Rootie, we still can lick the Nazis in America. At any odds! We got the heart and we got the people. We've even got Sinatra. And now we've got you, Rootie!"

Part Five

From *The Honorable Pete*

Unpublished manuscript, c. 1950.

In July of 1932, twenty thousand veterans of World War I, jobless and desperate, journeyed to Washington to demand payment of a promised bonus for their military service. Calling themselves the "Bonus Army," they set up camps on public property and held demonstrations and parades dressed in remnants of the uniforms they'd worn in Europe.

President Hoover, worried by the popularity of a Democrat named Roosevelt, wanted to look strong and ordered the veterans evicted. On July 28, US infantry and cavalry, supported by tanks and commanded by General Douglas MacArthur, mustered near the White House and marched down Pennsylvania Avenue. The Bonusers thought they were marching in their honor until the infantry fixed bayonets, put on gas masks, and started lobbing tear gas grenades. They drove the veterans across the Anacostia River into a muddy field where their wives and children, many of them sick and hungry, were living in a tent city. That night, MacArthur's forces set fire to the Bonus encampment. Families fled as a hellish blaze lit up the sky. Two veterans were killed and at least sixty injured.

Among the historical accounts of the Bonus incident, few are written from the perspective of the victims. An exception is Gold's The Honorable Pete, *a two-act play that dramatizes the life of Pete Cacchione, a beloved New York City councilman whom Gold often called "the first Communist to be elected to a major legislative position in the United States." In Scene 7, Cacchione and the veterans witness MacArthur's appalling crackdown.*

~

Act I, Scene 7

(*In the darkness we hear the voices of schoolchildren singing "America the Beautiful." This is interrupted by the single voice singing the refrain of "Brother Can You Spare a Dime." On the screen we see the veterans' encampment at Anacostia Flats. Dominating everything is the Capitol, Washington, D.C. Now we hear "Over There" sung by many men's voices. As the picture fades the singing fades out like a tired phonograph.*

The light reveals: A corner of the veterans' encampment. Off one side, a pup tent, with a line of washing suspended thereto. The bandaged head of a woman—Mrs. Russo, shows out of the tent. Joe Russo, of Sayre, kneels beside his wife.

At other side, ORLANDO, PETE CACCHIONE, MIKE SHEEHAN *and* ROCKY *are staring off into the distance at some great event. They wear assorted pieces of old army dress; all wear their overseas caps.*)

CARMELA. Get us a doctor, Joe!

JOE RUSSO. How can I, honey? They got the tanks and the troops here! They're chasing us out!

CARMELA. It's pneumonia, Joe! The kids will die!

JOE RUSSO. No, it's only the flu, Carmela! The whole camp got it after that last rain.

CARMELA. Don't let the kids die.

JOE RUSSO. (*holding his head*) Oh my God, my God!

CHILD'S VOICE. (*from the tent*) Daddy, I want an orange.

JOE RUSSO. Yes, babe! (*A bugle sounds, he straightens up, looks around wildly.*) Daddy'll get you an orange! (*He joins Pete and others.*) Pete, I gotta get a doctor! They're dying.

PETE. (*bitterly*) Why did you bring them to this battlefield? It was wrong Joe, wrong!

JOE RUSSO. Honest, I couldn't leave her alone. She was sick, and that crowd of vets from Buffalo came through in the truck and Mike and me suddenly decided to go. There were other families. I explained it all to you, Pete.

MIKE. Have some sense. Joe lost his house, I told yuh. He had to do something. Joe and me has got a right to the bonus, too. Don't get so damn bullheaded, Pete.

PETE. Do kids have to suffer in this swamp—and now MacArthur's tanks coming on?

ORLANDO. Joe has got a right to be here—that includes his family.

PETE. All right, Orlando—excuse me, fellas—this waiting gets me down—

JOE RUSSO. I got to have a doctor, Pete.

PETE. We're waiting for Carl. He went to headquarters.

JOE RUSSO. Headquarters is loaded with stoolies. What's the use waiting for them?

PETE. We can't break up squad by squad. We've gotta hold together.

JOE RUSSO. Can you get me an orange, Pete? For God's sake, fellas—(*He joins the others in looking out.*)

ROCKY. (*staring into distance*) Look, Pete—they're lining up—it must be the whole army—

ORLANDO. Them kids was in diapers while we was in France—

MIKE. That general there—who's that?

ORLANDO. Eisenhower, I think.

MIKE. Look at that other one—dressed up like a Christmas tree—Wow—what a tailor he's got . . .

ROCKY. That's MacArthur—Garibaldi was never dressed up so good—or General Grant.

MIKE. Mac's twice as brave as them—you have to be very brave to drive out us vets—and the kids—

ORLANDO. Look at all them tanks—Guys with torches—what are they doin'?

MIKE. Burning us out like rats—we're rats to them—

PETE. I still don't think anything'll happen—It's another bluff.

ORLANDO. Not this time, Pete—

PETE. They want to scare us out—it's worked before—

MIKE. This time it's for keeps—it's war—and I've carved me a shillelagh—

ROCKY. I agree—let's get ready, Pete—I need a good fight to cheer me up—

PETE. It's a bluff—how could they dare—how could they even fight another war—get soldiers again, if they starve and attack their veterans—no, you just can't shoot down your veterans—no country does—

ORLANDO. I never made the mistake of creditin' our lynchers with havin' a heart—

MIKE. Or brains—they ain't got that either—

ROCKY. (*clowning*) Who me?—I'm Mr. America himself—look at all my muscles, my frigidaires, my ottermobiles and flush toilets—I'm so strong I can conquer Anacostia Flats—yes, the whole damn world . . .

MIKE. You can't do it Uncle—(*taps his forehead*) You ain't got enough stuff up here—

ROCKY. Who me? Hoover, the great engineer?

CHILD'S VOICE. Daddy, you said you'd get me an orange!

JOE RUSSO. (*wildly*) Pete, Pete, you're our captain—get us to a doctor!

PETE. I told you, Joe, we have to wait for Carl. We can't wander off one by one. We have to follow some organized plan.

ORLANDO. Pete, I'll go and look for Carl. We have to get a doctor for Joe's kids.

PETE. All right. (ORLANDO *slips out.*) If they're not back in five minutes, Joe, we'll take you and the family through the lines.

MIKE. Rocky and me ain't giving up yet. We was at the Marne. We got a right to be here. We'll stay.

ROCKY. I earned my bonus the hard way.

PETE. First help us get Joe's family through.

MIKE AND ROCKY. Oh sure, Pete, of course.

PETE. (*staring out at the right*) It's organized like a battle. They're burning the tents. I can't believe it. They can't dare treat their vets that way. It don't make sense. The country's behind the vets—

ROCKY. Vets or no vets—they're treating us like they do the unemployed councils. And guys on the waterfront. It's the same gang, Pete.

PETE. There's a difference—veterans are the country itself—not a class—they're attacking America—the bastards won't dare . . .

MIKE. I see you still got illusions about the bastards—

(ORLANDO *runs in, followed by* CARL. *Shots. The mean, dangerous clanking of tanks. Bugles, screams and curses as of a battleground.*)

ORLANDO. I found him.

CARL. (*taking a drink*) Headquarters is shot, Pete. Ain't no such animal. The attack's begun. We better get moving.

ORLANDO. They're setting fire to the whole camp.

PETE. I can't believe it—

CARL. Tanks, bayonets, tommy guns—it's war—with plenty of generals.

JOE RUSSO. How'll we get out—they're surrounding us—they're using tactics.

PETE. Yes, it's regular war—organized, planned—I can't believe it . . .

CARL. The stoolies bust up everything at headquarters—let's move Pete—it's each group for itself now . . .

PETE. I can't believe it—tactics—war on veterans—(*pulls himself together with a sudden gesture of rage*) To hell with brooding! It's war. All right, let's start planning our retreat. The first thing is for us to get Joe's family out to a hospital. Any discussion?

ORLANDO. No, we're all for that.

PETE. Joe, you'll carry your wife. I'll take the boy. Orlando, you carry the little girl.

(*As they start arranging and preparing, shots are again heard, the tanks roll, flames flare. The bugle calls to action. Screams. A young soldier stalks in, bayonet at the ready.*)

SOLDIER. Get outa here. We're burning this row down next.

PETE. Wait a minute. There's a sick woman and two sick kids in that tent.

SOLDIER. The guys with torches are right behind me. They don't wait for nobody. Git going!

(*He goes to tent and pokes his bayonet inside. A scream of pain from* CARMELA.)

Scram, I told yuh!

(*The kids cry—*JOE RUSSO *knocks the soldier down—soldier fires a shot—* JOE *kicks the gun out of his hand—picks it up and in his rage wants to bayonet the soldier—*PETE *prevents him—*JOE *bends down to his wife, after kicking the soldier.*)

CARMELA. He stabbed me—

CHILD. Daddy, where's my orange?

SOLDIER. (*whimpering*) He broke my arm. I didn't mean to hurt nobody.

PETE. Then why did you stab her, damn your puny soul?

SOLDIER. It was orders. I had to. None of us like fighting you vets.

PETE. That makes it all the worse. Where are you from?

SOLDIER. West Pennsylvania. My old man's a coal miner—

MIKE. A miner's kid, huh—your old man's ashamed of yuh, I bet—

SOLDIER. I had to enlist—the family was starving—I enlisted for the grub—

PETE. The rich hire the poor to jail and murder the poor—they don't soil their hands—(*He goes off to right and looks out.*) Whenever you're ready, Joe, we'll start—(*The others are helping* JOE *bandage his wife's wound,* MIKE *stands over the soldier—kicks him.*)

MIKE. Stupid kids. Comic books, radio, ice cream sodas, baseball. You lousy little superman. Murdering your own people for a hot dog. How can I get an idea in that comic-book skull of yours? (*lifts his club.*)

PETE. Let him alone, Mike. You can't solve it that way.

(*He stares out at the field below.*)

She's making war on us. I still can't believe it. It's so well organized, tactics and big brass generals! Can a nation make war on its people? I loved her like a mother. Look what she's doing to us. We're the Huns—they treat us like Huns . . .

ORLANDO. She's treated her Negro children like this for a long time—now you know Pete.

CARL. You still get surprised Pete, don't you—let's go, Pete—

PETE. All right, you elected me captain—Now's the real test of how we stick by each other—Are you ready, Joe—take Carmela—Orlando takes the little girl—I'll take the boy—Carl, you and Mike form a rear guard—Rocky Greco, you go in front—grab stones, a chunk of wood—anything—nobody lays a finger on Joe's family—d'ye hear—nobody lays a finger on them while we're alive—Dammit, let's go—

BLACKOUT

"Spring in the Bronx"

In the July 1952 issue of Masses & Mainstream, *Gold published a series of six verses under the title "Spring in the Bronx." From a notably global perspective that scorned the cultural egocentrism of the United States, he weighed varied phenomena including McCarthyism, a booming consumer economy, a new wave of immigration, and the war in Korea.*

~

1. The Killers

A mother wheels her baby down the street
he wears the stylish two guns and western holster
made so fashionable by toy merchants this year
the baby shoots and shoots at his proud mother
nobody is surprised to see a baby shoot his mother
he shoots at dogs at passing strangers autos and the sky
all the kids are shooting now in their games of kidnap and murder
they read comic books and study shooting sadism and shooting
the sun of truth is rarely seen by child or adult
millions of locust lies darken our sky
television and the newspapers movies radio and comic books
the cocaine peddlers lurk around every Bronx school
wagging their mouths like advertising men
anxious to infect for a dollar
it is free enterprise

the murder of truth and innocence
it is big business
my heart is troubled when I see
this baby shoot a mother in Korea

2. The Buds Are Open

Spring came to our street this morning
dressed in five lovely shades of new green
bearing lilac buds and a pink magnolia
our janitor's wife sang like a thrush
so the neighbors heard her up the airshaft
"Glory to God and the bursting buds
my son is coming back from the war!"
Lee was born in our basement
he worked in a garage and was popular
he played second base on a local team
played sax and folk guitar and collected opera records
the neighbors mourned when Lee was taken
his parents are tall stately and silent folk
who sweep the halls and stoke the furnace
and shift the daily garbage
thinking their own secret thoughts
but the neighbors hear the secret
"Mister Faraway President
a man can be forced into war
a man and his wife can shift dirty garbage
but not all the garbage in the Bronx
is as dirty as your war
your napalm massacre war
your son-destroying war!"
break out O buds of half-thought
pushing in silence amid the garbage
announce the people's glory and power
the whole world waits for an American spring
and our people at last in flower!

3. Boom Industry

The churches call with a sweet clang of bells
the Bronx worships Christ in its best Sunday clothes
long ago this man was betrayed by an informer
today the people worship Christ and not that "ex-Christian"
America's number one informer has been given another award
just made Professor of Christian Ethics in a Bronx university
can Christ hope to build brotherhood on such rotten foundations
the project is dubious I do not see how it can succeed

This informing has become a new American boom industry
boom fortunes are being made by many a rotten sneak and Judas
but such silver always vanishes and the informers' children will curse their fathers
will want to change their names and hide from the rotten heritage

things will be different in the future there will be brotherly love
informers have no love and without love you cannot create the world
the future belongs only to workers and creators rich in brotherly love
these Sunday bells promise an end to sterile informers and the coming of a world of love

4. The Happy Corpse

Doggedly all day he climbs
up and down the steep apartment houses
a gray little Chaplin refugee
escaped from the Hitler furnaces

to become a Fuller Brush salesman here
now he is 100 per cent American
with stern faith in our toilets frigidaires and autos
he worships in the chromium temple of success
Hitler's victim now believes in the Chase National Bank
it was not the bad people who won for Hitler
they were always a minority
it was the good people the meek and law abiding
the smug and petty bourgeois brush salesmen the blind
the egotists dwelling in family caves warm secure and rotten

5. Bronx Express

Though chewing gum ads shed much bright hope
and big healthy blondes show triumphant teeth from the
cigarette posters
humanity suffers in these subways
the fathers and mothers of New York
are pushed and cursed here like stockyard cattle
be they sick or well strong humble or foolish
all are kneaded into a dough of exploited flesh
of legs arms buttocks and souls
buttons rubber rayon and the subway spit and slime
roar and scream of tortured subway metals
and unhappy subway faces that submit
God wants us to suffer in subways
under the optimistic loud ads
peddling ten brands of adulterated whiskey
life is crushed and sorrowful
for a bunch of working people from the Bronx
traveling to the daily job
truckmen in eisenhower jackets
Jewish Italian Puerto Rican needle trade workers
reading newspapers that preach atombomb war
low-wage clerks in neat blue suits doing crosswords
and crisp young stenos with silken legs
dodging reality in a brave Hemingway novel
a longshoreman dozes darkly in his dungarees

electricians teachers domestics and bookkeepers
nobody is a tall elegant Hemingway hero
caught in a tunnel by their bread necessities
they read lunatic newspapers preaching war
in the sick green subway light
the flickering light of a diseased social system
but do not stop halfway with the subway gloom
this is the womb
these are the producers
necessity is the mother of history
only out of necessity
will the new heaven and earth get born
not made by tourists parasites or informers
but by producers in dark subways
traveling to the necessary job ahead

6. Ode to a Landlord

New York is mine
New York is my village
every street has known my grief and joy
my loved ones sleep in these cemeteries
my children talk with a Bronx accent
landlord of the white eyelashes and fat nervous mouth
you really can't evict me from my home
I was born over a Bowery saloon
and peddled papers along that street of the damned
I worked in offices factories and on trucks
I raised corn peas and roses by Raritan Bay
and dug clams for the nightly chowder there
lived too by the Coney Island beach
where Walt Whitman once chanted Homer
to the startled seagulls of Brooklyn
landlord of the many capitalist fears and manias
you own the skyscrapers factories and tenements
but you can't own Walt Whitman or his people
you own banks but you don't own me
I have marched in many picketlines against you

made speeches in all the five boroughs
written plays poems and cries of my heart
if I am poor I know why I chose it
poverty is my military medal of valor
it says I was loyal to my people
my mother my father my brothers and the poor
I know the soul of New York
my people rallied to Lincoln's call
though all the rich and the politicians were copperheads
my people rallied to Roosevelt
though the slave owners cursed and abused him
I was with my people in the famine of 1930
they showed their great mettle then
they rose like the trampled grass
never imagine you have safely duped or suppressed them
we are always getting reinforcements
now the Puerto Ricans are arriving to our help
starved and persecuted and exploited
like earlier immigrant Jews or Italians
they bring us new valor and song
hurrah for the brave Puerto Ricans
with their bright colors and lovely girls
they renew our song and solidarity
my family is a big brave family
with new births and weddings for every sad death
how can a man be disloyal to his mother
maybe you will evict me into one of your jails
where you are throwing my family nowadays
as a magic cure for your fatal disease
but I will still be happier than you
more secure and with healthier roots in life
owning more of New York than you
landlord with the white fearful eyes and fat face
though I cannot pay my rent
yes we suffer and sweat and are too noisy
you may fool or evict us
yet we survive like the trampled grass
that lives between two lifeless stones
along an old pier where the gulls are flying
landlord my people are bigger than skyscrapers

Autobiographical Manuscripts

(notebook fragment, c. 1952)

It is only a few weeks since two clean-cut young men rang my doorbell. They looked like college graduates just started on a well-rutted bourgeois career. But this time the career was the F.B.I. They said they had come to find out what I was doing and what theories I now held about proletarian literature and socialist realism, and the names of many literary people I knew, and such matters. I refused to share my thoughts with these bourgeois intellectuals. It is still one's technical right, under the poor old Constitution. So they went away.

Such visits are becoming terribly commonplace in the land of Walt Whitman. If a writer ever emitted in the past a single feeble poem against fascism or lynching he is on the big permanent FBI list of suspects containing, it is said, such names as Eleanor Roosevelt.

Writers are being sent to prison for their opinions, the first time it has happened in America. The American writer begins to understand the feelings of European and Asian writers during their own time of fear, shame and fascism.

"Americans Want to Be Loved"

(unpublished poem, c. 1953)

We wear second hand shirts and shoes and we eat poorly
And a knock on the door often sets our blood beating
I am a man of heart and therefore suspect in America
Women and men of heart and socialism are prey now of the FBI
I have diabetes to suffer as well as the FBI
So the problem remains will I and my petty troubles outlast
Wall Street America and its grandiose conflicted contradictions
You see I still have a sense of humor
And make a joke or two on my gallows
Behind these ribs I have still a heart
I am proud of its warm glowing newness
I have been cheated in life I have been betrayed
I have seen hundreds of stronger men than I go down
Dead of poverty and lack of faith
But I have been loyal to the people
And it has kept my heart in good repair
I am proud I can still feel it glow
It grows old strongly for justice
And burns with rage anew.

"The Rosenberg Cantata"

Touted as "the first American literary work of stature fixing Ethel and Julius Rosenberg where history will assuredly place them—in the gallery of martyred heroes with Joe Hill, Sacco and Vanzetti and the men of Haymarket," this piece appeared in The National Guardian *of June 21, 1954. The editors of* Jewish Life *magazine observed, "Mike Gold's Rosenberg Cantata ranks with the best writing of the 60-year-old people's poet and essayist."*

"The final answer is always with the people."

—Julius Rosenberg

History

From their cells in the dark death house
Ethel and Julius Rosenberg saw the sun go down
The sun of justice was going down in America
And in the darkness a Beast hunted the People
He poisoned the green Jefferson fields
He shattered the cities of Roosevelt
He was armed with a Bomb and a Lie.

The Beast

It is the American Century!
The Rosenbergs stole our Bomb!
Kill!   kill   kill   kill!

Ethel

How can you live without love?
There is no love in a prison
Julius where are you?
Have we lost the darling boys?

Julius

Our love grows through life and death
And the People will set us free.

The Beast

I have muddied the People's brain with movies and
television
I have deadened their hearts with money and dead art
I have deafened them to the great voices
The People can never hear you
And every bank and steel mill has sworn
That this is the American Century
And the Rosenbergs must die.

The Children

Mummy and Daddy please come home.
The house is so lonesome.

Ethel

We'll be home in the spring
With the flowers and joyful birds.
Wait for us darlings!

Children

Daddy and Mummy does it hurt
To die in an electric chair?

Congregation of Old Jews

And the rulers worshipped a Golden Calf
And they worshipped a Hydrogen Bomb

And they killed the Prophets and burned the Jews
And murdered Sacco-Vanzetti and Willie McGee—
O God of Justice spare the Rosenbergs!
Thy humble prophets of the poor!

The People

We are the People
In song and suffering
And blood of martyrs
We are the People
Steadfast in sorrow
We build a new world.

History

The stench of a dying world
Poisons the streets and homes and schools and courtrooms
Imperialist decay rots the young promises of America
Yet slowly a miracle deeply stirs
The world can never end.
In every age and in every clime
Miracles of the People are born
To save man's world anew.
In a dark death cell the Rosenberg miracle is born
To testify that Lincoln still lives,
And their name still rings like a sacred bugle through the world.

Children

Mummy and Daddy tell us the wedding story again.

Ethel

Your father was so thin and poor and serious
Like a pale young East Side prophet
That I loved him for his hunger and dreams.

Julius

Your mother was a beautiful Queen Esther
And her singing so moved my heart

I thought the tenements were a green forest
And she the sweetest singer there.

Ethel

The Rabbi married us under the canopy
We began in joy! We lived in joy!

Julius

I waltzed my bride around the hall
The guests applauded and drank red wine
O beautiful swan with white wings
Where is our family joy?

Both Rosenbergs

Beast! Give us back our children!

The Beast

All are at the feast of life but you
The auto roads and sunny beaches swarm with happy
  Americans
They rejoice in their autos and frigidaires
And their children play around them in joy
But you have sacrificed your family joy
To your beehive bitter god.
(a silence)
Confess only that you stole the Bomb.
I need your confession
It is a battle won
In the war for the American Century.
(a silence)
Here is the key to your prison
Confess and live.
You can gain the bright crown of success
Confess daily at treason trials and on television
Become famous informers rich and admired like Hollywood stars
And your children will have joy.
(a silence)

Be practical, make a deal and live,
Justice and truth are commodities
The world is a jungle,
Its only law victory or death.

Congregation of Old Jews

And they tortured the Jews to confess
That we had betrayed the State and drunk Christian blood
at our Passovers
They burned and tortured us through the centuries
But we never surrendered to their great lie
Or gave up our Jewish song in man’s symphony.

The Rosenbergs

We cannot take the road of the beast and informer
We will follow the road of brotherhood
That leads to the shining festival
Where every child will be loved
And hearts are united and a Bomb no longer is God.
Man is the meaning of the universe
And Brotherhood is the meaning of Man
And here in the lonely prison dark
Our cells are alight with faith.
We will persist in love
And if the Beast crushes our hearts
Our dark agony may bring a bright blessing
To all the children of Man.
Oh happy children of tomorrow remember the Rosenbergs
Who were steadfast on the road of Man.

The Beast

Executioner
Set up the Chair.

History

The Rosenbergs have chosen
As all must choose in this hour

Man who has fought upward from the primeval slime
Now comes to his final hour of birth and death
This is the turning point
Here the roads part forever
Man must choose hate and grief and the Hell Bomb death
The final fascist flame and explosion of the world—
Or world brotherhood.

The Beast

They are trapped in a mine
They are alone.

History

No stars shone down there was only silence
In that dark night when Spartacus died on the cross
But man is awake now at last
And millions of hearts beat with the Rosenbergs on their
   cross
It is the century of Man
And on the five continents the People are marching
Take heart take heart we have come a long way!

The Rosenbergs

Listen children! The People are marching!
Take heart we are coming home
With the lilacs and joyful birds!

The People

The world conscience is marching on picketlines
All the cities stand watch with bared heads in the sunlight
         squares
On the sacred hills of Rome and in the vineyards of Chile
Miners scholars and priests unite for the Rosenbergs
Great China arises, the people of a new planet of labor
         and peace
The mothers and soldiers of China cry out for the New York
         martyrs

And Africa rises in her wrath and affirms her ancient
freedom
And joins humanity's watch over the Rosenbergs
The Latin Americans the brave oppressed peoples declare
their fierce love for the Rosenbergs
The France of Joan of Arc and the Bastille unites again
As against the Nazi to thunder with the voice of resistance
for the Rosenbergs
And the great world pioneers ever faithful to the human
hope
The Soviet people the heroes of Stalingrad march for the
Rosenbergs
Man is awake he pleads in a hundred tongues
For the Rosenbergs for the pure souls of the Rosenbergs.

History

I History tell you again America
America stands alone
Free the Rosenbergs to save America.

The Beast

Executioner make ready the Chair
America can stand alone.

The People

Our picketlines ringed the White House
Jefferson and Lincoln America spoke to the America of
Eisenhower
We the People were rejected
American mothers machinists doctors and seamen
We the delegates of the People
Clothing workers miners and brave sharecroppers
From Florida to Canada and California to Maine
Dishwashers steelworkers and poets
Beautiful young girls with their hearts aflame
The hungry the strong the young and the old the Negro
and white Americans

All marching for justice in the American dark
To save the Rosenbergs.

The Beast

Executioner are you ready?
In the name of the American Century
Throw the switch FOREVER
(a sudden scream, the cry of the children,
the anger and weeping of masses)

The People

It is done. The Rosenbergs are dead. A cry of horror rises
from the earth
The Beast has won another battle. He has flung the bodies
of the Rosenbergs at the People.
He roars his challenge to the stars.
If he cannot rule the earth he will end it in flame and gas
As he did with the Rosenbergs.
He murdered Spartacus and Joan of Arc. He killed Joe Hill
and Sacco and Vanzetti and the men of Haymarket.
But the rivers still flow to the sea.
The sun rises each morning and the People are marching on.
The great revolutions come like strong winds into
his house of death.
Miracle of the People renew the dying world.
His faithless informers his lying teachers scientists and writers
His sneaks and whores and human monsters born of money
Rally behind the standard of the Hydrogen Bomb and Death
But they cannot build a world.
And the People rally about the flag of Life.
Americans do you hear the voice of the Rosenbergs
Calling you to brotherhood and joy?
The Bomb cannot build a world!
Only joy can build a world!
We are the People
We are the People
We are the builders.

"The Troubled Land"

Masses & Mainstream, July 1954

The writing Gold produced in the McCarthy era and after has either been ignored or viewed disrespectfully as the "tired" scribblings of a declining writer. In fact, an argument can be made that the 1950s accounted for some of his most affecting prose. A case in point is "The Troubled Land," Gold's account of his "American Tour" for Masses & Mainstream. *Here Gold presents an alternative view of America at mid-century, a vision more honest than the conformist fantasy of prosperity that has been adopted as a substitute for real knowledge of that decade.*

~

American Tour: 1954

1.

The speaking tour lasted a month, and was the result of my sixtieth birthday. I had avoided thinking about the approaching anniversary, because I had always felt young, and now was I supposed to feel venerable and old? But the editors of *Masses & Mainstream* together with International Publishers discovered the secret. They arranged a surprise party that proved to be the most wonderful day of my life. Thanks, dear friends everywhere! This speaking tour was a good approach to the solemn sixties, a fond hand clasp with my America!

2.

Chicago looked even shabbier and filthier than twenty years ago, when I had visited during the depression. Certainly in the South Side, the Negro ghetto, the tenements were still the same rotten, unpainted wrecks, paying superprofits to criminal landlords and their bought politicians.

Chicago is the capital of heavy industry, and it is feeling the first blows of the "recession." There were more men on the streets of the South Side than a month ago, or two months ago. The Negro workers are always the first to pay.

It was in the South Side that I first got to know and admire that monumental figure—the Negro worker of heavy industry. Resistance to the American famine on the South Side was a folk movement, with its own songs and heroic legends. Everyone was in it, men, women and children, preachers, saloon keepers and steel workers, mothers with babies in arms, and the slaughterers from the packinghouses.

Every day in Ellis Park there was held a great forum lasting from morn to midnight. Thousands of families would sit there and listen to a never-ending stream of speakers. I remember the eager kids who climbed into the trees and sat and listened, too. And in the barbecue joints, in saloons and churches, one heard the great debate raging on the question of socialism versus capitalism. And the sadist cop cars prowled the streets, and there were hourly battles around evictions or relief stations.

Now the Korean war boom had given the people jobs but not houses or equality. But the layoffs had begun again and Ellis Park may soon have to re-open its folk forum.

The progressive movement has lost numbers in Chicago. People have been frightened by McCarthyite fascism. It is obviously dangerous to think, to read liberal papers like the *Nation* or *National Guardian*, to sneak into a movie house for a French, Russian, Italian or other foreign movie. Government boondogglers are everywhere like roaches in the neglected house—tapping phones, gathering auto license numbers, watching the mails, frightening employers into firing the victims of informers.

Prison is not the worst thing that happens to people in America today. The walking death of being made jobless because of a fascist frameup is often worse than jail.

But in spite of the fascists, and a sudden cloud-burst that dropped millions of tons of water, there were 800 people at the *Freiheit* anniversary where I spoke. It was a typically warm and soulful meeting of the Jewish workers, these brave, good veterans of the struggle, the garment workers, carpenters, house painters and small businessmen. At such meetings every night all over Chicago people brave the blacklist to fight the fascist danger.

Chicago is as corrupt at the top as ever, but the bearing of its people remains solid and reassuring. I like that proletarian look of Chicago, the big men and women doing big things, a match for the roaring fires and metal monsters of industry.

It is interesting that all the newspapers of Chicago, from the pale, liberal *Sun* to the vile old reactionary *Tribune*, are opposed to American intervention in Asia. This is more than the old midwest isolationism; it is the new disgust of the people with futile, costly and risky adventures like Korea.

The Hell Bomb, too, haunts the minds of the people of Chicago. The papers carry columns of their letters expressing univeral fear.

In Chicago high schools and colleges the youth are wearing the Green Feather. This movement began in Indiana, I believe, as a protest against a stupid board of education that had taken Robin Hood out of the school libraries, because Robin stole from the rich and gave to the poor. *He was a subversive Communist!* The youngsters wore his Lincoln green feather, however, and now the feather has come to mean a protest against McCarthyism. This is the way movements often happen in America, without organization, without theories, sudden fiery eruptions of a deep old democratic volcano.

I visited Haymarket Square for the first time. The authorities have placed there the cast-iron ugly statue of a squat policeman with uplifted club. Was this the hero of the event that launched May Day in the world?

3.

My host in Minneapolis was a machinist, with a wonderful Finnish wife, and a college daughter engaged to a young soldier and half-sick with the separation.

Their hospitable home was in a working-class neighborhood of pleasant tree-lined streets and yards. Through the hours a troop of friends and neighbors daily visited there—carpenters, farmers or railroad workers, millers and visting miners down for the day from the Mesabi iron range. They drank coffee and beer and they talked about the fascist threat and the trade union struggle, or the books they read, and movies they'd seen. They talked about the Hell Bomb and about the crazy rulers who still dream of war and profit. And they argued and reminisced about hunting and fishing.

They all were fishermen. They fished in summer and in winter, by day and by night. I have never been in a city where people were so infatuated with fishing. I was invited often to join a fishing party, and there were daily gifts of walleyes, sunfish and other trophies to be fried and eaten.

There was a Finnish miner, a husky with pink cheeks, clear blue eyes and an engaging grin. He drove in weekly from the Iron Range, 150 miles away, to pick up books and magazines and any other literature he could distribute among the miners.

He was a volunteer sower of thought, an American bee spreading the pollen of progress, an intellectual in the mine, a Jimmy Higgins. There are thousands of him through America, anonymous as the workers who built the grand cathedrals of the Middle Ages. Now they are building the House of Man amid capitalist greed, war and chaos!

So he looked at me with his baby blue eyes and grinned: "Come back to the Iron Range in deer season, Mike. I will arrange meetings for you among the miners and farmers every night. And every day we will go hunting and fishing."

The biggest, broadest, most beautiful boulevard in Minneapolis is named after Floyd Olson, the farmer-labor governor elected a decade ago in a people's revolt against the capitalist parties.

The farmer-labor movement still lives in Minnesota. Delegations of workers and farmers who come to government offices to protest some new outrage committed by creeping fascism will sternly remind the officials that they were elected with farmer-labor support. They must not betray the democratic traditions of the state of Minnesota. Democracy still is a potent word in this state, if it isn't in Washington.

Sinclair Lewis grew up in Sauk Centre, not far from Minneapolis. His *Babbitt* and *Main Street* are based on Minnesota life, and I thought of Babbitt, that go-getting real estate salesman whom Lewis satirized for boastful and vulgar optimism.

That was thirty years ago, but now it seemed far away as the landing of Columbus. What! A bourgeois American who was an optimist? Today the rulers of America can offer the people only three pessimisms: world suicide via the Hydrogen Bomb, or a new depression, or McCarthy fascism, or all three in one last dismal Gotterdammerung!

As I walked the pleasant streets of Minneapolis I almost wished for the return of Babbitt. He had dreamed of happy homes and a reasonable profit, not imperialist super-profits and hydrogen bombs. Babbitt was folksy, he liked people, he wasn't a mad dog Pegler, Winchell or McCarthy. He believed in the right of every American to choose his own wife and his own church and political party. Come back, Mr. Lesser Evil, boastful, folksy, optimistic Mr. Babbitt!

Minnesota is a workingclass state, and Sinclair Lewis and F. Scott Fitzgerald, another native son, simply never saw or described the region. They were as far from the basic life of its masses as the first-class passenger on some ocean liner from the reality of engine room and fo'cs'le.

Meridel Le Sueur, who chaired my meeting in Minneapolis, is a true voice of this people. Her dark, noble, majestic beauty reveals her French and Indian ancestry and helps her understand this French and Indian region. Meridel is an example of what a people's writer should be. She is involved in the freedom struggles of her people today, she is also the bard of their past and herald of their future. Meridel has written many fine, lyrical books of folk lore, reportage and history of the North Star country. Hers is a regionalism filled with a socialist spirit—the regional roots sustain a great living tree, not the artificial roses of the college regionalism.

4.

When I was last in Detroit, in the Thirties, it was like a French city occupied by the Nazi devil. Henry Ford's storm troopers dictated every minute of a worker's life. They were an army of trained thugs, spies and informers. They watched the worker in the factories, supervised his saloons, movies and churches; were a witness even in his bedroom adventures.

The worst crime, under a Nazi occupation, is to dream of independence, and of heresies such as free trade unions. That was the supreme crime in Henry Ford's Detroit and too frequently it was punished by torture or death. I visited a worker in a hospital who'd been trampled by Ford thugs until near death. He had passed out some leaflets agitating for a trade union. He was a Communist. The Communists led the resistance to Ford fascism in Detroit, as they led it against Hitler in Europe. It was they who smuggled leaflets into the plants, then placed them on the assembly lines to reach other workers. They organized secret meetings in the woods, in churches, homes. It seemed like a lost cause. But the people won. And Communist pioneers paid with their blood and suffering for the rights now enjoyed by all.

Some cunning opportunists in the great union are cashing in on the wounds of better men. Yet the vision of the Communist pioneers stamped itself deeply on the union. And the union today exerts a wide progressive influence on Detroit. It has changed the city. For example, Negro segregation has been dealt some heavy blows here.

I visited Local 600, the Ford branch that has 60,000 members and is said to be the biggest union local in the world. Negro workers like Coleman Young have wielded a mighty influence here for years. Recently, this valiant local resisted a witch-hunting committee from Washington, practically chased the bloodhounds out of town.

I was told that concentration of big capitalism is still moving fast in Detroit. Detroiters are saying that Chrysler and Kaiser, like other "smaller" producers, are being squeezed out. Ford and General Motors remain the Big Two and have the monopoly on ninety percent of auto production. And General Motors, whose cabinet sits in Washington, may soon be swallowing its rival dinosaur of the primitive age of industry. Show me some "free enterprise" in Detroit, Professor!

The bosses concentrate on super-profit, the workers think about schools, segregation, decent homes, parks, and peace. The auto workers know Detroit is in the front line of any Hydrogen Bomb sucidal war. Detroit is a main center of war production. But listen to the words of Carl Stellato, president of Ford local 600: "Our members would rather stand in breadlines again than see a single American boy killed in the dirty war in Indo-China."

Detroit has the highest proportion of jobless of any industrial city. It is the first place I've seen where you find many apartments for rent.

At the University of Michigan, Ann Arbor, where I spoke off the campus, the influence of the mighty trade union of auto workers seemed to have spread. How else explain the fact that this university leads the nation's schools in resistance to fascism? The students showed me a page ad that had appeared the day before in the campus daily. The ad was an outspoken manifesto against the congressional smear committee that had been persecuting several instructors and students. The manifesto defended their right to the Constitution and its Fifth Amendment. The document was signed by 250 faculty members, including famous professors and heads of departments.

5.

Wherever you find a healthy trade union functioning, on its fringes you will find man-eating jackals of the Immigration Department, hunting and harassing.

It was surprising to hear about so many deportation cases through the midwest and far west. This obviously has become an important weapon of the bosses. It is intended to cow the workers, sabotage the unions, keep down wages. Half of the country is foreign-born or the children of foreign-born.

There is a case pending against Stanley Nowak, Polish-American worker of Detroit nationally known for his brilliant statesmanship and courage. He was one of the original founders and fighters in the Auto Workers' Union. For some years he served in the State Senate, where he made a record comparable to that of Vito Marcantonio in Congress.

It was an honor to spend an afternoon with this warm and generous leader of his people. We discussed the culture of the national minorities in America, among other topics.

There is a rich literature writtten by immigrants in their native tongues, and completely unknown to English-speaking America. A multinational culture would have deepened and enriched American culture. It's hard to believe that the first non-Anglo Saxon to become a major novelist in America was Theodore Dreiser, son of German immigrants. But there are other American novelists who write in Armenian, Yiddish, Lithuanian, Norwegian, Hungarian and different tongues of the nation of nations.

I asked Nowak if there were novels by American Polish authors. He named a recent novel he thought had social content and artistic craft. "Do you think these national cultures will survive?" I asked.

"Yes, but in English," was the opinion of Mr. Nowak. "Our young Polish-Americans may lose the language of their parents, but still retain a deep pride when they hear the names of Chopin or Copernicus. They will express these special feelings for their Polish heritage in English, I believe."

6.

Los Angeles has grown fabulously since I lived there from 1934 to 1936. You can drive fifty miles in a straight line and be within the city limits. It is all planless, like a cancer; it is the usual chaos, greed and profiteering. The transportation is terrible; almost every worker needs a car to get to his job, and to maintain a car takes about a fourth of the average wage.

A giant embryo striving to be born! A Coney Island with palm trees! A distorted chop suey of all the architectural styles ever conceived by man—the Gothic, the Japanese, the Iowa farmhouse and Greek temple and Spanish ranch house! The home of Theosophy! The home of slimy Nixonism! Los Angeles is also the home of steel mills, auto assembly plants, and the great airplane factories!

One of my greatest surprises on this tour was to behold the industrialization of Los Angeles. Mockingbirds still sing in the streets; roses, lilies and blue lupines bloom in the front yard. But it has become a Pittsburgh with palm trees! A majority of America's planes are manufactured here! There are steel mills belching yellow sulphur fumes, there are hundreds of dirty, noisy, ruthless gangsters of big industry fouling up the white city!

If Los Angeles didn't have enough trouble, now it has SMOG! I caught a whiff one afternoon of this gripping, choking industrial poison that Angelenos must breathe half the year. The city once attracted people with its claims to be a health resort. But smog is a killer as bad as the stuff that killed many people in Donora, Pa. The Angelenos have been fighting to have it controlled. But the big corporations fight back and, with the help of their fascists, have won thus far. Smog in the air, smog in the brain!

L.A. knows the depths of human degradation, it knows the heights of human grandeur! The coming of the factories and a working class has changed the spiritual climate. It used to be the premier open shop city of America, run by a lynch mob of millionaires. "Red" Hynes, sadist cop, headed the Red Squad that raided, slugged and ruled the city. Now he has died and gone to the hottest part of hell. There have been changes made. The working class brings progress.

Only this week there came news of the defeat of Jack Tenney, the little tin fascist McCarthy of Los Angeles. For eighteen years he had managed to wriggle his way into the State Senate. He was California's chief inquisitor. But he has been licked this time. James Roosevelt too was nominated, despite the opposition of every political boss of both parties. California has its ups and downs; but its people remain solid. They have always been one of the cornerstones of American democracy. They come through in every emergency.

It was a pleasure to renew old friendships in Hollywood. Filmland has been through the fascist wringer since I last was here. The Hollywood film has sunk to its lowest and most boring level since its only conscience, both artistic and social, was jailed and smeared. The persecution of the Hollywood Nine cost the industry many millions of dollars. Hollywood films are almost bankrupt, both in money and art. But the persecutions have brought a new and wonderful reserve to the struggling people's art in America. *Salt of the Earth*, that miracle, first proletarian epic of our film culture, is the first fruit of Hollywood terror. Its making is an epic story in itself, an epic of the underground. What courage, what will to create was aroused in the former employees of Hollywood! They are refinding the path to human greatness, and laying foundations of the new American art.

In the Hollywood upheaval there were stool pigeons, boot-lickers, degenerates and opportunists galore. But the best of humanity was revealed, as well as its worst. I can't express all my admiration for the outlawed Hollywood people I met on this visit. Some are driving taxis or working as carpenters and machine hands. Nobody is whining or looks back with regret at the fleshpots. They are really good people, with a real faith in humanity. They have proved to themselves and others what they are. It is wonderful to see people at their moral best. This colony of the exiled in Hollywood is producing new books, plays and poems. Their creativeness burns bright. It will shine through America and the world. Wait and see!

We had a warm and inspiring May Day meeting in Los Angeles, with 1800 in attendance. I spoke also in several homes and smaller halls. Beautiful mixed-up city of smog and orange blossoms, of stool pigeons and moral heroes, of the people's genius struggling and degeneracy of the masters! I have never been one of those to reproach you for bursting out with such extremes of good and evil! I believe you to be a confused young giant, on the way to glory as one of the centers of American truth and people's culture. *Avanti,* Los Angeles!

7.

At the meeting in Seattle there appeared yet another one of the big birthday cakes that had followed me around the country. A troupe of young actors presented an hour of dramatized selections taken from my writings for thirty years. It was really touching to feel these cords of sympathy and comradeship here by Puget Sound, in the rugged city of fishermen, lumberjacks, and Alaskan cannery workers. This is the city that made the first general strike in American labor history, a protest against government repression during World War I.

Down by the waterfront, located between a saloon and a barbershop, one finds the Frontier Bookshop. Its manager is Marion Kinney, and all day the longshoremen and sailors browse in and around, and Marion advises them on their reading.

The working people and the monopoly capitalists are the two decisive classes of our time. In an industrial state, workers are at the sources of power. But without the moral, social and progressive idea, power is but a blind and often destructive force. Hence, the worker reading a book, the worker who incarnates the socialist idea, is the man of our century. He is the gauge of progress, and herald of the bright future. He is the one who changes the world.

Marion Kinney is quiet and amiable, with the sturdy common sense of a pioneer woman. I have noted on this trip that more and more women seem to be taking over places of responsibility in the anti-fascist fight. It was that way in resistance Europe, too. The emergency brings out the hidden reserve of the people.

In Los Angeles there were two fine bookshops, progressive centers managed by women. One in the Negro region had an interesting story. It is called the Hugh Gordon Bookshop, after a Negro janitor whose evenings were given to education. He was a true scholar and lecturer and taught and spread the light. When he died, Mr. Gordon left his life-savings to found a bookshop in the Negro neighborhood. Its manager is a Negro social worker with great initiatitive and love of people. The shop has become a success.

8.

I had lived and worked in San Francisco long ago, from 1923 to 1925. My heart beat fast when I stood again on Telegraph Hill and looked down over the Bay and its shining expanse of blue water, amid sensuous hills covered in spring with poppies and lupine, in summer tawny as lions.

This beauty has one cancer on its face. It is Alcatraz. The Rock can be seen wherever you stand. Morton Sobell is chained to that Rock like a modern Prometheus. The tragedy haunts the city.

How I had come to love this city and its people! I still believe that it is just about the best all around American town. It was a romantic city in my youth, or was it that my youth was romantic? There were legendary figures whom I knew intimately, like Fremont Older, my editor, the last of the old buffalos. He had grown from a ruthless newspaper sensationalist into the defender of Tom Mooney. And Colonel Charles Erskine Scott Wood, bearded and majestic as a god, had fought the Indians, then resigned his army commission as a protest against government betrayal. He became a wealthy corporation lawyer, then turned fighting pacifist against the world war and wrote *The Poet in the Desert* and the satires of *Heavenly Discourse*. Colonel Wood was a true man of the Renaissance, and a passionate champion of civil rights!

Lincoln Steffens, George Sterling and a host of other original figures remain in my memory. California was original. Now the originality had gone into the union of the longshoremen, led by Harry Bridges. They had led the great general strike, they have turned San Francisco into the best union town in America. Once it was a graft-ridden city, now it is clean. Once there were romantic individual rebels and a labor movement fallen under the domination of dull, business reactionaries. Now progress has a solid base among the people, it has mass strength and organization.

It is better so. I remember poor George Sterling, poet laureate of the city, with his beautiful face of a ravaged Dante. He was a great friend of Jack London, and told me many stories about Jack. He told me about the money-making and the lust for bourgeois ostentation, the show ranch with its forty saddle horses and its gaudy weekends when bankers, generals and industrial barons came out to booze and fraternize with the proletarian writer, with the former bard of the people and fighting Socialist—ah, the American tragedy! Jack London was cynical and burned out at forty. He killed himself. Dear, gentle George Sterling killed himself for other reasons. And the People has its ebbs and flows but never kills itself. It inches on. It will change the world.

California still has the blood of pioneers in its veins. It will be, I prophesy, the first state where the new People's Front will be born, leading America to crush fascism before it traps us into the hydrogen bomb end of the world!

9.

The tour is over. It was a speaking tour, not a profound study of America today. I offer these hasty impressions for what they are, yet must believe they can have a little value.

I can report that I felt better about the country after seeing it again at close hand. An image from a cartoon by Daumier occurs to me. It was made after the betrayal by the tinpot dictator, Louis Napoleon. Daumier drew a majestic tree trunk that had been stripped by a blast of lightning. "Poor France, the trunk is shattered, but the roots are still sound," wrote Daumier.

The roots are still sound in America. The fascist rottenness is at the top. Nowhere did I hear or see mass demonstrations for war and fascism. The people want peace. But it is a silent prayer in the heart, a cry on the lips. It is not an organized, effective national movement. But pioneers are working everywhere like bees to fertilize and organize the people.

They are part of the people, these pioneers, bone of its bone—everyday machinists, housewives, lawyers, fishermen, miners, doctors, farmers—geniuses!

We must find a new definition for genius—the old confines it to a rare and special superman. It is true that great individuals can speed history, but it is the people alone who can change the world.

Like some of the persons I met on this tour, whose homes I stayed in or visited. Ordinary Americans, bearing the common burdens, getting up at six to go to work at a job. They must make a living. They have children to take care of, old parents and relatives and friends to help. Their bodies break down with worry and sickness—they have doubts, fears, hesitations.

Yet they persist in their pioneering. They overcome the downpull that keeps the average person passive and neuter. They have an extra share of energy and faith, and give it to the cause of liberation. What is this outgiving but a form of social genius?

I believe in the American people. Nothing on this trip made me change my belief. Slowly, in confusion, groping in the fog of malice made by opportunists and saboteurs, the People's Front against Fascism is being born in America. It is the green signal in the desert. It is the American spring, it is the resurrection of our McCarthyized democracy.

“A Reply to William Faulkner’s ‘Thinking with the Blood’ ”

The National Guardian, April 9, 1956

Gold saw hopeful signals in the early civil rights movement but could not ignore the violent Southern resistance to the 1954 Brown v. Board of Education decision. In 1956 he turned his attention to William Faulkner’s public comments on integration. Exposing Faulkner’s vacillation and hypocrisy, Gold took sophisticated positions far in advance of conventional thinking at the time.

~

The Manifesto of Retreat Belongs to the Past

William Faulkner has published a strange manifesto of retreat in a recent issue of *Life*. It is like a queer, hopeless letter from a suicide. “I was formerly against segregation,” he writes. “Now I am just as strongly against compulsory integration.”

He and others, he says, had occupied a middle ground, but “where will we go now if that middle ground becomes untenable?” He would be forced “to become a segment of that white embattled minority who are our blood and kin,” since now they would have become the “underdog,” and the Negro the new “topdog!”

This surely is thinking with the blood, not with the heart or mind, the sort of “thinking” that loomed large in Nazi ideology, and has long kept the South in pauperism.

WHAT HE'S TELLING US: How painful that a writer of Faulkner's great stature should so easily desert reason and be ready to accept the leadership of Kluxers and Dixiecrats, the vile Eastlands and Milams! For that is what he is telling us, this strong, honorable artist, the Southern man who had groped for justice and understanding! Are these really his kinfolk, these haters of culture, and torturers and killers of little boys? They would burn his books, if they had their way. They would burn him too. He can never fit into their totalitarian system of organized cruelty and ignorance. Faulkner was never a Nazi.

But here is the crisis at last in Negro-white relationships, and he can't face it, evidently. It isn't easy to face. Only after a soul struggle does any white Southern intellectual join the 20th century. Feudal dogmas weigh him down as they do a Bedouin Arab, a clerical-fascist Irishman, or an extremist-orthodox Jew. He had grown up, too, biologically conditioned by a group fixation that the Negro is an inferior, the Negro is his born servant. He can feel tenderly toward the Negro servant, but the Negro who rejects that historic status and demands his full humanity wounds the fixated white to the core. It is a great shock; the foundations of his psychology seem to be crashing.

BACK TO THE CLAN: Yet Faulkner had wrestled with his split Southern soul. He had broken through in some of his books, and when he also spoke for Willie McGee, that tragic victim of Southern hate. Faulkner also denounced the rat-like killers of Emmett Till, and his latest novel, *A Fable*, is a new departure, a powerful parable against war, a parable of the peasant and worker Christs crucified in capitalist wars for profit.

It looked as though in Faulkner the Southern people were finding a strong new voice in a time of the agony of change. Now he may be going back to the clan and the blood-thinking. In a recent *Reporter* interview he was quoted as saying that even if the Negroes were morally right on segregation, if the government stepped in he would "fight for Mississippi against the United States even if it meant going out into the streets and shooting Negroes."

This may be a crude misquotation, yet the *Life* article contained some of the same Dixiecrat argument for state's rights. It is the familiar old evasion of the slaveowners of 1861, who couldn't face the ugly fact that they were fighting to preserve a slave system. They, too, built up a state's rights mythology to conceal the reality from even themselves. They pictured the fight, like Dixiecrats today, as a holy war for people's freedom against a brutal dictatorship. This is just demagogy.

IT'S NO WATER TAP: "Stop now for a time," Faulkner demands of the North in his *Life* article. Wait, delay the movement. The implication is that that movement can be turned on and off like an electric lamp, or a water tap. It's made to sound like a palace conspiracy, a plot by a few envenomed leaders. Henry Luce and his cabal of fellow-millionaires and their hired segments of intellectual castrates, often explain in the same manner those vast movements and upheavals of history, outcome of a long evolution, that are now changing China, Russia, and more than a third of man's world. All this is made out as the plot of a few discontented bums in a Hollywood cellar. It would all stop if they could be bribed or stopped.

But what we are beholding is a new stage of American history, the rolling tide of a new consciousness among Negroes. The Negro is no longer a plantation serf; a majority of the Negroes now live in cities, where it is harder to isolate them, to crush them with naked force. The Negro has developed a big working class in the industries who are entering the trade unions en masse. This means a new way of thinking. The Negroes have developed an educated, ambitious middle class. And how many thousands of white Americans have learned to venerate and love such giants as George Washington Carver, W.E.B. DuBois, or Paul Robeson! Such noble figures have lent a new spiritual glory in the eyes of the world to the nation that has so long kept them in Jim Crow.

YOU CAN'T HALT HISTORY: Can any leader order the Negro people to stop producing such majestic figures of light and moral beauty? That is really what Faulkner is asking of them—to halt their history. Can anyone advise Negro writers like Langston Hughes, Lloyd Brown and John Killens—men of deep indignation and love and artistic powers—to stop making literature about their kinfolk? All such requests are as futile as to ask the Negro people of Montgomery to stop the mass protest against the Jim Crow buses. They are inspired with a Gandhi-like flame. They are praying. It is the first mass resistance to jimcrow. They are using passive resistance. They do not hate the whites. They are praying to live together in peace. But they can no longer wait. They will not.

I should like to point out another aspect of the crisis which Faulkner and so many others seem to ignore. This is the role of the Wall Street monopolies. They own the South. They are internal imperialists, and the South is their exploited colony.

THE SUPER-OCTOPUS: Take Faulkner's own state of Mississippi. Its Jim Crow politics, education and wage system are completely dominated by a giant utility, the Mississippi Power and Light Corp., according to the report of the Senate Committee that recently investigated the crooked Dixon-Yates Power contracts.

This public utility in Faulkner's state keeps 20 of the state's leading lawyers (they are also politicians, no doubt) on a fat monthly retainer. The corporation controls the racist newspapers, radio and TV stations in Jackson, the capital, thus influencing every Mississippi mind. The company spends over a third of its total operating expenses on this outlay for corruption, the Senate Committee discovered.

But a super-octopus of the North, the Electric Bond & Share Corp. of New York, owns this Mississippi octopus, the committee also found. One Southern official testified that the Northern satraps "did everything around the place but lick the stamps." They used Southerners only as their stooges, their working front. So much for kinfolk!

The textile industry of the South, the great petroleum industry and the oil fields, the steel plants, the auto plants, the great chemical industry, nearly every bit of southern production and the natural resources of the South are almost entirely owned by northern monopoly capital. The South is another Puerto Rico.

THE POWER THAT PAYS: Even the agriculture has been largely taken over. Metropolitan Life, that eleven billion dollar octopus, with the biggest assets in America, now has heavy investments in Southern plantations. Wall Street controls the price of the fertilizer every little sharecropper must buy, and fixes the prices in tobacco, and in cotton and other agricultural fields.

And it is they who preserve jimcrow. They have the power to stop it, but it pays. They came into the South, as the British once entered India, and exploited the native prejudices for their own profit. Divide and rule!

The lowest wages in America are found in the South. This is the famous "southern differential." A recent bulletin by the Labor Research Assn. estimated that A.T.&T, the octopus that owns all the telephone lines in America including Southern Bell and the phones of the South, makes a million dollars a week out of the differential. They pay Southern workers 30% less for the same work done by their employees in the North. The Northern unions are compelled from self-interest to lift the standards of life in the South.

OLD, SICK TRAGEDY: Is Faulkner against higher wages for his kinfolk, the good food and shelter, the music and books and happy children, the better schools, that higher wages would mean? Does he really want to preserve that old, sick, mean pessimist tragedy of Southern life, that he has chronicled with so much poetic realism in his bitter tales?

Take the poll tax situation. It deprives more white southerners of their votes than it does Negroes. Congressmen and Senators from the South are elected, as everyone knows, by a tiny segment of the population. It is a great fraud, and the legislators thus elected become Janissaries of Northern imperialism. These Dixiecrats now form a permanent fascist core in our nation's government.

William Faulkner has spoken some hot and whirling words in this crisis that shakes the South. His mind, his heart and his blood-prejudices are in deadly conflict with each other. One could almost reverse his warning and in turn say to him:

> "Stop now. Think. Study. It is not a simple situation, like a dog fight or a vendetta. It is the agonizing birth of a new and better South. The South needs democracy as the parched fields need the healing rain. The Negroes are fighting for democracy. The trade unions are fighting for it. The Eastlands and Milams and the Klan politicos are fighting against it. The Northern monopolies that own the South don't want it.
>
> "Which side can one choose? It seems to me, an outsider, that any Southerner who truly loves his oppressed people must choose the side that will elevate their lives."

Under the dirt and savagery that came with a century of terrible poverty, the Southern folk still retain so much human beauty. They are a people of deep feelings, who want to believe in something good, and ready to sacrifice themselves for it, if necessary.

THE QUIET ONES CHANGE: If there were no Northern monopolies in the South, and the Southern demagogues they employ, the people would soon forget jimcrow. It is a vileness that has to be constantly stirred up with lies, as Iago poisoned the innocent Othello. In the Autherine Lucy case the white college students showed much good-will. Their elders, the calloused old hack politicians, were the bitter-enders. These problems can be solved. All over the South, in hundreds of communities, there are quiet people who are changing in the new day.

I am willing to prophesy that one of these days the South will be fired by a great revival spirit as it enters modern times. Democracy in the

South will be almost a religion. It will pray and fight, sing ballads and dance reels—fathers, mothers, and children. And the Negro will be one of the kinfolk, as by white rape through the years, he actually is. It is coming. Where the greatest struggles rage, look for the birth of human greatness. It doesn't come from the well-fed sophisticates, the well-fed professional pessimists of the bourgeois academies. It will come from necessity and from the dark, deep, blood-stained earth of the people.

William Faulkner should study his people. He knows everything about them except that they have a great democratic future.

“A Word to ‘Tired Radicals’ ”

The Worker, November 24, 1957

The final iteration of Gold's syndicated “Change the World” column ran from 1957 to 1966. Observing the life around him from the streets of Haight-Ashbury to Vietnam, he wrote about the civil rights “freedom fight” that was then reaching a climax in the South and about the beatniks and hippies outside his window, who never bathed but were “morally cleaner than the makers of the dirty wars, in the Congo, Vietnam and Santo Domingo.”

In the 1930s, Gold the firebrand would have condemned and castigated “tired radicals,” but in changed times his message was deeper.

~

“Tired Radicals,” an essay by Walter Weyl that appeared some thirty-five years ago in the weekly, *New Republic*, has a curious timeliness today. Mr. Weyl was giving friendly and fatherly advice to the disillusioned radicals of that epoch.

There were plenty of them, heaven knows, because of liberal disappointment with Woodrow Wilson's war “to make the world safe for democracy,” and because of the great Coolidge boom.

The liberals had gone overboard for that war. Many had red-hunted, informed and served as propagandists in the government. Their sacrifice of principle did not change the character of the imperialist peace that followed the war. So they packed the bar rooms of Paris and New York pitying themselves enormously with Hemingway.

Many were infected by the Boom with the usual arrogance and the theory of American exceptionalism. They became bar room supermen and Nietzscheans with H.L. Mencken, who taught them to despise the American "mob"—the booboisie—in short, democracy and the people.

Mr. Weyl's essay was meant to save that generation from fascism, the only logical end of such cynicism and nihilism.

~

With the bedside urbanity of a *New Republic* editor, Mr. Weyl advised those intellectuals to retire gratefully from the political scene. They were sick, and should recognize that they were sick. If they looked their sickness in the face, it might prevent them from turning into sour, bitter renegades, a menace to the democracy they once had faith in. Let's have a quiet divorce, Mr. Weyl was pleading in effect. Don't slander and publicly defame the mother of your children whom you once loved. You don't have to turn into a warped and dirty informer; just step aside, and let the democracy keep rolling along.

~

He advised them to take up some cheerful hobby, to learn the piano, to cultivate a garden, to collect rocks, postage stamps, or books.

In America today we have once again a period of crazy boom nearing a possible bust, as well as heartbreak and political disillusionment such as followed the Khrushchev revelations.

The Renegades are about the same sick, and venomed breed as yesterday. The host of "tired radicals," on the other hand, are decent people who have just lost their way. Many are veterans of decades of social struggle, in which they have always remained loyal and courageous. The pressure of McCarthyism, the breakdown of all leadership in this country, added to the Khrushchev horror, have set up a true moral fatigue.

Thirty-five years later they have taken the kindly advice of Dr. Weyl and without venom or hatred, have stepped to the sidelines. Quietly, gracefully they have taken up hobbies and personal interests, in an attempt to deaden the pain in hearts that once beat strongly for progress and the human dream.

It can't work, of course. It is like a premature old age which one isn't yet ready to accept. It is a vacuum, and the heart of man rejects any such vacuum. Man is happy only in struggle and creation.

Whatever it is, the feelings of such people are honest, and their wounds are the wounds of a friend. This places a heavy responsibility on those who remain in the left movement, particularly the Communist party.

"A Long Day in a Short Life"

The Worker, December 11, 1957

In 1946, novelist-screenwriter Albert Maltz published in New Masses *the essay "What Shall We Ask of Writers?," in which he asserted that leftist writers had been for years producing inferior work because they were placing political concerns above artistic ones. "Much of left-wing artistic activity," Maltz wrote, "has been restricted, narrowed by a vulgarized version of the 'art is a weapon' theory." For creative writers, party doctrine was in Maltz's view "not a useful guide, but a strait jacket." In response, Gold and others publicly scolded Maltz. Gold's invective was perhaps the harshest; he looked like a bully.*

A decade later the old quarrel seemed insignificant, and in 1957 Gold took pleasure in celebrating Maltz's latest novel, along with the younger writer's strong stand against McCarthyism.

~

Look back at your youth; did some book greatly influence you on the side of the people? Did it touch your heart and crystallize your ambiguities then to a new life-pattern?

I am almost certain it wasn't a book of political theory or statistics, but some novel or book of poetry. Today it might even be the folk songs of a Woody Guthrie sung to the guitar.

Theory and science come later, as they do in the evolutionary history of man. First comes the emotion, the personal experience. Yet the science and maturity that come later are worthless without first emotional roots in the character. As Maxim Gorky says in one of his novels: "without love of people you can't be a true socialist." This love must be learned in life, but a fine novel of socialist realism can help crystallize it, help give it form.

The novel, whether printed or shown on TV and radio, is the university of the people. I think the novel that most influenced my own youth was "Les Miserables" by Victor Hugo. In the memoirs of such world leaders of socialism as William Z. Foster, Maurice Thorez and Chu The, one finds them saying that "Les Miserables" had a profound influence in shaping their youth.

Today as never before, a literature of socialist realism is needed in America. The boom has dulled the finer feelings of our people. The kids are singing those horrible TV commercials as though they were the folk songs of today. Their parents are knee deep in the things you buy on the installment plan. They worship the gadget. Their love has been turned toward four-wheel brakes and the hydromatic drive. Also the high fins on the broad bottomed cars. But behind the boom a third of the nation still lives in the old poverty. Visit the skid rows and slums of any city. Visit the free wards in the hospitals, the insane asylums, the runaway sweatshops, the lonely hardscrabble farms, or the great Western ranches where thousands are still kept in bondage.

It seems a miracle, but a small band of dedicated writers still produces works of socialist realism in America. They are the living nerve of our land, over which, in Shelley's phrase, creep the wrongs otherwise unfelt. Albert Maltz is one of this group of valiant and lonely pioneers. He was one of the Hollywood Ten, served a term in prison, and has just published his newest novel, "A Long Day in a Short Life." It relates the story of some Americans in prison today. The book has been reviewed in the press, and I am not attempting another review. I want only to point the book out to readers, and to fervently exhort them to wake up to life, to reality, to the truth and necessity of such novels. It is almost a political crime to neglect such literature, and like the practical business "Babbitt," not to understand their effect on the youth, their ability to change human nature through an appeal to the heart.

There isn't a single mention of the word "socialism" in Maltz's book, yet it leads there as surely as did the humanitarian epic, "Les Miserables" because such novels testify to the fundamental goodness of man. That is what makes them so different from bourgeois literature, most of which reflects the pessimism of a dying system and is based on the now fashionable philosophy of original sin, the very convenient faith that man is incapable of progress and evolution to a higher stage. He is doomed by his nature never to achieve peace and brotherhood. The same damned great lie of Hitler, though wrapped up in so many new complicated aesthetic veils.

In a setting that is all evil, against the sleepless tensions and terrors of a prison in Washington, D.C., Maltz portrays a group of Americans in trouble—the typical troubles of America today. One prisoner is a young high school student, a Negro who was attacked by a gang of white students and almost killed. A passing stranger, a southern white now working in a Ford plant in Detroit, impulsively saves the boy. He and the Negro youth are arrested and charged with serious crimes in their fight against school segregation. Huey Wilson is charged with having pulled a knife on the whites. McPeak, who saved him, is offered his freedom by the police if he will swear to the lie.

McPeak is a martyr, no crusader. He is a family man, who only wants to be left alone. He goes through a long agony of indecision. The youth, Huey Wilson, is no crusader, no hero. He only has the great ambition to become a lawyer, and is ready to sacrifice anything to that. But the forces of change, and the forces of the human conscience, meet on the battleground of the hearts of the two prisoners.

It is a beautifully told story, full of excitement and humor and authentic American talk. A masterly piece of work that will deepen your knowledge of America. This book, started several years ago, is almost a guide to the way people of the South are feeling today in the integration fight. It will help you understand the changes going on in the minds of Negro and white. That is the function of a novel—to furnish you with a chart to progressing human nature in motion and struggle to evolve.

"A One-Man United Front: Du Bois for President"

People's World, January 11, 1958

Gold and W. E. B. Du Bois were friends from the 1940s forward. Their families spent Thanksgiving together in 1952, and on Gold's next birthday, his sixtieth, Du Bois wrote with encouragement: "Square yourself for the next sixty years Mike, we'll win yet!" Gold was fond of referring to the United States as "the land of Lincoln and Dr. Du Bois." In 1958 he shared a dream that was fifty years ahead of its time.

~

Friends in New York tell me that plans are already being laid to celebrate in 1958 the 90th anniversary of our great and good Dr. William E. B. Du Bois.

Wonderful news! Let the stars be polished anew to serve as lamps at the festival! Let the free winds be rehearsed as an orchestra! Open all the doors! Let everyone be invited to the party! For this will surely be a festival of human reason and brotherhood, a holiday of progress!

~

If America but knew her truly great sons, would not this birthday of Dr. Du Bois be celebrated in every public square and meeting place in the land?

I can imagine how France or any other European nation would have honored Dr. Du Bois, were he their own proud possession. He would have long been the head of some great university, or institute of historic research. His writings would be part of the cultural heritage, known to all. Dr. Du Bois would have long assumed his right place as a national sage, a national treasure. Here that role is played by a vulgar, ignorant Wall Street crap shooter named Barney Baruch. No wonder we have trouble with our educational system.

~

As Americans have first been discovering, the Negro is the key to our history, our education, our democracy.

Dr. Du Bois has been a Columbus in the discovery of all the carefully buried secrets of the Negro's part in American history.

Is there any period in American history that has been more slandered, more falsified, more hated, than the Reconstruction period after the Civil War?

I was brought up, like every other American student, on the myth that the newly freed Negroes made this a time of debauchery. But Dr. Du Bois was one of the first to give a true picture of the progressive ideals of the Negro legislator.

~

The events in Little Rock have shaken the world. They are the climax of a struggle of many years, that began in the historic contest of Dr. Du Bois and Booker T. Washington.

The latter was the foremost leader of the Negro people around 1900. He believed that the Negro could best advance himself by concentrating first on the acquiring of wealth and industrial status. Mr. Washington strongly opposed cultural colleges for the Negro. But Dr. Bu Bois led a group that fought for higher education and full cultural life, for a complete humanity. His theories led to the Negro renaissance, to figures like Dr. George Washington Carver, to Paul Robeson and the struggles in Little Rock and Montgomery, Alabama.

~

I read his "The Souls of Black Folk," way back in 1914, when I first was coming into the radical movement. Dr. Du Bois with these poetic essays taught thousands of us the inner beauty and courageous humanity of the Negro soul. Much that was said there still needs to be studied and pondered by the backward whites of America. He is still a passionate teacher, a sociological poet, a stern soldier of truth and justice in America.

Life is hard on the American Left today. We are being split from within; sometimes for reasons that contain too much heat and very little light or common sense, it seems to me.

I should like to nominate Dr. Du Bois for President on a United Front ticket. He is a one-man united front and worthy to lead the great cause.

Part Six

"Message of New Epoch: 'Freedom Is Indivisible' "

People's World, June 15, 1963

That historic demonstration for human rights here in San Francisco seemed too silent, even solemn. Though 12,000 citizens were in line, one heard none of the songs, cheers and chanted slogans that usually overflow the freedom parades.

For the first time in a life-time of demonstrations I was now marching in a parade where black and white Americans walked in equal numbers. It gave one a wonderful feeling of hope. Was a new nation, a new brotherhood, being born out of the flames of these giant struggles in the South?

But why this solemnity, this strange silence? It puzzled me for some blocks. Then the marcher beside me, a dignified tall man of about 40, with a cheerful little wife and three children, asked me in soft tones: "Friend, did you ever march before in a freedom parade?"

"Yes, it happens that I have," I answered.

"I've seen a few," he reflected solemnly, "but never thought myself would be marching in one of them. It's a great feeling, isn't it, Rosie?"

"Yes, yes indeed," said his wife. A sudden tear rolled down her face.

And then I understood the silence and reserve. Most of these paraders were marching for the first time in their persecuted lives. They were new at it, and were carrying a great load of grief, defense, and other emotions.

We are passing into a new epoch. Such a vast movement for human rights could not have happened ten years ago in the ugly reign of McCarthyism.

History is a zigzag. Did not McCarthy seem immortal? But as long as capitalism exists, it will produce these McCarthys and the war, racism and fascism that is their fatherland. Yet McCarthy is dead today with his great lies and infamies, while the people keep coming on, in Birmingham as in San Francisco.

Ten years ago, on June 10, 1953, I stood in a tragic demonstration in New York. The police had closed a block leading off Union Square, where some 5,000 of us waited in weird silence for news from Sing Sing prison.

A last appeal was being made to the President for the lives of the pure young idealist radicals, Ethel and Julius Rosenberg. The chairman, a veteran clothing worker, read bulletins arriving every few minutes. Our foolish hopes were followed by bulletins of despair. It was a hot New York day. In the west, an immense red sun stood on the rim of the Jersey shore. We had been waiting and hoping since noon. The sun of justice was constantly going down. And then the chairman, his rugged face of an old worker twisted in sudden sobs, read the last bulletin. The Rosenbergs had finally been murdered in the electric chair.

To the end of my life I shall always remember the cry of the crowd. It was a sob of collective heartbreak, a shriek of despair and rage, bitter as though one's own child had been murdered by a sadist. I wept with the others.

The Rosenbergs had become precious to me as my own family. I suffered over them as I had over Sacco and Vanzetti, the betrayal of the Spanish Republic and the slaughter by Nazi beasts of six million Jews. Such tragedies tear a vital piece out of the heart. How does one ever survive such defeats? They seem like the end of the world.

The Negro people have lost thousands of sons and daughters through frame-ups and legal lynchings like that which destroyed the Rosenbergs. Jim Crow and lynchings are respectable institutions because they are the means to keep the wages of Negro labor down to a third of the northern white wage.

The Rosenbergs were framed and murdered by the same profiteers in blood. Their cold war was at its height. The armament billionaires needed constant fear and panic in the land. That was growing weather for war billionaires.

When in 1950 the sensational news came that Russia also had the bomb, the billionaires whipped up a new panic: "They Stole the Bomb from Us!" With all the army of thieves and liars of their Establishment, a spy hunt was started. The Rosenbergs, because they were radicals, fell like Sacco and Vanzetti into the reeking devil's pit of frame-up.

At every step of their long martyrdom, vulturous government agents swarmed eagerly around the martyrs, begging them to confess, promising their lives if they did. Such a confession would have meant an ever greater war budget. Up to the last hour, agents hung around the death cells urging the victims to confess to a lie and live.

Morton Sobell, another tortured victim of the Cold War, has had the same devil’s choice constantly pressed upon him. But he could not lie and for that has spent thirteen years in solitary, including five years in the horrible Alcatraz, once our Devil’s Island for bandits and gangsters.

On June 21 in San Francisco and in New York about the same time, memorial meetings will be held for the Rosenbergs and for the release of Morton Sobell. Let every free voice be raised in the land!

I hope these meetings can be as impressive as the Negro demonstrations. They are part of the same struggle for human rights and American freedom. Freedom is indivisible, and I know the Rosenbergs were marching with us that happy day of Human Rights in San Francisco.

"What Tereshkova Accomplished Here"

People's World, July 20, 1963

Perhaps few Americans know the name Valentina Tereshkova. She was a cosmonaut, the first woman in orbit, and she remains the only woman ever to complete a solo space mission. Gold's column about Tereshkova called out chauvinists, stood up for women, and celebrated the courage of a space pioneer.

~

The flight of Valya Tereshkova, that beautiful young Soviet girl, through a million miles of mysterious space aroused more emotion in America than had any other such event.

For one, the VIP poobahs and Colonel Blimps of our space program were too obviously disturbed that a mere girl amateur who got herself a permanent before taking off, should have doubled the number of orbits made by the best male American astronaut.

But why not keep the famed stiff upper lip of a military chief, and in the sporting tradition, congratulate the winner of the current race, knowing that America was sure to catch up and have its own day?

No, they were very bum sports, it seems, and snarled to the public press that the whole thing was a propaganda gimmick. Lt. General Leighton Davis, commander of the Air Force Missile Test Center at Cape Canaveral, called the flight "merely a publicity stunt."

It had no scientific value whatever, Congressman Celler and scores of other American architects of the space race and Cold War muttered with a petty snideness unworthy of a great country.

The top general in charge of the biggest of all these space projects added, with no doubt a snicker, "If it had had any scientific value, we could have been the first to send up a woman. Hadn't we already sent up a chimpanzee?"

These typical remarks of the male supremacist seemed to infuriate a group of splendid American women who are professional air pilots. Some of them fly jets, others are instructors, thirteen of them have passed grueling physical tests given to would-be astronauts and had been vainly waiting and agitating for a place on the team.

But the summons never has come through several years. "The talk of an American space woman makes me sick at my stomach," an unidentified NASA spokesman is reported to have said. The Negro people have often met such sick stomachs.

"Life" magazine, biggest national slickie in the stable of Emperor Henry Luce, came out last week with a progressive and passionate blast at the silly cave men who run the space show and distrust women as much as did their Victorian granddads.

What a surprise it was to see that the spokesman of the air women was Claire Booth Luce, wife of emperor Hank himself, and a shrewd aggressive blonde dripping with diamonds, as the saying goes. In her public life so far as I can remember, she has never been more progressive than that barefoot country millionaire, Barry Goldwater himself. What was she doing in this gallery?

Under that iron armor of reactionary ideology there beat a woman's heart, it seemed. Call it enlightened self-interest, if you will, but with a progressive passion Madame Luce defended the discriminated-against American airwomen.

In defending them, Madame Luce had to break down the charge that the flight of a Soviet woman was merely a propaganda dodge. She did it by first informing millions of Americans that "the progress of women, in all Communist countries, but especially in the USSR, has been spectacular."

She gave some spectacular statistics of emancipation of Soviet women: 53% of all professionals in the USSR were women; 31% of all engineers were women; 26% of the Supreme Soviet that ruled the immense land were women; 24% of all the doctors too, were of the "weaker sex" (332,000 women physicians and surgeons as against 1400 in all America.)

The fiery author James Baldwin, who has become the Tom Paine of the Negro revolution, has often accused white America of having lost its sense of reality. It cannot recognize the human dimensions of the Negro who has been so permanent and so central in American history. Male supremacists suffer from the same blind stupidity. They are obsessed with a defunct image of what America is and fail to recognize the modern reality. Thus, they dogmatically and blindly believe that a woman cannot have all the talents and endurance necessary for a space pilot.

Many a talent, many a spark of human genius, certainly a great Niagara of useful human energy, is sure to be found among the 110 million Soviet girls and women. It is equally to be found among the 93 million American females. But the Soviets, liberated from male stupidity by their Marxism, are freely developing all that wealth of human power while we in America hedge it around with insult and frustration.

Claire Booth Luce is determined to surpass the Soviet Union in every field. That is "peaceful coexistence." It will bring progress and peace, not nuclear war. It will make for women's rights, for Negroes' rights, for justice to the poor and oppressed in America.

The race against socialism has already stimulated the modernization of our school system. If continued, the race can make socialism itself seem necessary to America.

“The Birmingham Bomb Was Warning to America”

People’s World, October 12, 1963

The thinkers of the American Revolution early perceived that the American rebellion had an international significance. It wasn’t only the struggle of an oppressed backwoods colony against the monopolist taxes imposed by an arrogant king. It was the first revolt against world feudalism and its old rotten slave system.

The future of democracy depended on the fate of the young colony, they said. Thirteen years after 1776, the great French revolution also threw off the feudal chains and joined the heralds of the coming age of democracy, and the centuries of the common man.

Today, in a parallel manner, it seems to me that the great epic now unfolding in America that some have named “the Negro Revolution,” is not the personal affair of the Negro American alone, but affects for life and for death the future of all Americans.

As one example, we have just seen how the group of Southern Dixiecrats in Congress lined up against the U.S.-Soviet test-ban treaty. In coalition with the Northern Wall Streeters, they have made the Cold War possible all these bitter years.

This reactionary alliance also is the same evil, anti-democratic force that has passed innumerable bills against labor, in a ceaseless “cold war” whose open aim is to destroy the labor movement.

It is responsible for all the drift toward American fascism that can be found in the numerous “anti-communist” skullduggeries and disguises, such as the various oaths and witch-hunts.

~

All of this drive in the high places is based, one cannot repeat often enough, on the Dixiecrats. By deserting their own Democratic Party, they have seized the balance of power in Congress.

It also needs to be endlessly repeated, that they are in this place of power where they can endanger all of our American lives and destinies, only because they were able to rob the Southern Negro of his vote.

To get themselves elected by a tiny section of the southern population, they have used hundreds of shyster tricks, also murder and arson, to cheat the Negro of his voice and ballot in the elections.

Now "the Negro Revolution" has broken out, and is fighting for the Negroes' democratic rights. Can the Wallaces and Eastlands ever allow that? It would mean the end of their political lives and ambitions. These 14th century minds would rather perish than give up their slaveholder's theory and practice.

As I write these lines, it is only a few days since the insane rightists of Birmingham threw sticks of dynamite into a Negro church, and murdered four small and innocent little girls being taught in their Sunday school class.

The murder has shocked the country. It also shocked the Southern moderates and a number of the more naive racists. They never meant harm to the Negro, they say, but somehow manage to do nothing against such deeds as this.

It was an act that resembled in its crazy meaningless horror those frequent crimes with plastic bombs committed by French fascists during the struggles over Algeria.

Fascists do these things deliberately. Horror is their only weapon to terrorize the people and prevent the resistance they fear. I think a shudder passed through all decent Americans at the thought that this might be the signal for a chain of fascist atrocities such as flooded Algeria and France.

And I hope and believe that the terrible deed opened the eyes of many a "neutral" to the danger of fascism creeping into America in this fashion.

With this vile slaughter of the innocent children of Birmingham fascist-like reaction has unfurled its flag. Let every loyal trade unionist now prepare to defend his trade union. Let every honest teacher, artist, scientist make sure to see that American culture is on guard against the American fascists.

Imagine what would happen now if the Negroes are defeated in their struggle. Imagine the waves of repression that would be set in motion against everything free, and true, and beautiful and democratic in this, our native land.

And imagine what it would be like if all in America who supported Roosevelt in the years of need in the great depression, would now rise again and join the Negro in the present hour.

The unholy alliance in Congress would end. The Eastlands and Wallaces would not be our masters. It would not only be a "Negro Revolution," but a national resistance to fascism, a struggle of all Americans for equality in school and factory and home, for jobs, for peace in the world and an end to nuclear war, for justice and brotherhood in the land of Lincoln and Doctor Du Bois.

“A Vivid Recollection of Elizabeth Flynn”

People’s World, September 26, 1964

Our beloved Elizabeth Gurley Flynn has passed into history. For many decades she had blessed us with her serene courage, her noble leadership. Her life was spent in the harsh dangers of her struggle for human rights, but she remained so human, so poetic and youthful in spirit.

She was the veteran leader of the great strikes marked by the barbarian violence of the great corporations. Whatever the odds she remained true to the People.

Dear Elizabeth, I wish I could write something worthy of your great soul. But all the words sound so puny.

In looking through some old notes, I found one of a 1914 mass meeting in Union Square, New York. Let me place it here as the poor and inadequate symbol of my long regard for you. Dear Elizabeth, rest in peace.

The year 1914 is regarded by most historians and school children only as the year when the first of the world wars struck the rolling star which is now our home.

But another terrible thing was also happening that year in America—a great crisis of joblessness.

I was among the millions of unfortunate bastards who tramped the streets of New York looking for the job that wasn’t there. Since my twelfth year I had been working in a succession of unskilled, badly paid jobs that lead youth nowhere. I often dreamed of running away to the free West but my father had been an invalid for years. I was the main support of a family.

~

The date was April 11, 1914. A cold, spring rain fell on the dirty tenements and skyscrapers of our imperial city. I opened my eyes reluctantly and saw the ugly dawn of another jobless struggle.

Deprived of a job and place in life, what hope was there left in the world? What good is an old sardine can rusting on a pile of garbage? My head was filled with disgusting images, my lips were feverish and I thought again of suicide. I dreamed of death as though it were a wonderful vacation in the Catskill mountains.

~

My mother gave me a dime, which I tried to refuse, but finally I took it with some shame. I bought a *New York World*, the great want-ad paper of the time, and laid out a route for the job hunt. From a "Strong Boy" want ad I wandered to "Shipping Clerk" ads and "Busboy Wanted."

I tried this job and that one, hung around in the rain, tramped miles of cold sidewalks of New York. Around noon I ate the hunk of black bread my mother gave me for lunch.

Union Square was about halfway to my tenement. Choking with the usual hatred, disgust, and self-loathing of the jobless man, I sat on the bench in the cold mist. The big trees were still naked as winter skeletons. They dripped icy drops on hundreds of anxious people passing restlessly to and fro.

I heard a woman's voice sounding clear and sweet as a great bell through the Square where Lincoln's boys had volunteered in 1861 to save the Union. Timidly I pushed into the great crowd and asked a young fellow in a teamster's pea jacket what it was all about. He told me it was a demonstration for jobs. Curious, I pushed closer to the platform and then I could see the speaker.

She was a young girl with a classic beautiful face and blue eyes. She spoke so earnestly and inspiringly about the human rights that belonged to every man, woman and child in America. Work and education were to be fought for, if necessary. We must change the world. We had the power to. It was the first time I had heard that there was an economic system that belonged to all! And could be changed by all.

That vast idea, spelled out by a majestic young woman in a voice that filled the Square like a golden bell of freedom, plunged me into a trance almost esthetic in delight.

The speaker was Elizabeth Gurley Flynn, since her 15th year a fearless and inspiring spokesman for the American working class. So a little Italian in the crowd told me, proudly.

But I was startled out of my poetic trance by the sudden rush of a line of husky cops with red inflamed faces. Their eyes glared madly, and for no reason at all they fell upon us with their cruel clubs. They broke human skulls and crippled human legs and arms. People shrieked, ran, fought, cursed, fell and lay still on the wet stones.

I saw an enormous cop with a bushy mustache club down a frightened little woman in a black peasant shawl. She looked like my mother. Instinctively I tried to help her to her feet. The cop hit me a terrible whack over the spine.

And that was how I was introduced to Karl Marx—by the club of a police brute and by the golden words of a beautiful young Irish goddess named Elizabeth Gurley Flynn.

"Paean to Pete Seeger and American Music"

People's World, February 8, 1958

Gold and his family would long maintain personal and public ties with Pete Seeger and Toshie Ohta, who became Seeger's wife in 1943. In the decades of World War and Cold War that followed, Seeger often spoke of Gold with admiration, not only in acknowledgment of their well-aligned political views, but in gratitude for his friend's work to propagate folk music, helping immeasurably to curate the cultural space for Seeger's long career.

By the 1950s Seeger was a strong influence and honorary uncle for Gold's two sons, Nick and Carl. When Carl showed an interest in music, his father encouraged him and told him to pick an instrument. Carl said, "I want to learn guitar and banjo because I love Pete Seeger."

Pete Seeger recently packed Carnegie Hall with a concert of his folk singing and guitar and banjo playing—the first time, I believe, a folk singer has ever done this. Though far from New York, I could understand. There is nobody like Pete in all the world. He is a master musician with music in his bones, nerves, fingers. This lanky Pete, with his big hybrid American-French nose and radiant smile, can play any instrument divinely. The humblest folk instrument sings for him as though transformed and awakened to its own latent genius.

Pete does that to people, too; he transforms them at his concerts. However beat up, jaded, ingrown they may be, he gets them to sing together. They open up for him; it is a mystery of social therapy. He even gets them singing in four-part harmony, people who have probably never sung in their sophisticated and commercialized lives.

Pete is also a notable scholar of research in folk music. He has been a great directing force in the renaissance of folk music that has been ranging through America during the past several decades. It has remained one of the few healthy movements in cold-war America. It is touched by contradictions, of course, like the fact that these old cowboy and rural songs that go far back into feudalism are sung by young city people speeding in cars and incongruously rigged up in blue jeans and blucher boots to make them look like the honest toilers who once sang in their harvest fields.

Just the same, the folk movement has done much to bring Negro and white together in a simple and unforced brotherhood of song. It has given youth a feeling for the older, uncommercial America of farmers, weaver and railroad worker, miner and sailor.

But I am laboring the obvious—every reader of this newspaper has seen or heard Pete Seeger. He wrote a piece in "Sing Out," recently, that got me to thinking of him. In this piece Pete discusses a problem that has been gnawing at all our minds. It is the terrible degeneration and commercialism that has been taking place in mass culture, notably in our popular music. Everyone now has an electronic device in the home—radio, TV or record player. The record player has taken the place with youth of the former book and movie. And Tin Pan Alley (and the singers it spawns) is the main fountainhead of American mass culture.

In his piece in "Sing Out," Pete Seeger gives us a little dialogue on pop music between a Purist and a Hybridist. The Purist is indignant at the way Tin Pan Alley kidnapped and then mutilated and degraded some of the fine old ballads.

The Hybridist tells his indignant purist friend that this thieving is legitimate and has always been practiced. There is no such thing as cultural purity, any more than there is any racial purity. Cross-fertilization in biology as well as culture is one of nature's means of renewing the vitality of life. America is the supreme example of hybridization of cultures.

So the good hybrid experiments in pop music will live, the bad ones will die. "Some of it is swell music, even though it may not be folk music in the old sense. Certainly some of America's hybrid music has proved so powerfully popular that it is sweeping the world: jazz, for example."

"Yes, that's just the trouble," says the poor old Purist. "It's like the starling population in some of our cities. This bird, introduced from overseas, soon became a plague, wiping out many beautiful local varieties of birds. Thus, in country after country, local musicians are fighting for the right of their own loved traditions to stay alive. They are being swamped by jazz."

So the Hybridist again defends the mingled glory of our great American goulash of cultures—though truly, we never gave the different cultures a real chance to make their contribution, but killed them from the start.

Pete of course is giving both sides of the argument. Which side he prefers is obvious from his own activities—he is on the side of purism but understands pop, too, and has dabbled in it in the later days of The Weavers. What a sad period that was—one could watch the corruption commercial music can cause in even the most healthy group.

Pete, however, is an undaunted optimist and says to us, "Don't worry about the American people. They are OK—like a healthy man who gets sick once in a while, or has an accident, but then recovers. Music comes from the people. There will always be music in America."

Loving music as I do, and loving America because it is my mother, however drunk at times, or foolish and crazy, I will go along with Pete and believe in the people. What else is there to believe in?

“The Songs of Hope, and Their Singers”

People’s World, March 28, 1964

Almost everyone in America has by now chuckled over that saucy little ballad, “Little Boxes.” Written by Malvina Reynolds, for years a writer of people’s songs, and sung on a hit-parade record by Pete Seeger, pathfinder of the nation’s music, the song is a barbed satire of the suburban bourgeoisie. From cradle to grave they let themselves be locked into the “little boxes” of a sterile conformism.

They all live on hillsides in ticky tacky little boxes, and box their children into the right summer camps and universities, and they all come out of the boxes looking and acting and thinking just the same.

In his story, “Man in a Box,” the Russian author Chekhov satirized the Czarist version of Malvina’s hero. Sinclair Lewis did it so memorably with his novel, “Babbitt,” and there have been many others to attack the sterile hero of capitalist culture and money-getting and status. But the hero is still with us in life, status-ridden and sterile as ever, and everyone who hears the song recognizes him at once and gives him the horse-laugh. Malvina struck a gold mine of public recognition in that song.

To the status heroes this little song, with its tinkly music-box melody, must seem like a frightful piece of atheist, non-American “radicalism.” If they could stop it, I suppose they would. But it has become deeply embedded in the entertainment industry. It has earned its own status and has been used by preachers in their sermons, pirated by smart realtors for their advertising gimmicks, sung over TV by prominent entertainers, etc., etc. It has been on the Hit Parade, highest accolade of the music industry. The people obviously want this merchandise, meaning big profit for the music merchants—and profit, not Christ, Mohammed or Moses, is the sacred god of capitalism, its only core of meaning, as everyone knows.

I say it's wonderful that the climate in America has changed so much, and that "radical" songs are now again spreading everywhere, and the people's song movement, that forgotten voice of our democracy, has risen from the grave where senator McCarthy thought he had forever buried it.

~

One of the big flaws of the capitalist system is that nobody has ever been able to write a song of love and devotion to Mr. Rockefeller's chain of banks or the Bank of America for instance. But songs of love and devotion to the people's cause get written every day by young enthusiasts in every state of the union. For periods, the dead hand of capitalist fascism is able to throttle that singing voice of the true democracy, then capitalism sickens of its own contradictions, and the beautiful song of the birds of freedom is heard again in the woodlands and swamps of the returning spring.

It is good to be alive in such an inspiring moment of history, whatever its danger and uncertainty. This is what we were born for—this is the basic law of our biology—to constantly progress, to grow from hour to hour, to be creative and free and fearless—not safe little bumps on a status log, or residents of a tight little box.

And what is a poetical movement without a touch of poetry, without the great freedom songs that have inspired mankind through its darkest years?

~

We are hearing today in a hundred mass demonstrations in America the deep, proud, fervent songs of the millions of Americans who had been persecuted and submerged for the past century.

"They are singing beautifully," Malvina Reynolds told her interviewer recently on a TV program. She had come the day before from a massive picketing and sit-down by a thousand black and white youth at the plushy Sheraton Palace Hotel. Stately, white-haired, the kindly face of the maker of people's songs glowed with maternal pride.

"Yes, American freedom is singing again," she said. "As a writer of freedom songs I stirred in all my being. I want to write and write every moment of the day. I now have begun to think in songs—after the hotel picketing I went home and wrote a new song. I believe in this generation of youth. They are great—they will free not only themselves, but all of us."

I have known Malvina for some years, but somehow never guessed she was Jewish, like myself. When the interviewer asked where and when she had first tried to write songs, she answered: "I guess it must have been at home, in my childhood. My father, a Jewish immigrant tailor, was crazy about music. At five, he bought me a violin which I really never tried to play. But it started me on my path, I suppose. Also my parents loved the old Jewish folksongs, and I, too, have loved their tender beauty all my life, and they brought me to the love of all folk songs."

Her father was a working-class Socialist who opposed the first World War and was persecuted for it. Malvina, a high school girl, was also persecuted. At the last minute the authorities withheld her graduation diploma, but she and her family fought and the injustice was rectified.

"The Jews had their freedom songs, too," she said in the interview. "So did the white workers of America through bitter years of struggle against the corporations. All the peoples of the earth are united in the family of the folksong. And as Walt Whitman said, the greatest songs of the people are still to be written."

"Bob Dylan—Voice of America's Youth"

People's World, November 13, 1965

Ralph Gleason, jazz critic of The *San Francisco Chronicle* and perceptive writer in his field, says the following about Bob Dylan: "The most popular single performer in this country, perhaps in the world today, is Bob Dylan, the poet and singer whose songs are dominating the popular music hit parade, who can draw 15,000 people in the Forest Hills arena and the Hollywood Bowl all by himself and whose albums are among the best-selling discs in the music business . . . Dylan's music is a powerful voice raised in the world-wide moral disaster area. His lyrics are poetry pure and simple, and represent for the first time in our society a merger of poetry and popular music which can have a deep and lasting effect on our entire society."

No, jazz cannot do that much. It cannot quite change the battlefields of the social conflict, any more than a song like "John Brown," however marvelous, popular and significant, could have won the Civil War. Yet popular music is a great force. It is significant that just now, a renaissance of folk music and an elevation of its tone has taken place in America.

Dylan justifies the praise of Mr. Gleason, however, in that his songs, poetry and themes are having a great effect on American youth. He is their intellectual leader, their artistic guide, with whom they can share every emotion, every modern image, every bewilderment, and the feeling of reversal for all grown-up, so-called mature logic.

Dylan is a small young man who looks sometimes like a Charlie Chaplin walking with a broken heart into the sunset. He is even more fragile during his saddest moments. He has let his hair grow so that he is no longer an actor who stops acting when he is off stage. His hair identifies him with that curious world of beatnikism and surrealism that squares, or ordinary people of America, have not yet caught up with.

Statisticians have been telling us that in ten years the majority of the population of the USA will be under the age of twenty-five. In other words, in a decade, the youth will be actually forming the thinking of this country. Now the juvenility of popular music has been, up to the advent of the Bob Dylan epoch, a pretty terrible thing: maudlin, illiterate, infantile in its emotional self-pity, weepy like a spoiled child or an abandoned orphan. Dylan walked into this world and gave it a new character. It is a character full of violent contradictions which, I think, will sooner or later turn upon itself and demand some new synthesis. But whatever the future holds, Dylan has already done something as popular with youth as the Beatles, but a lot more profound.

Most of Dylan's themes are concerned with the poor people of the gutters of our monstrous cities; with the injured and despised of our cold society everywhere. Several years before President Johnson directed an alleged war on poverty, Dylan was portraying the victims of the great American social desert.

There is one of his songs called, "I Don't Want To Work On Maggie's Farm No More," that has clung to my memory. In a dazed, almost incoherent whine of protest of a lost soul, Dylan's little farm-hand tells of the cruelties and insults he suffers from the family of rich farmers for whom he is the wage-slave. The refrain goes: "I don't want to work for Maggie's father because he has done such and such a thing. I don't want to work for Maggie's mother, sister, brother . . ." and it goes on and on. Somehow, hearing it, you don't know whether to laugh or cry. And that's the effect, no doubt, Dylan wanted to give you.

Dylan's songs are on the model of the French Surrealists that are still fashionable in the posh and plush cafes of Paris. Their work may have struck Dylan for their weird mixtures, for the America he knows is also jumbled up in a crazy pattern of contradictions. But whatever the source of his inspiration, the fantastic attempt to clutch at the essence of this upside-down society and to put it in songs, really succeeds in Dylan's own American surrealist expression. Dylan's songs are not all melancholy strains. Positive assertions that life is going to be good someday, despite everything, despite the destruction which now hangs over all of us, emerge throughout the young poet's work.

In addition, there is also the rock and roll music that Dylan writes. He is actually a fine composer in this expression of youthful America. It takes an old square like myself time to catch up with the rock and roll. But I think that I have made it. All you have to do is try to be as natural as Bob Dylan, let your hair grow long, sing when you feel like singing, sleep when you have to sleep, love, protest, be a natural man in an unnatural time. I have become a partisan, in my late years, of rock and roll, for the reason that it is also a positive music with a strong life beat in its veins. It is a great music to get up to in the morning, and do a little exercise, when all your bones are creaky.

You don't get old gracefully unless you do keep up with the youth. And I assure you that anybody over fifty who will invest in an album or two of Bob Dylan's music and verses, will find again that there is hope and humor in this nuclear surrealistic world of the squares and the exploiters.

Dylan's stupendous popularity should teach us all a lesson in communication. The moral of his technique is perhaps his breadth and continental generosity. It reminds one of Walt Whitman. Yet, he is himself and brand new, and no critic has been able really to define the essence of his art. Keep going, friend.

"We're a Long Way from Lincoln's Dream"

People's World, February 27, 1965

Early in the Vietnam War, Gold issued warnings and prophecies that were later validated. In the article below, written a month before the first US Marines landed at Da Nang, Gold depicts the Vietnam intervention as a racist colonial war that could not be won. In a second piece written nine months later, he considers the meaning of a great cry of anti-war protest. In a third article from January 1966, he wades into the bloodstained mud of the Vietnam quagmire.

~

For technical printshop reasons, this column has to be written two weeks before it appears in print. I am writing on February 12, which is the anniversary of the great liberator, Abraham Lincoln. However, if Americans are excited and emotionalized on this day, it is not because old honest Abe, the rail-splitter president, led the nation in the Civil War of 1861 that abolished slavery from free American soil.

No, today America is too worried over President Johnson's announcement of his invasion of North Vietnam by air and fear of the nuclear disease that threatens to make a world Hiroshima that might well abolish the human race.

Abe Lincoln has always been very real to me, since the time I was a boy in the great ghetto of the Jewish immigrant in New York. My father and grandfathers came to this promised land in search of freedom and justice; they had a genuine faith in American democracy, so different from the despotic persecution they knew under Europe's czars and kings.

I grew up on the legendry of the Civil War. Many of the veterans of that conflict were still alive. The principal of my grammar school, P.S. 20, was a white-bearded stately veteran, Col. Robert Smith. The popular author, Harry Golden, also was a student at P.S. 20. He mentioned the soldierly old principal who often reminisced at the morning assembly. In vigorous language, full of the homely and personal realism of life that rarely gets into the books, he wanted most to make his students feel that the issues of the Civil War were close to us, that we too were the children of a poor and oppressed folk, denied human rights like the Negro. The old principal, to whom the cause of democracy was as real and personal as it was when he shed his young passionate blood at Shiloh, Vicksburg and Gettysburg, was the finest teacher I have ever had in the great principles on which American was founded: "A man's a man for a' that."

So it is Lincoln's day again and I remember the Jewish immigrant exploited in reeking sweatshops and living with his hungry family in the tenements. I remember how they revered Abe Lincoln. They even had concocted a legend that Lincoln was a Jew. He had a Jewish beard, didn't he? And his first name was Abraham? And his sad, strong face—wasn't it the face of leaders and "wise men" famous in the old world ghettos?

The kinship they felt to Lincoln was as real as the desire the majority of Jews still feel for full citizenship in America. Our country, which made the first democratic revolution in history, has not yet fulfilled the promises of its Constitution, nor has it yet fused its various peoples into a new and glorious free and equal nation. That is the meaning of the vast struggle of the Negro people raging on this Lincoln day. That is the essence of the struggle of Jews against the ugly anti-semitism of the racist-fascists, the struggle of the Mexican-Americans against the same bigots, and the defense of other minorities held in the snake-pit.

"America was promises," wrote Archibald MacLeish, and Lincoln day is surely the day of the American President who most believed and fought hardest for the fulfillment of all the great promises that spell America.

Does the current president believe as strongly as Lincoln in the fulfillment of those sacred promises? Or to put the question in another form: Would President Lincoln have sent jet-planes to tear up the humble villages and towns and destroy the peasant fathers and mothers and children of Asia and Africa?

No, Lincoln would never have done it. He would have denounced the Administration that performed such atrocities on the body of world democracy. Lincoln denounced the American war and robbery of its neighbor Mexico. Lincoln fought against slavery, not for it. Lincoln fought to preserve the great principles of the American and French Revolutions—"All men are created free and equal," as the Declaration of Independence definitely states for all the world to hear.

President Johnson, at this late date in history, is fighting a colonial war against the great continents of the colored majority of the human race. How else can you call this war?

And it is a war that cannot be won. American boys must die as well as their colored victims, and for what? For a foolish program that is as impossible of fulfillment as the return to the throne of the last Czar of Russia or the final Empress of China.

The chicken is out of the egg and can never be returned there. The world now belongs to the people, though the President and his cabal still preach the faded McCarthyite lie that this movement of the world's peoples, vast as the tides of the ocean, is nothing but a mean little cellar conspiracy of a few obscure beatniks and Communists.

“About Broad Humor and Intense Tragedy”

People’s World, November 27, 1965

The waving of militant and humorous placards is one of the forms of protest taken by thousands of youth in their effort to stop war. One slogan popular in student demonstrations and seen also on the front of shirts and sweaters and car bumper strips says briefly, “Make Love, Not War.”

Recently I heard some people grumble against such slogans. They say it is frivolous and they are right. The stake of the peace movement is too huge and terrible to be joked about. At the same time, could you really have a youth movement that did not joke on the very threshold of hell? I think that the health of all youth movements can be measured by this reservoir of joviality on the surface.

Every struggle for human rights takes on a different aspect, even though the fundamental facts remain the same, whether it be struggle for free speech in the streets or on the campuses, or the fight for social justice everywhere. “The silent generation” now speaking again, as youth should, freely and independently, is feeling all the slanders repeated by the baffled reactionaries unable to abide the fact that the young people have principles which they are willing to fight for.

This new generation of youth always impresses me with its remarkable maturity, wisdom and gift for action and strategy when battling all the gigantic odds thrown against it by the capitalist establishment.

Some amazing pages of history being written now will have the American historians of the future rummaging about and blinding themselves in libraries in order to run down all the legends of the present youthful nobility.

With the death, last week, of Norman Morrison, who burned himself alive with kerosene under the very windows of our belligerent minister of war defense, Generalissimo McNamara, I think this is something too terrible to become a popular force. It is especially so, since he was a young man, father of three small children and the husband of a beautiful and brave wife. Norman Morrison was a Quaker, and before had been a preacher of another denomination. He held his baby girl close and let go of her only seconds before igniting himself, as if he had wanted to awake in us the feeling of what war and napalm bombs are doing to all children when we don't care enough to stop the madness. This action was the last sermon of a man who fought without rest to obey his own conscience in the struggle for peace upon which all our existence now depends.

Last spring, in Detroit, Mrs. Alice Hertz, an 82-year-old Hitler refugee, first chose to die a fiery death to arouse in the American people the sense of outrage she felt in the genocidal war conducted against the Vietnamese people. The actions of these noble suicides, who gave their lives for the cause of peace, are a signal of the intensification of feeling across the country against the escalation of our "dirty little war." We can see now that the peace struggle is an earnest one, not a folly of some wild and unresponsible persons.

Yet, reflecting on those deaths, I do not believe that such emulations are necessary, and I think it may repel Americans who do not wish to be dragged into a struggle so terrible, and yet, as their conscience tells them, so necessary. It is the jolt to their conscience that brings up all the opposition of the average American. He has to come into the peace struggle in his own natural way. And the average American, unlike the Vietnamese Buddhists, had not had a history of such martyrdom for religion or for justice.

Still, a struggle for conscience began in America in the days of Tom Paine and the American revolution. It started in England with the Puritans and other Protestant sects fighting the persecution of the State and its State religion.

But it seems to me that the individual deed is not productive of collective organization. The Quakers, dedicated brothers of Norman Morrison, do not rush out to burn themselves with gasoline. What is most necessary is to organize the people against war and to give them the wisdom that comes from collective action and experience. Collective action, united front, is the key that unlocks all the jails of the world.

Of Norman Morrison it can finally be said that his great sacrifice has not gone unheard, all the newspapers of America noted the act. It will never be forgotten in our history, and will start a new current, perhaps, toward organized action for peace.

If there is a Quakers' heaven, I hope the keeper of the gate will have shaken this brave man's hand warmly, and sat him at the head of the table where all the good things the Quakers love best are spread, and that he was given a hero's welcome in his heaven.

"No Songs and Flowers for Vietnam Slaughter"

People's World, January 22, 1966

Some weeks ago, on the CBS Evening News report, there was flashed the terrible scene of a field dressing station of the U.S. Army. Young men were undergoing the familiar lonely agony of soldiers fighting a war they never wanted or understood. We at home viewed the horrible gaping flesh, the amputated limbs, the whimpers of the farm boy away from home for the first time in his life, the deaths of greenhorns, the business-like surgeons with weary eyes, the curses, the sighs, the blood, sweat and tears of which the vain-glory statesmen are so proud, they who are not ashamed to be heroes on another man's wounds.

It was all there—a bleeding slab of the dark truth about war, with no parades, no brass bands, no medals or unlimited drunk fests and visits to brothels which are the paradise prescribed for the fighting forces, as a reward.

No, the invention of the movie machine had made it unnecessary to join the army to witness, with one's own eyes and beating heart, the messy corpses in the humid rain back in an Asian battlefield. It was all there, in the movie theater and on TV, and it is like being disillusioned out of the romance of your love by some ghastly professional whore. I wonder that government censors allow this shattering realism to sneak into the fairyland of No Substitute for Victory propaganda. Truth, more sacred than all the gods and religions, is always mighty, and always prevails.

Amid the blood-stained mud—an unforgettable detail of the dressing station—the orderlies deposited a young officer with a haggard western face and tortured eyes. His right leg was about to be amputated, and he had lost control. Exhausted by pain and fear, he broke down and wept like a little girl who had lost her mother.

He beat his forehead with his fists, no longer the disciplined soldier of Mr. Kipling's tradition. He sobbed his deep agony, and the words came clear over the TV box: "We slaughtered them! We wiped out their villages! We destroyed them with napalm, the women and the kids and the cattle, even the rice! Oh, my suffering Christ! Oh my God!" And more of it. There was more of that truth which alone can set us free, if that hellish institution on which the capitalist system still rests, is ever abolished. Without a war every ten years, the profit system would wither away for lack of its war boom life blood.

There are a thousand arguments that can be made for war, pro and con, large and small, wicked or just.

Yet the total sum always comes out the same: war is the greatest crime against mankind and unless it is abolished now, man can scarcely hope to survive and the planet may burn up like the little peasant huts of Vietnam or Korea.

It is a sign of man's progress that war is no longer glorified, even here among the less sophisticated Americans. The two past world wars have been the cause of so much destruction that even the dumb sadist is frightened, for he knows he may be the first to go in nuclear world war.

The stakes of war are too high for gambling with all humanity on a single throw of the dice. Yet the sensible people with honest constructive fear of war are only beginning to organize themselves at this late hour, to make their majority consensus the sacred law of the earth.

I am old enough to remember the senseless idiot joy that flared through all the capitals as the guns opened the hellish rhapsody of the First World War. The young bank clerks, mechanics, longshoremen and salesmen were covered with flowers and kissed by the pretty girls as they paraded along the avenues and sang "Over There" and other battle hymns, and hustled to their tombs and mustard gas. Everyone wanted to buy them sandwiches and a shot of bourbon, and repeated the idiotic wisdom that the official brain-washers of the Establishment had injected into the empty spaces of the U.S. brain: "The war will be over in three months, by the end of the summer!"

"And who told you?"

"The same one who told you, our genial landlady, the morning papers, Crazy Joe, the barber, the president of the corner bank, our preacher, our school-marms, our garbage collector."

But all these worthy joyful and patriotic authorities were proven, in reality, to have been more foolish than the most unfortunate cretins.

So by the time the Second World War rolled around, the American people no longer sang or threw flowers at the young draftees. The bloom was off the war romance. Hitler was regarded as a maniac, and it was our job, along with our allies, to place him in an asylum. There was little belief that a victorious war would help democracy. Much cynicism prevailed in America, much of it well justified by the grafting and profiteering, the racism and all the familiar furniture in a century run by capitalists seeking big money out of another man's wounds.

And today, in the shadow of nuclear weaponry, as they crouch in the mental fog of the great cold war boom, in a time of creeping inflation and manipulation by the Texas and Wall Street tycoons, the people of the United States are confused and show not the slightest enthusiasm for war. The people of the richest country in the world speak of war gloomily as one does of a funeral.

Not much of a spark of hope about a war taking place 9,000 miles away. The tone is pessimistic. There are no flowers, there are no songs.

Autobiographical Notes

By the mid-1960s Gold's eyesight had deteriorated from the effects of diabetes. Nearly blind, he continued to write for the People's World, *dictating articles to his wife Elizabeth and using a tape recorder to work on a never-completed autobiography. A sampling of thoughts recorded for those memoirs, typed up by Elizabeth less than a year before his death and left among the author's papers, do not reveal anything close to a political change of heart. But they do reveal a bit of the unmasked Mike Gold he intended to make public in his autobiography: a man capable of introspection, self-criticism, and some regret.*

At one point Gold contemplated his "Greenwich Village period," which was really another term for his youth.

I have often thought about that period of my life and have not liked that period too well. I felt like I wasted many years of strong feeling, of useless emotion, of misunderstanding of the general world and confinement to a narrow little beatnik society. . . . It seems such a waste of life as I look back on it later. I should have kept on writing hard and furiously and writing about the things that moved me the most. The Village did not move me as the strikes did at the time, the great social injustices. I really felt that with all my heart and soul, as I did not feel the prettiest woman in the Village.

—1966

The aging writer thought also about a part of himself he had repressed or left undeveloped, one that happened to be tender and human.

In thinking over these things, I came on a curious fact, that I had never really written one love poem in all my writing. [. . .] I wrote quite a few poems, and they were all poetry of the class struggle. This will make me out to be sort of a freak, I suppose, but it is a form of freakishness which has seized hundreds of writers since that early time when I was one of the four or five writers of proletarian poetry in America.

As I look back I see that one of the troubles of my character was formed then. I began to have too much of the outlaw temperament. I didn't think I had any friends so I became too extreme in my self-defense, too extreme in my attack on people who believed in capitalism. I did not learn to judge them by their own special character. I have found so many kindly, good and talented people who were not radicals since that time, that I feel I must explain it sometime or other and I will in this book, I hope.

—1966

On another occasion, he looked back on literary history to take a long view on the fates and factors that, he felt, had made him a scapegoat. He likened his literary life to forced estrangement from a "family"—a painful process that was, thankfully, only temporary.

During the time of McCarthyism in America a great vacuum was formed in the thinking of the Left. Actually the only political party who was haunted by McCarthy was the Communist Party. That party was practically driven underground by the endless persecutions and its publications were not seen any more on college campuses or otherwise, and this created an intellectual vacuum in the type of great debate on history that continuously goes on in a healthy nation. Into the vacuum flocked the numerous little splinter parties and groups whose chief aim in life seemed to be to help the McCarthyites destroy the Communist Party. The strange thing was, after McCarthyism had been wiped off the scene, the intellectual vacuum still went on for years, and for instance one of the things that was taught in many of the English departments of the colleges, was the confidently and elaborately conceived fiction that there had been no literature of the thirties. Yes, these teachers of truth had actually created a fiction that so many in the collegiate world took for gospel. Another less important fiction that was widely spread was that proletarian literature was a mechanical literature written on formulas which had no art or science. I was somehow mixed up in this fiction by reason of the fact that every anti-communist intellectual needed a whipping boy for the theory that no literature was produced and that it was a mechanical literature, and that I was the chief commissar of the conspiracy to destroy real literature and to substitute proletarian literature for it. This was also widely believed by hundreds of innocent young freshmen who had taken their first classes in literature and world literature. It is not a pleasant thing to be a scapegoat. I can testify I got sick of reading these descriptions of myself as a beetle-brow gangster commissar snapping the whip over the innocent victims of a party of commissars who were taking over American literature by every manner of brutal means.

In the last four or five years, however, I had the delightful luxury of seeing this myth peter out like dying in the desert of thirst. It just withered away and I had quite a few young college students writing a thesis on some form of literature of the thirties come to see me as if I was a grandfather, which I am, telling them stories of the old battle. The thirties has been rediscovered by the American youth, . . . I felt often a new pride burning in my veins when I came across evidence that they didn't look down on me and my writing, but accepted it as a worthy specimen of a new time. Yes, it is a wonderful feeling to have your family reunited.

—1966

"*Change the World!* A Warm Farewell"

People's World, July 30, 1966

Gold's final column. He chose his moment and bowed out gracefully. Mike Gold died nine months later, on May 14, 1967.

Dear Friends, dear Readers, dear Editors:

I am giving up, with your permission, the writing of future columns for at least a year. The project of an autobiography that I have been working on from time to time has become so compelling that I find myself unable to get my teeth into a column again. I think it would be better for everyone if I don't attempt the impossible at this moment.

I am and I will always remain loyal to the tradition of working class journalism in which I have labored for almost 50 years.

At this moment, let me join in the fervent welcome of all good people to Esther and Art Shields, those grandest of proletarian journalists who have just come back from the assignment of several years in the Soviet Union.

With a warm comradely handshake to the young and old readers, to the wise, witty, militant, optimistic and fearless ones who read this paper and guarantee that it will never fail to survive the storms of social change,

Your friend,

MIKE GOLD

Bibliography

During a career that lasted from 1914 to 1966, Gold contributed hundreds of articles, stories, poems and essays to commercial, academic and political publications including the *Masses*, *Revolt*, the *Liberator* the *Daily Worker*, the *New York Call*, *New Masses*, the *San Francisco Call*, the *Boston Journal*, *The One Big Union Monthly*, *The Morning Freiheit*, *Masses & Mainstream*, the *Oakland Post-Enquirer*, *The Worker*, and the *People's World*. He also wrote introductions to books by a handful of leftist writers including Langston Hughes and Albert Maltz.

Works by Michael Gold

The Damned Agitator and Other Stories, Daily Worker Publishing, 1924.

Life of John Brown. Haldeman-Julius Publications, 1924, reprint, Roving Eye Press, 1960.

Hoboken Blues: The Black Rip Van Winkle; A Modern Negro Fantasia on an Old American Theme. *The American Caravan: A Yearbook of American Literature*, edited by Van Wyck Brooks, Alfred Kreymborg, Lewis Mumford, and Paul Rosenfeld, Literary Guild of America, 1927, pp. 548–626.

120 Million. Modern Books, 1929.

Money, in *One-Act Plays*, edited by D. H. Clark and T. R. Cook, D. C. Heath Co., 1929.

Jews Without Money. H. Liveright, 1930, 2nd ed., Carroll & Graf, 1996.

Charlie Chaplin's Parade (children's book), New York: Harcourt Brace, 1930.

Change the World! Edited by Robert Forsythe, International Publishers, 1936.

Battle Hymn: A Play in Three Acts, Prologues, and an Epilogue, with Michael Blankfort. Samuel French, 1936.

The Hollow Men. International Publishers, 1941.

The Mike Gold Reader. Edited by Samuel Sillen, International Publishers, 1954.

Mike Gold: A Literary Anthology. Edited by Michael Folsom, International Publishers, 1972.

Manuscripts

Unpublished memoirs. Gold-Folsom Papers, University of Michigan, Ann Arbor.

Fiesta (play). 1929, Gold-Folsom Papers, University of Michigan, Ann Arbor.

Moscow Love (play), c. 1929, Gold-Folsom Papers, University of Michigan, Ann Arbor.

Song for Roosevelt (play). C. 1948, Gold-Folsom Papers, University of Michigan, Ann Arbor.

The Honorable Pete (play). C. 1952, Gold-Folsom Papers, University of Michigan, Ann Arbor.

Selected Critical and Biographical Studies of Michael Gold

Aaron, Daniel. *Writers on the Left: Episodes in American Literary Communism.* Avon Books, 1961.

Berman, Paul. "East Side Story: Mike Gold, the Communists, and the Jews." *Village Voice*, Mar. 1983, pp. 39–53.

Bloom, James D. *Left Letters: The Culture Wars of Mike Gold and Joseph Freeman.* Columbia UP, 1992

Brogna, John J. *Michael Gold: Critic and Playwright*. 1982. University of Georgia, PhD dissertation.

Calverton, V. F. *The Liberation of American Literature.* Charles Scribner's Sons, 1932.

Chura, Patrick. *Michael Gold: The People's Writer.* SUNY Press, 2020.

Denisoff, Serge. *Great Day Coming: Folk Music and the American Left*. U of Illinois P, 1971.

Foley, Barbara. *Radical Representations: Politics and Form in U.S. Proletarian Fiction, 1929–1941*. Duke UP, 1993.

Folsom, Michael. "The Book of Poverty." *Nation*, 28 Feb. 1966, pp. 242–45.

———. "The Education of Mike Gold." *Proletarian Writers of the Thirties*, edited by David Madden, Southern Illinois University Press, 1968, pp. 221–51.

———. "Introduction: The Pariah of American Letters." *Mike Gold: A Literary Anthology*, by Michael Gold, International Publishers, 1972, pp. 7–20.

Freeman, Joseph. *An American Testament. A Narrative of Rebels and Romantics.* Farrar & Rinehart, 1936.

Klein, Marcus. *Foreigners: The Making of American Literature, 1900–1940.* U of Chicago P, 1981.

Lawson, John Howard. "The Stature of Mike Gold." *Political Affairs*, vol. 46, no. 6, Jun. 1967, pp. 11–14.

Lieberman, Robbie. *"My Song Is My Weapon": People's Songs, American Communism, and the Politics of Culture 1930–1950.* U of Illinois P, 1989.

Madden, David, editor. *Proletarian Writers of the Thirties*. Southern Illinois UP, 1968.

Maxwell, William J. "The Proletarian as New Negro: Mike Gold's Harlem Renaissance." *Radical Revisions: Rereading 1930s Culture*, edited by Bill V. Mullen and Sherry Linkon. U of Illinois P, 1996, pp. 91–119.

Pyros, John. *Mike Gold: Dean of American Proletarian Writers*. Dramatika Press, 1979.

Reuss, Richard A., with JoAnne C. Reuss. *American Folk Music and Left-Wing Politics, 1927–1957*. Scarecrow Press, 2000.

Roessel, David. " 'What Made You Leave the Movement?': O'Neill, Mike Gold, and the Radicalism of the Provincetown Players." *Eugene O'Neill and His Early Contemporaries: Bohemians, Radicals, Progressives, and the Avant Garde*, edited by Eileen J. Hermann and Robert M. Dowling, McFarland, 2011, pp. 234–49.

Shields, Art. "Mike Gold, Our Joy and Pride." *Political Affairs*, vol. 51, no. 7, Jul. 1972, pp. 126–28.

———. *On the Battle Lines, 1919–1939*. New York: International Publishers, 1986. Sillen, Samuel. Introduction. *The Mike Gold Reader*, by Michael Gold, International Publishers, 1954.

Tuerk, Richard. " 'Jews Without Money' as a Work of Art." *Studies in American Jewish Literature*, vol. 7, no. 1, spring 1968, pp. 67–79.

Wald, Alan. *Exiles from a Future Time: The Forging of the Mid-Twentieth-Century Literary Left*. U of North Carolina P, 2002.

Name Index

Subject Index

Communism

The Depression/1930s

Fascism

Folk Music

Heroes of the Left

Higher Education

Korean War

Labor

Literary Criticism/ Commentary

Lynching

www.ingramcontent.com/pod-product-compliance
Lightning Source LLC
Chambersburg PA
CBHW020641030726
47498CB00002B/308

9781438495347